ABOUT THIS PUBLICATION

FOR SERVICE ASSISTANCE

Customer Service
1.704.898.0770

North Carolina General Statues is published by The Muliti-Media Group of Greater Charlotte in Charlotte, North Carolina. Copyright 2015 by the Multi-Media Group of Greater Charlotte. This book or parts thereof may not be reproduced in any form, stored in a retrieval system, or transmitted in any form by any means—electronic, mechanical, photocopy, recording or otherwise—without prior written permission of the publisher, except as provided by United States of America copyright law.

The records required by U.S. Code 2257(a) through (c) and the pertinent regulations 28 C.F.R. Cli. 1, Part 75 with respect to this publication and all materials associated with such records are maintained by The Multi-Media Group of Greater Charlotte, Publisher and available for review by Attorney General.

www.visionbooks.org

Copyright © 2015 by MMGGC
All rights reserved!

TID: 5107809
ISBN (10) digit: 1503243664
ISBN (13) digit: 978-1503243668

123-4-56789-01239-Paperback
123-4-56789-01239-Hardback

First Edition

090520140547

Printed in the United States of America

2015 EDITION

North Carolina Criminal Law And Procedure-Pamphlet # 77

Printed In conjunction with the Administration of the Courts

North Carolina Criminal Law and Procedure
Pamphlet Reference Guide

Chapters	Pamphlet
Chapter 1 Civil Procedure	1
Chapter 1 Civil Procedure (Continue)	2
Chapter 1A Rules of Civil Procedure	2
Chapter 1B Contribution.	2
Chapter 1C Enforcement of Judgments.	2
Chapter 1D Punitive Damages.	2
Chapter 1E Eastern Band of Cherokee Indians.	2
Chapter 1F North Carolina Uniform Interstate Depositions and Discovery Act.	2
Chapter 2 - Clerk of Superior Court [Repealed and Transferred.]	3
Chapter 3 - Commissioners of Affidavits and Deeds [Repealed.]	3
Chapter 4 - Common Law	3
Chapter 5 - Contempt [Repealed.]	3
Chapter 5A - Contempt	3
Chapter 6 - Liability for Court Costs	3
Chapter 7 - Courts [Repealed and Transferred.]	3
Chapter 7A – Judicial Department	3
Chapter 7A – Continuation (Judicial Department)	4
Chapter 7A – Continuation (Judicial Department)	5
Chapter 7B - Juvenile Code	5
Chapter 8 - Evidence	6
Chapter 8A - Interpreters for Deaf Persons [Recodified.]	6
Chapter 8B - Interpreters for Deaf Persons	6
Chapter 8C - Evidence Code	6
Chapter 9 - Jurors	6
Chapter 10 - Notaries [Repealed.]	6
Chapter 10A - Notaries [Recodified.]	6
Chapter 10B - Notaries	6
Chapter 11 - Oaths	6
Chapter 12 - Statutory Construction	6
Chapter 13 - Citizenship Restored	6
Chapter 14 - Criminal Law	7
Chapter 14 –Criminal Law (Continuation)	8
Chapter 15 - Criminal Procedure	9
Chapter 15A - Criminal Procedure Act (Continuation)	10
Chapter 15A - Criminal Procedure Act (Continuation)	11
Chapter 15B - Victims Compensation	11
Chapter 15C - Address Confidentiality Program	11
Chapter 16 - Gaming Contracts and Futures	11
Chapter 17 - Habeas Corpus	11

Chapter 17A - Law-Enforcement Officers [Recodified.]	11
Chapter 17B - North Carolina Criminal Justice Education and Training System [Recodified.] Chapter 17C - North Carolina Criminal Justice Education and Training Standards Commission	11 11
Chapter 17D - North Carolina Justice Academy	11
Chapter 17E - North Carolina Sheriffs' Education and Training Standards Commission	11
Chapter 18 - Regulation of Intoxicating Liquors [Repealed.]	12
Chapter 18A - Regulation of Intoxicating Liquors [Repealed.]	12
Chapter 18B - Regulation of Alcoholic Beverages	12
Chapter 18C - North Carolina State Lottery	12
Chapter 19 - Offenses against Public Morals	12
Chapter 19A - Protection of Animals	12
Chapter 20 - Motor Vehicles	13
Chapter 20 - Motor Vehicles (Continuation)	14
Chapter 20 - Motor Vehicles (Continuation)	15
Chapter 20 - Motor Vehicles (Continuation)	16
Chapter 21 - Bills of Lading	17
Chapter 22 - Contracts Requiring Writing	17
Chapter 22A - Signatures	17
Chapter 22B - Contracts Against Public Policy	17
Chapter 22C - Payments to Subcontractors	17
Chapter 23 - Debtor and Creditor	17
Chapter 24 – Interest	17
Chapter 25 – Uniform Commercial Code	18
Chapter 25 – Uniform Commercial Code (Continuation)	19
Chapter 25A – Retail Installment Sales Act	20
Chapter 25B - Credit	20
Chapter 25C - Sales of Artwork	20
Chapter 26 - Suretyship	20
Chapter 27 - Warehouse Receipts [Repealed.]	20
Chapter 28 - Administration [Repealed.]	20
Chapter 28A - Administration of Decedents' Estates	20
Chapter 28B - Estates of Absentees in Military Service	20
Chapter 28C - Estates of Missing Persons	20
Chapter 29 - Intestate Succession	21
Chapter 30 - Surviving Spouses	21
Chapter 31 - Wills	21
Chapter 31A - Acts Barring Property Rights	21
Chapter 31B - Renunciation of Property and Renunciation of Fiduciary Powers Act	21
Chapter 31C - Uniform Disposition of Community Property Rights at Death Act	21
Chapter 32 - Fiduciaries	21
Chapter 32A - Powers of Attorney	21
Chapter 33 - Guardian and Ward [Repealed and Recodified.]	21

Chapter 33A - North Carolina Uniform Transfers to Minors Act	21
Chapter 33B - North Carolina Uniform Custodial Trust Act	21
Chapter 34 - Veterans' Guardianship Act	22
Chapter 35 - Sterilization Procedures	22
Chapter 35A - Incompetency and Guardianship	22
Chapter 36 - Trusts and Trustees [Repealed.]	22
Chapter 36A - Trusts and Trustees	22
Chapter 36B - Uniform Management of Institutional Funds Act [Repealed.]	22
Chapter 36C - North Carolina Uniform Trust Code	22
Chapter 36D - North Carolina Community Third Party Trusts, Pooled Trusts	23
Chapter 36E - Uniform Prudent Management of Institutional Funds Act	23
Chapter 37 - Allocation of Principal and Income [Repealed.]	23
Chapter 37A - Uniform Principal and Income Act	23
Chapter 38 - Boundaries	23
Chapter 38A - Landowner Liability	23
Chapter 39 - Conveyances	23
Chapter 39A - Transfer Fee Covenants Prohibited	23
Chapter 40 - Eminent Domain [Repealed.]	23
Chapter 40A - Eminent Domain	23
Chapter 41 - Estates	23
Chapter 41A - State Fair Housing Act	23
Chapter 42 - Landlord and Tenant	23
Chapter 42A - Vacation Rental Act	23
Chapter 43 - Land Registration	23
Chapter 44 - Liens	24
Chapter 44A - Statutory Liens and Charges	24
Chapter 45 - Mortgages and Deeds of Trust	24
Chapter 45A - Good Funds Settlement Act	24
Chapter 46 - Partition	24
Chapter 47 - Probate and Registration	25
Chapter 47A - Unit Ownership	25
Chapter 47B - Real Property Marketable Title Act	25
Chapter 47C - North Carolina Condominium Act	25
Chapter 47D - Notice of Settlement Act [Expired.]	25
Chapter 47E - Residential Property Disclosure Act	25
Chapter 47F - North Carolina Planned Community Act	25
Chapter 47G - Option to Purchase Contracts	25
Chapter 47H - Contracts for Deed	25
Chapter 48 – Adoptions	26
Chapter 48A - Minors	26
Chapter 49 - Bastardy	26
Chapter 49A - Rights of Children	26
Chapter 50 - Divorce and Alimony	26
Chapter 50A - Uniform Child-Custody Jurisdiction and	

Enforcement Act	26
Chapter 50B - Domestic Violence	26
Chapter 50C - Civil No-Contact Orders	26
Chapter 51 - Marriage	26
Chapter 52 - Powers and Liabilities of Married Persons	27
Chapter 52A - Uniform Reciprocal Enforcement of Support Act [Repealed.]	27
Chapter 52B - Uniform Premarital Agreement Act	27
Chapter 52C - Uniform Interstate Family Support Act	27
Chapter 53 - Banks	27
Chapter 53A - Business Development Corporations and North Carolina Capital Resource Corporations	28
Chapter 53B - Financial Privacy Act	28
Chapter 54 - Cooperative Organizations	28
Chapter 54A - Capital Stock Savings and Loan Associations [Repealed]	28
Chapter 54B - Savings and Loan Associations	29
Chapter 54C - Savings Banks	29
Chapter 55 - North Carolina Business Corporation Act	30
Chapter 55A - North Carolina Nonprofit Corporation Act	31
Chapter 55B - Professional Corporation Act	31
Chapter 55C - Foreign Trade Zones	31
Chapter 55D - Filings, Names, and Registered Agents for Corporations, Nonprofit Corporations, and Partnerships	31
Chapter 56 - Electric, Telegraph and Power Companies [Repealed.]	31
Chapter 57 - Hospital, Medical and Dental Service Corporations [Recodified.]	31
Chapter 57A - Health Maintenance Organization Act [Recodified.]	31
Chapter 57B - Health Maintenance Organization Act [Recodified.]	31
Chapter 57C - North Carolina Limited Liability Company Act.	31
Chapter 58 - Insurance.	32
Chapter 58 - Insurance (Continuation)	33
Chapter 58 - Insurance (Continuation)	34
Chapter 58 - Insurance (Continuation)	35
Chapter 58 - Insurance (Continuation)	36
Chapter 58 - Insurance (Continuation)	37
Chapter 58 - Insurance (Continuation)	38
Chapter 58A - North Carolina Health Insurance Trust Commission [Recodified.]	38
Chapter 59 - Partnership.	39
Chapter 59B - Uniform Unincorporated Nonprofit Association Act.	39
Chapter 60 - Railroads and Other Carriers [Repealed and Transferred.]	39
Chapter 61 - Religious Societies	39
Chapter 62 - Public Utilities	39

Chapter 62 - Public Utilities (Continuation)	40
Chapter 62A - Public Safety Telephone Service And Wireless Telephone Service	40
Chapter 63 - Aeronautics	40
Chapter 63A - North Carolina Global TransPark Authority	40
Chapter 64 - Aliens	40
Chapter 65 – Cemeteries	40
Chapter 66 - Commerce and Business	41
Chapter 67 - Dogs	41
Chapter 68 - Fences and Stock Law	41
Chapter 69 - Fire Protection	41
Chapter 70 - Indian Antiquities, Archaeological Resources and Unmarked Human Skeletal Remains Protection	42
Chapter 71 - Indians [Repealed.]	42
Chapter 71A - Indians	42
Chapter 72 - Inns, Hotels and Restaurants	42
Chapter 73 - Mills	42
Chapter 74 - Mines and Quarries	42
Chapter 74A - Company Police [Repealed.]	42
Chapter 74B - Private Protective Services Act [Repealed.]	42
Chapter 74C - Private Protective Services	42
Chapter 74D - Alarm Systems	42
Chapter 74E - Company Police Act	42
Chapter 74F - Locksmith Licensing Act	42
Chapter 74G - Campus Police Act	42
Chapter 75 - Monopolies, Trusts and Consumer Protection	42
Chapter 75A - Boating and Water Safety	43
Chapter 75B - Discrimination in Business	43
Chapter 75C - Motion Picture Fair Competition Act	43
Chapter 75D - Racketeer Influenced and Corrupt Organizations	43
Chapter 75E - Unlawful Activities in Connection With Certain Corporate Transactions	43
Chapter 76 - Navigation	43
Chapter 76A - Navigation and Pilotage Commissions	43
Chapter 77 - Rivers, Creeks, and Coastal Waters	43
Chapter 78 - Securities Law [Repealed.]	43
Chapter 78A - North Carolina Securities Act	43
Chapter 78B - Tender Offer Disclosure Act [Repealed.]	43
Chapter 78C - Investment Advisers	43
Chapter 78D - Commodities Act	43
Chapter 79 - Strays [Repealed.]	43
Chapter 80 - Trademarks, Brands, etc.	44
Chapter 81 - Weights and Measures [Recodified.]	44
Chapter 81A - Weights and Measures Act of 1975.	44
Chapter 82 - Wrecks [Repealed.]	44
Chapter 83 - Architects [Recodified.]	44

Chapter 83A - Architects	44
Chapter 84 - Attorneys-at-Law	44
Chapter 84A - Foreign Legal Consultants	44
Chapter 85 - Auctions and Auctioneers [Repealed.]	44
Chapter 85A - Bail Bondsmen and Runners [Recodified.]	44
Chapter 85B - Auctions and Auctioneers	44
Chapter 85C - Bail Bondsmen and Runners [Recodified.]	44
Chapter 86 - Barbers [Recodified.]	44
Chapter 86A - Barbers	44
Chapter 87 - Contractors	44
Chapter 88 - Cosmetic Art [Repealed.]	44
Chapter 88A - Electrolysis Practice Act	44
Chapter 88B - Cosmetic Art	45
Chapter 89 - Engineering and Land Surveying [Recodified.]	45
Chapter 89A - Landscape Architects	45
Chapter 89B - Foresters	45
Chapter 89C - Engineering and Land Surveying	45
Chapter 89D - Landscape Contractors	45
Chapter 89E - Geologists Licensing Act	45
Chapter 89F - North Carolina Soil Scientist Licensing Act	45
Chapter 89G - Irrigation Contractors	45
Chapter 90 - Medicine and Allied Occupations	45
Chapter 90 - Medicine and Allied Occupations (Continuation)	46
Chapter 90 - Medicine and Allied Occupations (Continuation)	47
Chapter 90 - Medicine and Allied Occupations (Continuation)	48
Chapter 90A - Sanitarians and Water and Wastewater Treatment Facility Operators	48
Chapter 90B - Social Worker Certification and Licensure Act	48
Chapter 90C - North Carolina Recreational Therapy Licensure Act	48
Chapter 90D - Interpreters and Transliterators	48
Chapter 91 - Pawnbrokers [Repealed.]	48
Chapter 91A - Pawnbrokers Modernization Act of 1989	48
Chapter 92 - Photographers [Deleted.]	48
Chapter 93 - Certified Public Accountants	48
Chapter 93A - Real Estate License Law	49
Chapter 93B - Occupational Licensing Boards	49
Chapter 93C - Watchmakers [Repealed.]	49
Chapter 93D - North Carolina State Hearing Aid Dealers and Fitters Board.	49
Chapter 93E - North Carolina Appraisers Act	49
Chapter 94 - Apprenticeship	49
Chapter 95 - Department of Labor and Labor Regulations	49
Chapter 95 - Department of Labor and Labor Regulations (Continuation)	50
Chapter 96 - Employment Security	50
Chapter 97 - Workers' Compensation Act	50
Chapter 97 - Workers' Compensation Act (Continuation)	51

Chapter 98 - Burnt and Lost Records	51
Chapter 99 - Libel and Slander	51
Chapter 99A - Civil Remedies for Criminal Actions	51
Chapter 99B - Products Liability	51
Chapter 99C - Actions Relating to Winter Sports Safety and Accidents	51
Chapter 99D - Civil Rights	51
Chapter 99E - Special Liability Provisions	51
Chapter 100 - Monuments, Memorials and Parks	51
Chapter 101 - Names of Persons	51
Chapter 102 - Official Survey Base	51
Chapter 103 - Sundays, Holidays and Special Days	51
Chapter 104 - United States Lands	51
Chapter 104A - Degrees of Kinship	51
Chapter 104B - Hurricanes or Other Acts of Nature	51
Chapter 104C - Atomic Energy, Radioactivity and Ionizing Radiation [Repealed and Recodified.]	51
Chapter 104D - Southern States Energy Compact	51
Chapter 104E - North Carolina Radiation Protection Act	51
Chapter 104F - Southeast Interstate Low-Level Radioactive Waste Management Compact [Repealed]	51
Chapter 104G - North Carolina Low-Level Radioactive Waste Management Authority Act of 1987 [Repealed]	51
Chapter 105 - Taxation	51
Chapter 105 - Taxation (Continuation)	52
Chapter 105 - Taxation (Continuation)	53
Chapter 105 - Taxation (Continuation)	54
Chapter 105A - Setoff Debt Collection Act	55
Chapter 105B - Defaulted Student Loan Recovery Act	55
Chapter 106 - Agriculture	55
Chapter 106 - Agriculture (Continue)	56
Chapter 106 - Agriculture (Continue)	57
Chapter 107 - Agricultural Development Districts [Repealed.]	57
Chapter 108 - Social Services [Repealed and Recodified.]	57
Chapter 108A - Social Services	57
Chapter 108B - Community Action Programs	58
Chapter 108C Medicaid and Health Choice Provider Requirements.	58
Chapter 108D Medicaid Managed Care for Behavioral Health Services.	58
Chapter 109 - Bonds [Recodified.]	58
Chapter 110 - Child Welfare	58
Chapter 111 - Aid to the Blind	58
Chapter 112 - Confederate Homes and Pensions [Repealed.]	58
Chapter 113 - Conservation and Development	58
Chapter 113 - Conservation and Development (Continuation)	59

Chapter 113A - Pollution Control and Environment	59
Chapter 113A - Pollution Control and Environment (Continuation)	60
Chapter 113B - North Carolina Energy Policy Act of 1975	60
Chapter 114 - Department of Justice	60
Chapter 115 - Elementary and Secondary Education [Repealed.]	60
Chapter 115A - Community Colleges, Technical Institutes, and Industrial Education Centers [Repealed.]	60
Chapter 115B - Tuition and Fee Waivers	60
Chapter 115C - Elementary and Secondary Education	60
Chapter 115C - Elementary and Secondary Education (Continuation)	61
Chapter 115C - Elementary and Secondary Education (Continuation)	62
Chapter 115C - Elementary and Secondary Education (Continuation)	63
Chapter 115D - Community Colleges	63
Chapter 115E - Private Educational Facilities Finance Act [Recodified]	63
Chapter 116 - Higher Education	63
Chapter 116 - Higher Education (Continuation)	63
Chapter 116A - Escheats and Abandoned Property [Repealed.]	64
Chapter 116B - Escheats and Abandoned Property	64
Chapter 116C - Continuum of Education Programs	64
Chapter 116D - Higher Education Bonds	64
Chapter 116E -Education Longitudinal Data System	64
Chapter 117 - Electrification	64
Chapter 118 - Firemen's and Rescue Squad Workers' Relief and Pension Funds [Recodified.]	64
Chapter 118A - Firemen's Death Benefit Act [Repealed.]	64
Chapter 118B - Members of a Rescue Squad Death Benefit Act [Repealed.]	64
Chapter 119 - Gasoline and Oil Inspection and Regulation	64
Chapter 120 - General Assembly	65
Chapter 120 - General Assembly (Continuation)	66
Chapter 120 - General Assembly (Continuation)	67
Chapter 120C - Lobbying	67
Chapter 121 - Archives and History	67
Chapter 122 - Hospitals for the Mentally Disordered [Repealed.]	67
Chapter 122A - North Carolina Housing Finance Agency	67
Chapter 122B - North Carolina Agricultural Facilities Finance Act [Repealed.]	67
Chapter 122C - Mental Health, Developmental Disabilities, and Substance Abuse Act of 1985	67
Chapter 122C - Mental Health, Developmental Disabilities, and Substance Abuse Act of 1985 (Continuation)	68

Chapter 122D - North Carolina Agricultural Finance Act	68
Chapter 122E - North Carolina Housing Trust and Oil Overcharge Act	68
Chapter 123 - Impeachment	69
Chapter 123A - Industrial Development [Repealed.]	69
Chapter 124 - Internal Improvements	69
Chapter 125 - Libraries	69
Chapter 126 - State Personnel System	69
Chapter 127 - Militia [Repealed.]	69
Chapter 127A - Militia	69
Chapter 127B - Military Affairs	69
Chapter 127C - Advisory Commission on Military Affairs	69
Chapter 128 - Offices and Public Officers	69
Chapter 128 - Offices and Public Officers (Continuation)	70
Chapter 129 - Public Buildings and Grounds	70
Chapter 130 - Public Health [Repealed.]	70
Chapter 130A - Public Health	70
Chapter 130A - Public Health (Continuation)	71
Chapter 130A - Public Health (Continuation)	72
Chapter 130B - Hazardous Waste Management Commission [Repealed.]	72
Chapter 131 - Public Hospitals [Repealed.]	72
Chapter 131A - Health Care Facilities Finance Act	72
Chapter 131B - Licensing of Ambulatory Surgical Facilities [Repealed.]	72
Chapter 131C - Charitable Solicitation Licensure Act [Repealed.]	72
Chapter 131D - Inspection and Licensing of Facilities	72
Chapter 131E - Health Care Facilities and Services	72
Chapter 131E - Health Care Facilities and Services (Continuation)	73
Chapter 131F - Solicitation of Contributions	73
Chapter 132 - Public Records	73
Chapter 133 - Public Works	74
Chapter 134 - Youth Development [Recodified.]	74
Chapter 134A - Youth Services [Repealed.]	74
Chapter 135 - Retirement System for Teachers and State Employees; Social Security; Health Insurance Program for Children	74
Chapter 135 - Retirement System for Teachers and State Employees; Social Security; Health Insurance Program for Children	75
Chapter 136 - Transportation	75
Chapter 136 - Transportation (Continuation)	76
Chapter 137 - Rural Rehabilitation [Repealed.]	76
Chapter 138 - Salaries, Fees and Allowances	76
Chapter 138A - State Government Ethics Act	76

Chapter 139 - Soil and Water Conservation Districts	76
Chapter 140 - State Art Museum; Symphony and Art Societies	76
Chapter 140A - State Awards System	76
Chapter 141 - State Boundaries	76
Chapter 142 - State Debt	76
Chapter 143 - State Departments, Institutions, and Commissions	77
Chapter 143 - State Departments, Institutions, and Commissions (Continuation)	78
Chapter 143 - State Departments, Institutions, and Commissions (Continuation)	79
Chapter 143 - State Departments, Institutions, and Commissions (Continuation)	80
Chapter 143A - State Government Reorganization	80
Chapter 143B - Executive Organization Act of 1973	80
Chapter 143B - Executive Organization Act of 1973 (Continuation)	81
Chapter 143B - Executive Organization Act of 1973 (Continuation)	82
Chapter 143C - State Budget Act	83
Chapter 143D - The State Governmental Accountability and Internal Control Act	83
Chapter 144 - State Flag, Official Governmental Flags, Motto, and Colors	83
Chapter 145 - State Symbols and Other Official Adoptions.	83
Chapter 146 - State Lands	83
Chapter 147 - State Officers	83
Chapter 148 - State Prison System	84
Chapter 149 - State Song and Toast	84
Chapter 150 - Uniform Revocation of Licenses [Repealed.]	84
Chapter 150A - Administrative Procedure Act [Recodified.]	84
Chapter 150B - Administrative Procedure Act	84
Chapter 151 - Constables [Repealed.]	84
Chapter 152 - Coroners	84
Chapter 152A - County Medical Examiner [Repealed.]	84
Chapter 152A - County Medical Examiner [Repealed.] (Continuation)	84
Chapter 153 - Counties and County Commissioners [Repealed.]	84
Chapter 153A - Counties	84
Chapter 153A – Counties (Continue)	85
Chapter 153B - Mountain Resources Planning Act	85
Chapter 153C - Uwharrie Regional Resources Act	85
Chapter 154 - County Surveyor [Repealed.]	85
Chapter 155 - County Treasurer [Repealed.]	85

Chapter 156 - Drainage	85
Chapter 156 – Drainage (Continuation)	86
Chapter 157 - Housing Authorities and Projects	86
Chapter 157A - Historic Properties Commissions [Transferred.]	86
Chapter 158 - Local Development	86
Chapter 159 - Local Government Finance	86
Chapter 159 - Local Government Finance (Continuation)	87
Chapter 159A - Pollution Abatement and Industrial Facilities Financing Act [Unconstitutional.]	87
Chapter 159B - Joint Municipal Electric Power and Energy Act	87
Chapter 159C - Industrial and Pollution Control Facilities Financing Act	87
Chapter 159D - The North Carolina Capital Facilities Financing Act	87
Chapter 159E - Registered Public Obligations Act	87
Chapter 159F - North Carolina Energy Development Authority [Repealed.]	87
Chapter 159G - Water Infrastructure	87
Chapter 159H - [Reserved.]	87
Chapter 159I - Solid Waste Management Loan Program and Local Government Special Obligation Bonds	87
Chapter 160 - Municipal Corporations [Repealed And Transferred.]	87
Chapter 160A - Cities and Towns	88
Chapter 160A - Cities and Towns (Continuation)	89
Chapter 160B - Consolidated City-County Act	89
Chapter 160C - Baseball Park Districts [Repealed.]	90
Chapter 161 - Register of Deeds	90
Chapter 162 - Sheriff	90
Chapter 162A - Water and Sewer Systems	90
Chapter 162B Continuity of Local Government in Emergency.	90
Chapter 163 Elections and Election Laws.	90
Chapter 163 Elections and Election Laws. (Continuation)	91
Chapter 164 Concerning the General Statutes of North Carolina.	92
Chapter 165 Veterans.	92
Chapter 166 Civil Preparedness Agencies [Repealed.]	92
Chapter 166A North Carolina Emergency Management Act.	92
Chapter 167 State Civil Air Patrol [Repealed.]	92
Chapter 168 Persons with Disabilities.	92
Chapter 168A Persons With Disabilities Protection Act.	92

Chapter 143.

State Departments, Institutions, and Commissions

Article 1.

Executive Budget Act.

§§ 143-1 through 143-3.5: Repealed by Session Laws 2006-203, s. 1, effective July 1, 2007, and applicable to the budget for the 2007-2009 biennium and each subsequent biennium thereafter.

§ 143-3.6: Repealed.

§ 143-3.7: Repealed by Session Laws 1997-443, s. 23(b).

§§ 143-4 through 143-10. Repealed by Session Laws 2006-203, s. 1, effective July 1, 2007, and applicable to the budget for the 2007-2009 biennium and each subsequent biennium thereafter.

§ 143-10.1: Repealed by Session Laws 1991, c. 689, s. 342.

§ 143-10.1A: Repealed by Session Laws 2006-203, s. 1, effective July 1, 2007, and applicable to the budget for the 2007-2009 biennium and each subsequent biennium thereafter.

§ 143-10.2: Repealed by Session Laws 2006-203, s. 1, effective July 1, 2007, and applicable to the budget for the 2007-2009 biennium and each subsequent biennium thereafter.

§§ 143-10.3 through 143-10.6: Repealed by Session Laws 2001-424, s. 12.2(a), effective July 1, 2001.

§ 143-10.7: Repealed by Session Laws 2006-203, s. 1, effective July 1, 2007, and applicable to the budget for the 2007-2009 biennium and each subsequent biennium thereafter.

§ 143-11.1: Repealed by Session Laws 1983, c. 717, s. 55.

§§ 143-12 through 143-16.4: Repealed by Session Laws 2006-203, s. 1, effective July 1, 2007, and applicable to the budget for the 2007-2009 biennium and each subsequent biennium thereafter.

§ 143-16.5: Repealed by Session Laws 1999-237, s. 19a, effective June 30, 1999, and applicable to agreements entered on or after November 15, 1998.

§ 143-16.6: Repealed by Session Laws 2006-203, s. 1, effective July 1, 2007, and applicable to the budget for the 2007-2009 biennium and each subsequent biennium thereafter.

§ 143-16.7: Repealed by Session Laws 2006-203, s. 1, effective July 1, 2007, and applicable to the budget for the 2007-2009 biennium and each subsequent biennium thereafter.

§ 143-17: Repealed by Session Laws 2006-203, s. 1, effective July 1, 2007, and applicable to the budget for the 2007-2009 biennium and each subsequent biennium thereafter.

§ 143-18: Repealed by Session Laws 2006-203, s. 1, effective July 1, 2007, and applicable to the budget for the 2007-2009 biennium and each subsequent biennium thereafter.

§ 143-18.1: Repealed by Session Laws 2006-203, s. 1, effective July 1, 2007, and applicable to the budget for the 2007-2009 biennium and each subsequent biennium thereafter.

§ 143-19: Repealed by Session Laws 2006-203, s. 1, effective July 1, 2007, and applicable to the budget for the 2007-2009 biennium and each subsequent biennium thereafter.

§ 143-20: Repealed by Session Laws 2006-203, s. 1, effective July 1, 2007, and applicable to the budget for the 2007-2009 biennium and each subsequent biennium thereafter.

§ 143-20.1: Repealed by Session Laws 2006-203, s. 1, effective July 1, 2007, and applicable to the budget for the 2007-2009 biennium and each subsequent biennium thereafter.

§ 143-21: Repealed by Session Laws 2006-203, s. 1, effective July 1, 2007, and applicable to the budget for the 2007-2009 biennium and each subsequent biennium thereafter.

§ 143-22: Repealed by Session Laws 2006-203, s. 1, effective July 1, 2007, and applicable to the budget for the 2007-2009 biennium and each subsequent biennium thereafter.

§ 143-23: Repealed by Session Laws 2006-203, s. 1, effective July 1, 2007, and applicable to the budget for the 2007-2009 biennium and each subsequent biennium thereafter.

§ 143-23.1. Repealed by Session Laws 1985, c. 290, s. 4, effective July 1, 1985.

§ 143-23.2: Repealed by Session Laws 2006-203, s. 1, effective July 1, 2007, and applicable to the budget for the 2007-2009 biennium and each subsequent biennium thereafter.

§ 143-23.3: Repealed by Session Laws 2006-203, s. 1, effective July 1, 2007, and applicable to the budget for the 2007-2009 biennium and each subsequent biennium thereafter.

§ 143-24: Repealed by Session Laws 2006-203, s. 1, effective July 1, 2007, and applicable to the budget for the 2007-2009 biennium and each subsequent biennium thereafter.

§ 143-25: Repealed by Session Laws 2006-203, s. 1, effective July 1, 2007, and applicable to the budget for the 2007-2009 biennium and each subsequent biennium thereafter.

§ 143-26: Repealed by Session Laws 2006-203, s. 1, effective July 1, 2007, and applicable to the budget for the 2007-2009 biennium and each subsequent biennium thereafter.

§ 143-27: Repealed by Session Laws 2006-203, s. 1, effective July 1, 2007, and applicable to the budget for the 2007-2009 biennium and each subsequent biennium thereafter.

§ 143-27.1. Repealed by Session Laws 1979, 2nd Session, c. 1137, s. 43.

§ 143-27.2. Repealed.

§ 143-28: Repealed by Session Laws 2006-203, s. 1, effective July 1, 2007, and applicable to the budget for the 2007-2009 biennium and each subsequent biennium thereafter.

§ 143-28.1: Repealed by Session Laws 2006-203, s. 1, effective July 1, 2007, and applicable to the budget for the 2007-2009 biennium and each subsequent biennium thereafter.

§ 143-29: Repealed by Session Laws 2006-203, s. 1, effective July 1, 2007, and applicable to the budget for the 2007-2009 biennium and each subsequent biennium thereafter.

§ 143-30: Repealed by Session Laws 2006-203, s. 1, effective July 1, 2007, and applicable to the budget for the 2007-2009 biennium and each subsequent biennium thereafter.

§ 143-31: Repealed by Session Laws 2006-203, s. 1, effective July 1, 2007, and applicable to the budget for the 2007-2009 biennium and each subsequent biennium thereafter.

§ 143-31.1: Repealed by Session Laws 2006-203, s. 1, effective July 1, 2007, and applicable to the budget for the 2007-2009 biennium and each subsequent biennium thereafter.

§ 143-31.2. Repealed.

§ 143-31.3: Repealed by Session Laws 2006-203, s. 1, effective July 1, 2007, and applicable to the budget for the 2007-2009 biennium and each subsequent biennium thereafter.

§ 143-31.4: Repealed by Session Laws 2006-203, s. 1, effective July 1, 2007, and applicable to the budget for the 2007-2009 biennium and each subsequent biennium thereafter.

§ 143-31.5: Repealed by Session Laws 2006-203, s. 1, effective July 1, 2007, and applicable to the budget for the 2007-2009 biennium and each subsequent biennium thereafter.

§ 143-32: Repealed by Session Laws 2006-203, s. 1, effective July 1, 2007, and applicable to the budget for the 2007-2009 biennium and each subsequent biennium thereafter.

§ 143-33: Repealed by Session Laws 2006-203, s. 1, effective July 1, 2007, and applicable to the budget for the 2007-2009 biennium and each subsequent biennium thereafter.

§ 143-34: Repealed by Session Laws 2006-203, s. 1, effective July 1, 2007, and applicable to the budget for the 2007-2009 biennium and each subsequent biennium thereafter.

§ 143-34.1: Repealed by Session Laws 2006-203, s. 1, effective July 1, 2007, and applicable to the budget for the 2007-2009 biennium and each subsequent biennium thereafter.

§ 143-34.2: Repealed by Session Laws 2006-203, s. 1, effective July 1, 2007, and applicable to the budget for the 2007-2009 biennium and each subsequent biennium thereafter.

§ 143-34.3. Repealed by Session Laws 1977, c. 802, s. 15.20.

§ 143-34.4: Repealed.

§ 143-34.5: Repealed by Sessions Laws 1985, c. 479, s. 160.

§ 143-34.6: Repealed by Session Laws 2006-203, s. 1, effective July 1, 2007, and applicable to the budget for the 2007-2009 biennium and each subsequent biennium thereafter.

§ 143-34.7: Repealed by Session Laws 2006-203, s. 1, effective July 1, 2007, and applicable to the budget for the 2007-2009 biennium and each subsequent biennium thereafter.

§ 143-34.8. Repealed.

§ 143-34.9. Repealed.

Article 1A.

Periodic Review of Certain State Agencies.

§ 143-34.10: Repealed by Session Laws 1981, c. 932, s. 1.

§ 143-34.11. Certain General Statutes provisions repealed effective July 1, 1979.

The following statutes are repealed effective July 1, 1979, (except for purposes of the winding-up period, as provided by section 5 of this act):

Chapter 87, Article 3, entitled "Tile Contractors."

Chapter 87, Article 6, entitled "Water Well Contractors."

Chapter 66, Article 9A, entitled "Private Detectives."

Chapter 93C, entitled "Watchmakers."

Chapter 74, Article 6, entitled "Mining Registration." (1977, c. 712, s. 2; 1979, c. 616, s. 9; c. 629; c. 712, s. 6; c. 713, s. 9; c. 736, s. 1; c. 740, s. 1; c. 744, ss. 1-3; c. 750, s. 1; c. 780, s. 3; c. 819, s. 7; c. 834, s. 13; c. 871, s. 2; c. 872, s. 6; c. 904, s. 15.)

§§ 143-34.12 through 143-34.21: Repealed by Session Laws 1981, c. 932, s. 1.

§ 143-34.22. Reserved for future codification purposes.

§ 143-34.23. Reserved for future codification purposes.

§ 143-34.24. Reserved for future codification purposes.

Article 1.2.

Legislative Committee on Agency Review.

§§ 143-34.25 through 143-34.27: Expired.

§§ 143-34.28 through 143-34.39. Reserved for future codification purposes.

Article 1B.

Capital Improvement Planning Act.

§ 143-34.40: Repealed by Session Laws 2006-203, s. 2, effective July 1, 2007, and applicable to the budget for the 2007-2009 biennium and each subsequent biennium thereafter.

§ 143-34.41: Repealed by Session Laws 2006-203, s. 2, effective July 1, 2007, and applicable to the budget for the 2007-2009 biennium and each subsequent biennium thereafter.

§ 143-34.42: Repealed by Session Laws 2006-203, s. 2, effective July 1, 2007, and applicable to the budget for the 2007-2009 biennium and each subsequent biennium thereafter.

§ 143-34.43: Repealed by Session Laws 2006-203, s. 2, effective July 1, 2007, and applicable to the budget for the 2007-2009 biennium and each subsequent biennium thereafter.

§ 143-34.44: Repealed by Session Laws 2006-203, s. 2, effective July 1, 2007, and applicable to the budget for the 2007-2009 biennium and each subsequent biennium thereafter.

§ 143-34.45: Repealed by Session Laws 2006-203, s. 2, effective July 1, 2007, and applicable to the budget for the 2007-2009 biennium and each subsequent biennium thereafter.

Article 2.

State Personnel Department.

§§ 143-35 through 143-47: Repealed by Session Laws 1965, c. 640, s. 1.

Article 2A.

Incentive Award Program for State Employees.

§§ 143-47.1 through 143-47.5: Repealed by Session Laws 1965, c. 640, s. 1.

Article 2B.

Notice of Appointments to Public Offices.

§ 143-47.6. Definitions.

As used in this Article, unless the context clearly requires otherwise:

(1) "Appointing authority" means the Governor, Chief Justice of the Supreme Court, Lieutenant Governor, Speaker of the House, President pro tempore of the Senate, members of the Council of State, all heads of the executive departments of State government, the Board of Governors of The University of North Carolina, and any other person or group authorized by law to appoint to a public office.

(2) "Public office" means appointive membership on any State commission, council, committee, board, including occupational licensing boards as defined in G.S. 93B-1, board of trustees, including boards of constituent institutions of The University of North Carolina and boards of community colleges operated pursuant to Chapter 115D of the General Statutes, and any other State agency created by law, where the appointee is entitled to draw subsistence, per diem compensation, or travel allowances, in whole or in part from funds deposited with the State Treasurer or any other funds subject to being audited by the State Auditor, by reason of his service in the public office; provided that "public office" does not include an office for which a regular salary is paid to the holder as an employee of the State or of one of its departments, agencies, or institutions. (1979, c. 477, s. 1; 1987, c. 564, s. 27.)

§ 143-47.7. Notice and record of appointment required.

(a)   Within 30 days after acceptance of appointment by a person appointed to public office, the appointing authority shall file written notice of the appointment with the Governor, the Secretary of State, the Legislative Library, the State Library, the State Ethics Commission, and the State Controller. For the purposes of this section, a copy of the letter from the appointing authority, a copy of the properly executed notice of appointment as set forth in subsection (c) of this section, or a copy of the properly executed Commission of Appointment shall be sufficient to be filed if the copy contains the information required in subsection (b) of this section.

(b)   The notice required by this Article shall contain the following information:

(1)   The name and office of the appointing authority;

(2)   The public office to which the appointment is made;

(3)   The name and address of the appointee;

(4)   The county of residence of the appointee;

(5)   The citation to the law or other authority authorizing the appointment;

(6)   The specific statutory qualification for the public office to which the appointment is made, if applicable;

(7)   The name of the person the appointee replaces, if applicable;

(8)   The date the term of the appointment begins; and

(9)   The date the term of the appointment ends.

(c)   The following form may be used to comply with the requirements of this section:

"NOTICE OF APPOINTMENT

Notice is given that _____ is hereby appointed to the following

        Name

public office:

Public Office:
_____

Citation to Law or Other Authority Authorizing the Appointment:
_____

Specific Statutory Qualification for the Public Office, if Applicable:
_____

Address of the Appointee:
_____

_____

_____

County of Residence of the Appointee:
_____

Date Term of Appointment Begins:
_____

Date Term of Appointment Ends:
_____

Name of Person the Appointee Replaces, if applicable:
_____

_____   _____

Date of Appointment   Signature

_____

Office of Appointing Authority

Distribution:

Governor

Secretary of State

Legislative Library

State Library

State Ethics Commission

State Controller" (1979, c. 477, s. 1; 1991, c. 542, s. 8; 2003-374, s. 2; 2009-549, s. 18.)

§ 143-47.8: Repealed by Session Laws 2003-374, s. 3, effective August 31, 2003.

§ 143-47.9. Subsistence, per diem compensation, and travel allowances conditioned on filing of notice.

No person who has been appointed to any public office and has accepted that appointment shall be entitled to receive subsistence, per diem compensation, or travel allowances unless and until compliance is made with the provisions of G.S. 143-47.7. (1979, c. 477, s. 1.)

§§ 143-47.10 through 143-47.14. Reserved for future codification purposes.

Article 2C.

Limit on Number of State Employees.

§§ 143-47.15 through 143-47.20: Repealed by Session Laws 1989, c. 752, s. 45.

Article 2D.

North Carolina Board for Need-Based Student Loans.

§§ 143-47.21 through 143-47.24: Repealed by Session Laws 1987, c. 738, s. 41(c).

Article 3.

Purchases and Contracts.

§ 143-48. State policy; cooperation in promoting the use of small contractors, minority contractors, physically handicapped contractors, and women contractors; purpose; required annual reports.

(a)   Policy. - It is the policy of this State to encourage and promote the use of small contractors, minority contractors, physically handicapped contractors, and women contractors in State purchasing of goods and services. All State agencies, institutions and political subdivisions shall cooperate with the Department of Administration and all other State agencies, institutions and political subdivisions in efforts to encourage the use of small contractors, minority contractors, physically handicapped contractors, and women contractors in achieving the purpose of this Article, which is to provide for the effective and economical acquisition, management and disposition of goods and services by and through the Department of Administration.

(b)   Reporting. - Every governmental entity required by statute to use the services of the Department of Administration in the purchase of goods and services, every local school administrative unit, and every private, nonprofit corporation other than an institution of higher education or a hospital that receives an appropriation of five hundred thousand dollars ($500,000) or more during a fiscal year from the General Assembly shall report to the department of Administration annually on what percentage of its contract purchases of goods and services, through term contracts and open-market contracts, were from minority-owned businesses, what percentage from female-owned businesses, what percentage from disabled-owned businesses, what percentage from disabled business enterprises and what percentage from nonprofit work centers for the blind and the severely disabled. The same governmental entities shall include in their reports what percentages of the contract bids for such purchases were from such businesses. The Department of Administration shall provide instructions to the reporting entities concerning the manner of reporting and the definitions of the businesses referred to in this act, provided that, for the purposes of this act:

(1)   Except as provided in subdivision (1a) of this subsection, a business in one of the categories above means one:

a.   In which at least fifty-one percent (51%) of the business, or of the stock in the case of a corporation, is owned by one or more persons in the category; and

b.   Of which the management and daily business operations are controlled by one or more persons in the category who own it.

(1a)   A "disabled business enterprise" means a nonprofit entity whose main purpose is to provide ongoing habilitation, rehabilitation, independent living, and competitive employment for persons who are handicapped through supported employment sites or business operated to provide training and employment and competitive wages.

(1b)   A "nonprofit work center for the blind and the severely disabled" means an agency:

a.   Organized under the laws of the United States or this State, operated in the interest of the blind and the severely disabled, the net income of which agency does not inure in whole or in part to the benefit of any shareholder or other individual;

b.   In compliance with any applicable health and safety standard prescribed by the United States Secretary of Labor; and

c.   In the production of all commodities or provision of services, employs during the current fiscal year severely handicapped individuals for (i) a minimum of seventy-five percent (75%) of the hours of direct labor required for the production of commodities or provision of services, or (ii) in accordance with the percentage of direct labor required under the terms and conditions of Public Law 92-28 (41 U.S.C. § 46, et seq.) for the production of commodities or provision of services, whichever is less.

(2) A female or a disabled person is not a minority, unless the female or disabled person is also a member of one of the minority groups described in G.S. 143-128(2)a. through d.

(3) A disabled person means a person with a handicapping condition as defined in G.S. 168-1 or G.S. 168A-3.

(c) The Department of Administration shall compile information on small and medium-sized business participation in State contracts subject to this Article and report the information as provided in subsection (d) of this section. The report shall analyze (i) contract awards by business size category, (ii) historical trends in small and medium-sized business participation in these contracts, and (iii) to the extent feasible, participation by small and medium-sized businesses in the State procurement process as dealers, service companies, and other indirect forms of participation. The Department may require reports on contracting by business size in the same manner as reports are required under subsection (b) of this section.

(d) The Department of Administration shall collect and compile the data described in this section and report it annually to the General Assembly.

(d1) Repealed by Session Laws 2007-392, s. 1, effective October 1, 2007.

(e) In seeking contracts with the State, a disabled business enterprise must provide assurances to the Secretary of Administration that the payments that would be received from the State under these contracts are directed to the training and employment of and payment of competitive wages to handicapped employees. (1931, c. 261, s. 1; c. 396; 1957, c. 269, s. 3; 1971, c. 587, s. 1; 1975, c. 879, s. 46; 1983, c. 692, s. 2; 1989 (Reg. Sess., 1990), c. 1051, s. 1; 1993, c. 252, s. 1; 1995, c. 265, s. 2; 1999-20, s. 1; 1999-407, s. 1; 2003-147, s. 6; 2004-203, s. 72(b); 2005-270, s. 1; 2007-392, s. 1.)

§ 143-48.1. Medicaid program exemption.

(a) This Article shall not apply to any capitation arrangement or prepaid health service arrangement implemented or administered by the North Carolina Department of Health and Human Services or its delegates pursuant to the Medicaid waiver provisions of 42 U.S.C. § 1396n, or to the Medicaid program authorizations under Chapter 108A of the General Statutes.

(b) As used in this section, the following definitions apply:

(1) "Capitation arrangement" means an agreement whereby the Department of Health and Human Services pays a periodic per enrollee fee to a contract entity that provides medical services to Medicaid recipients during their enrollment period.

(2) "Prepaid health services" means services provided to Medicaid recipients that are paid on the basis of a prepaid capitation fee, pursuant to an agreement between the Department of Health and Human Services and a contract entity.

(c) The Department of Health and Human Services shall: (i) submit all proposed contracts for a capitation arrangement or prepaid health services, as defined by this section, that exceed one million dollars ($1,000,000) to the Attorney General or the Attorney General's designee for review as provided in G.S. 114-8.3; and (ii) include in all agreements or contracts to be awarded by the Department under this section a standard clause which provides that the State Auditor and internal auditors of the Department may audit the records of the contractor during and after the term of the contract to verify accounts and data affecting fees and performance. The Department shall not award a cost plus percentage of cost agreement or contract for any purpose. (1993, c. 529, s. 7.4; 1997-443, s. 11A.118(a); 2010-194, s. 20.2; 2011-326, s. 15(v).)

§ 143-48.2. Procurement program for nonprofit work centers for the blind and the severely disabled.

(a) An agency subject to the provisions of this Article for the procurement of goods may purchase goods directly from a nonprofit work center for the blind and severely disabled, subject to the following provisions:

(1) The purchase may not exceed the applicable expenditure benchmark under G.S. 143-53.1.

(2) The goods must not be available under a State requirements contract.

(3) The goods must be of suitable price and quality, as determined by the agency.

(b) An agency subject to the provisions of this Article for the procurement of services may purchase services directly from a nonprofit work center for the blind and severely disabled, subject to the following provisions:

(1) The services must not be available under a State requirements contract.

(2) The services must be of suitable price and quality, as determined by the agency.

(c) The provisions of G.S. 143-52 shall not apply to purchases made pursuant to this section. However, nothing in this section shall prohibit a nonprofit work center for the blind and severely disabled from submitting bids or making offers for contracts under G.S. 143-52.

(d) For the purpose of this subsection, a "nonprofit work center for the blind and severely disabled" has the same meaning as under G.S. 143-48. (1995, c. 265, s. 3; 1999-20, s. 1.)

§ 143-48.3. Electronic procurement.

(a) The Department of Administration shall develop and maintain electronic or digital standards for procurement. The Department of Administration shall consult with the Office of the State Controller, the Office of Information Technology Services (ITS), the Department of State Auditor, the Department of State Treasurer, The University of North Carolina General Administration, the Community Colleges System Office, and the Department of Public Instruction.

(a1) The Department of Administration shall comply with the State government-wide technical architecture for information technology, as required by the State Chief Information Officer.

(b) The Department of Administration, in conjunction with the Office of the State Controller and the Office of Information Technology Services may, upon request, provide to all State agencies, universities, and community colleges, training in the use of the electronic procurement system.

(c) The Department of Administration shall utilize the Office of Information Technology Services as an Application Service Provider for an electronic procurement system. The Office of Information Technology Services shall operate this electronic procurement system, through State ownership or commercial leasing, in accordance with the requirements and operating standards developed by the Department of Administration and the financial reporting and accounting procedures of the Office of the State Controller.

(d) This section does not otherwise modify existing law relating to procurement between The University of North Carolina, UNC Health Care, community colleges, and the Department of Administration.

(e) The Board of Governors of The University of North Carolina shall exempt North Carolina State University and The University of North Carolina at Chapel Hill from the electronic procurement system authorized by this Article until May 1, 2003. Each exemption shall be subject to the Board of Governors' annual review and reconsideration. Exempted constituent institutions shall continue working with the North Carolina E-Procurement Service as that system evolves and shall ensure that their proposed procurement systems are compatible with the North Carolina E-Procurement Service so that they may take advantage of this service to the greatest degree possible. Before an exempted institution expands any electronic procurement system, that institution shall consult with the Joint Legislative Commission on Governmental Operations and the Joint Legislative Oversight Committee on Information Technology. By May 1, 2003, the General Assembly shall evaluate the efficacy of the State's electronic procurement system and the inclusion and participation of entities in the system.

(f) Any State entity or community college operating a functional electronic procurement system established prior to September 1, 2001, may until May 1, 2003, continue to operate that system independently or may opt into the North Carolina E-Procurement Service. Each entity subject to this section shall notify the Office of Information Technology Services by January 1 of each year of its intent to participate in the North Carolina E-Procurement Service. (2000-67, s. 7.8; 2000-140, ss. 95(a), 95(b); 2001-424, s. 15.6(b); 2001-513, s. 28(a); 2002-126, ss. 27.1(a), 27.1(b), 27.1(c); 2003-147, s. 7; 2004-129, ss. 40, 40A, 41; 2004-203, s. 72(b).)

§ 143-48.4. Statewide uniform certification of historically underutilized businesses.

(a)   In addition to the powers and duties provided in G.S. 143-49, the Secretary of Administration shall have the power, authority, and duty to:

(1)   Develop and administer a statewide uniform program for: (i) the certification of a historically underutilized business, as defined in G.S. 143-128.4, for use by State departments, agencies, and institutions, and political subdivisions of the State; and (ii) the creation and maintenance of a database of the businesses certified as historically underutilized businesses.

(2)   Adopt rules and procedures for statewide uniform certification of historically underutilized businesses.

(3)   Provide for the certification of all businesses designated as historically underutilized businesses to be used by State departments, agencies, and institutions, and political subdivisions of the State.

(b)   The Secretary of Administration shall seek input from State departments, agencies, and institutions, political subdivisions of the State, and any other entity deemed appropriate to determine the qualifications and criteria for statewide uniform certification of historically underutilized businesses.

(c)   Only businesses certified in accordance with this section shall be considered by State departments, agencies, and institutions, and political subdivisions of the State as historically underutilized businesses for minority business participation purposes under this Chapter. (2007-392, s. 2; 2009-243, s. 2.)

§ 143-48.5. Contractors must use E-Verify.

No contract subject to the provisions of this Article may be entered into unless the contractor and the contractor's subcontractors comply with the requirements of Article 2 of Chapter 64 of the General Statutes. (2013-418, s. 2(d).)

§ 143-49. Powers and duties of Secretary.

The Secretary of Administration has the power and authority, and it is the Secretary's duty, subject to the provisions of this Article:

(1) To canvass sources of supply, including sources of goods with recycled content, and to purchase or to contract for the purchase, lease and lease-purchase of all goods required by the State government, or any of its departments, institutions or agencies under competitive bidding or other suitable means authorized by the Secretary including, without limitation, negotiations, reverse auctions, a best value procurement method such as that defined in G.S. 143-135.9(a)(1), and the solicitation, offer, and acceptance of electronic bids. For purposes of this Article, the term "goods" includes, without limitation, all commodities, supplies, materials, equipment, and other tangible personal property.

(2) To establish and enforce specifications which shall apply to all goods and services to be purchased or leased for the use of the State government or any of its departments, institutions or agencies.

(3) To purchase or to contract for, by sealed, competitive bidding or other suitable means authorized by the Secretary including, without limitation, negotiations, reverse auctions, a best value procurement method such as that defined in G.S. 143-135.9(a)(1), and the solicitation, offer, and acceptance of electronic bids, all services of the State government, or any of its departments, institutions, or agencies; or to authorize any department, institution or agency to purchase or contract for such services.

(3a) To notify the Attorney General of pending contracts for contractual services exceeding a cost of five million dollars ($5,000,000) and that are not otherwise excepted by this subdivision. Upon notification, the Attorney General shall assign a representative from within the office of the Attorney General, the Contract Management Section of the Division of Purchase and Contract, Department of Administration, or other qualified counsel to assist in negotiation for the award of the contract. It is the duty of the representative to assist and advise in obtaining the most favorable contract for the State, to evaluate all proposals available from prospective contractors for that purpose, to interpret proposed contract terms and to advise the Secretary or his representatives of the liabilities of the State and validity of the contract to be awarded. An attorney from within the office of the Attorney General shall review all contracts and drafts of contracts, and the office shall retain copies for a period of three years following the termination of the contracts. The term "contractual services" as used in this subsection and G.S. 143-52.2 means work performed by an independent contractor requiring specialized knowledge, experience, expertise or similar capabilities wherein the service rendered does not consist primarily of acquisition by this State of equipment or materials and the rental of equipment, materials and supplies. This subdivision does not apply to contracts entered into or to be entered into as a result of a competitive bidding process. In order to be valid, a ny contract for services reviewed pursuant to this subdivision must include the signature and title of the attorney designated from within the office of the Attorney General to review the contract. If the contract commences without the required signature, the State has the right to terminate the contract, and the other party or parties to the contract shall only be entitled to the value of all services provided to the State prior to the termination. The Secretary is not required to notify the Attorney General for the appointment of a representative for any contracts for contractual services to be entered into by the constituent institutions of The University of North Carolina pursuant to G.S. 114-8.3(b), or for contracts to be entered into by the Department of Treasurer pursuant to G.S. 114-8.3(b1), unless requested to do so by the General Counsel of The University of North Carolina or the General Counsel of the Department of State Treasurer, respectively.

(4)   To have general supervision of all storerooms and stores operated by the State government, or any of its departments, institutions or agencies and to have supervision of inventories of all tangible personal property belonging to the State government, or any of its departments, institutions or agencies. The duties imposed by this subdivision shall not relieve any department, institution or agency of the State government from accountability for equipment, materials, supplies and tangible personal property under its control.

(5)   To make provision for or to contract for all State printing, including all printing, binding, paper stock, recycled paper stock, supplies, and supplies with recycled content, or materials in connection with the same.

(6)   To make available to nonprofit corporations operating charitable hospitals, to local nonprofit community sheltered workshops or centers that meet standards established by the Division of Vocational Rehabilitation of the Department of Health and Human Services, to private nonprofit agencies licensed or approved by the Department of Health and Human Services as child placing agencies, residential child-care facilities, private nonprofit rural, community, and migrant health centers designated by the Office of Rural Health and Resource Development, to private higher education institutions that are described as nonprofit postsecondary educational institutions in G.S. 116-280 and to counties, cities, towns, local school administrative units, governmental

entities and other subdivisions of the State and public agencies thereof in the expenditure of public funds, the services of the Department of Administration in the purchase of goods and services under such rules, regulations and procedures as the Secretary of Administration may adopt. In adopting rules and regulations any or all provisions of this Article may be made applicable to such purchases and contracts made through the Department of Administration, and in addition the rules and regulations shall contain a requirement that payment for all such purchases be made in accordance with the terms of the contract.

(7)   To evaluate the nonprofit qualifications and capabilities of qualified work centers to manufacture commodities or perform services.

(8)   To establish and maintain a procurement card program for use by State agencies, community colleges, and nonexempted constituent institutions of The University of North Carolina. The Secretary of Administration may adopt temporary rules for the implementation and operation of the program in accordance with the payment policies of the State Controller, after consultation with the Office of Information Technology Services. These rules would include the establishment of appropriate order limits that leverage the cost savings and efficiencies of the procurement card program in conjunction with the fullest possible use of the North Carolina E-Procurement Service. Prior to implementing the program, the Secretary shall consult with the State Controller, the UNC General Administration, the Community Colleges System Office, the State Auditor, the Department of Public Instruction, a representative chosen by the local school administrative units, and the Office of Information Technology Services. The Secretary may periodically adjust the order limit authorized in this section after consulting with the State Controller, the UNC General Administration, the Community Colleges System Office, the Department of Public Instruction, and the Office of Information Technology Services.

(9)   To include a standard clause in all contracts awarded by the State and departments, agencies, and institutions of the State, providing that the State Auditor and internal auditors of the affected department, agency, or institution may audit the records of the contactor during and after the term of the contract to verify accounts and data affecting fees or performance.

(10)   To monitor and enforce the terms and conditions of statewide term contracts. The Secretary of Administration shall not delegate the power and authority granted under this subdivision to any other department, agency, or institution of the State.

(11) To develop rules, regulations, and procedures specifying the manner in which departments, agencies, and institutions of the State shall monitor and enforce agency term and non-term contracts.

(12) To consult with the Attorney General or the Attorney General's designee in developing rules, regulations, and procedures providing for the orderly and efficient submission of proposed contracts to the Attorney General for review as provided in G.S. 114-8.3 and G.S. 143-52.2.

(13) Repealed by Session Laws 2013-234, s. 2, effective October 1, 2013, and applicable to contracts entered into on or after that date.

(14) To work in conjunction with the Office of State Human Resources to create a Contracting Specialist career path to provide for the designation of one or more employees within each department, agency, or institution of the State to serve as the Contracting Specialist for the department, agency, or institution. Employees on the Contracting Specialist career path shall receive training and guidance as to the provisions of this Article.

(15) To work in conjunction with the Office of State Human Resources, the Division of Purchase and Contract, and the University of North Carolina School of Government to develop a rigorous contract management training and certification program for State employees. The program shall be administered by the Office of State Human Resources.

(16) To work in conjunction with the University of North Carolina School of Government to study and recommend improvements to State procurement laws, including the feasibility of adopting the provisions of the American Bar Association Model Procurement Code. The recommendations shall be reported by the Secretary to the Joint Legislative Commission on Governmental Operations and the Program Evaluation Division by June 30, 2014.

(17) To establish procedures to permit State government, or any of its departments, institutions, or agencies, to join with any federal, State, or local government agency, entity, or subdivision, or any nonprofit organization in cooperative purchasing plans, projects, arrangements, or agreements if the interest of the State would be served thereby. (1931, c. 261, s. 2; 1951, c. 3, s. 1; c. 1127, s. 1; 1957, c. 269, s. 3; 1961, c. 310; 1971, c. 587, s. 1; 1975, c. 580; c. 879, s. 46; 1977, c. 733; 1979, c. 759, s. 1; 1983, c. 717, ss. 60, 62; 1985 (Reg. Sess., 1986), c. 955, ss. 79-82; 1989, c. 408; 1991, c. 358, s. 1; 1993, c. 256, s. 1; 1995, c. 265, ss. 1, 5; 1996, 2nd Ex. Sess., c. 18, s. 24.17; 1997-443,

s. 11A.118(a); 1999-20, s. 1; 2000-67, s. 10.9(a); 2001-424, s. 15.6(a); 2001-424, s. 15.6(d); 2001-513, s. 28(b); 2003-147, s. 8; 2004-203, s. 72(b); 2005-213, s. 2; 2006-203, s. 82; 2010-194, s. 21; 2011-145, s. 9.18(h); 2011-326, s. 15(w); 2011-338, s. 1; 2013-234, s. 2; 2013-382, s. 9.1(c).)

§ 143-49.1. Purchases by volunteer nonprofit fire department and lifesaving and rescue squad.

In consideration of public service, any volunteer nonprofit fire department, lifesaving and rescue squad in this State may purchase gas, oil, and tires for their official vehicles and any other materials and supplies under State contract through the Department of Administration, and may purchase surplus property through the Department of Administration on the same basis applicable to counties and municipalities.

The Department of Administration shall make its services available to these organizations in the purchase of such supplies under the same laws, rules and regulations applicable to nonprofit organizations as provided in G.S. 143-49. (1973, c. 442; 1991, c. 199.)

§ 143-50. Certain contractual powers exercised by other departments transferred to Secretary.

All rights, powers, duties and authority relating to State printing, or to the acquisition of supplies, materials, equipment, and contractual services, now imposed upon or exercised by any State department, institution or agency under the several statutes relating thereto, are hereby transferred to the Secretary of Administration and all said rights, powers, duty and authority are hereby imposed upon and shall hereafter be exercised by the Secretary of Administration under the provisions of this Article. (1931, c. 261, s. 3; 1957, c. 269, s. 3; 1971, c. 587, s. 1; 1975, c. 879, s. 46.)

§ 143-50.1. Division of Purchase and Contract; Contract Management Section.

(a) The Contract Management Section (CMS) is established in the Division of Purchase and Contract, Department of Administration. The CMS shall include legal counsel with the duties and responsibilities included in this section.

(b) Unless otherwise provided in G.S. 114-8.3(b) or (b1), or in this section, for all proposed solicitations for supplies, materials, printing, equipment, or contractual services that exceed one million dollars ($1,000,000), the CMS shall:

(1) Participate and assist in the preparation of all proposed solicitations, and review all available proposals from prospective contractors, with the goal of obtaining the most favorable contract for the State.

(2) Interpret proposed contract terms and advise the Secretary or the Secretary's designee of the potential liabilities to the State.

(3) Review all proposed contracts to ensure that the contracts:

a. Are in proper legal form.

b. Contain all clauses required by law.

c. Are legally enforceable.

d. Require performance that will accomplish the intended purposes of the proposed contract.

The review and evaluation required by this subsection does not constitute approval or disapproval of the policy merit or lack thereof of the proposed contract.

(c) With respect to proposed contracts for services that exceed five million dollars ($5,000,000), the CMS shall perform the duties required under G.S. 143-49(3a).

(d) The CMS shall:

(1) Assist State departments, agencies, and institutions to establish formal contract administration procedures and functions.

(2) Advise personnel in contracting specialist roles as to appropriate contract management and administrative techniques and activities.

(3) Act as a general resource to State agencies on contracting issues related to procurement, including contract drafting, clarification of terms and conditions, proper solicitation and bid evaluation procedures, contract negotiation, and other matters as directed by the State Purchasing Officer.

(4) Assist representatives of the Attorney General, agency counsel, and other legal staff, as requested, in matters related to contracting for goods and services.

(e) The Department of Administration shall adopt procedures for the record keeping of the information provided by State agencies and that has been received by the Secretary or the Secretary's designee pursuant to G.S. 114-8.3(c). The Department shall keep the records, and shall include a log with information that provides identification of individual contracts and where the contract documents are located. The Secretary is authorized to require that entities reporting pursuant to G.S. 114-8.39(c) provide additional information that may be required to identify the individual contracts.

(f) The CMS shall consist of personnel designated by the Secretary and perform other functions as directed by the Secretary that are not inconsistent with this section. (2013-234, s. 3.)

§ 143-51. Reports to Secretary required of all agencies as to needs and purchases.

(a) It shall be the duty of all departments, institutions, or agencies of the State government to furnish to the Secretary of Administration when requested, and on forms to be prescribed by him, estimates of all goods and services needed and required by such department, institution or agency for such periods in advance as may be designated by the Secretary of Administration.

(b) In addition to the report required by subsection (a) of this section, all departments, institutions, or agencies of the State government shall furnish to the Secretary of Administration when requested, and on forms to be prescribed by him, actual expenditures for all goods and services needed and required by the department, institution, or agency for such periods after the expenditures have been made as may be designated by the Secretary of Administration. (1931, c. 261, s. 4; 1957, c. 269, s. 3; 1971, c. 587, s. 1; 1975, c. 879, s. 46; 1981, c. 602, s. 1; 2011-338, s. 2.)

§ 143-52. Competitive bidding procedure; consolidation of estimates by Secretary; bids; awarding of contracts; cost plus percentage of cost contracts strictly prohibited.

(a) The Secretary of Administration shall compile and consolidate all estimates of goods and services needed and required by State departments, institutions and agencies to determine the total requirements of any given commodity. Where the total requirements will involve an expenditure in excess of the expenditure benchmark established under the provisions of G.S. 143-53.1 and where the competitive bidding procedure is employed as hereinafter provided, sealed bids shall be solicited by advertisement in a newspaper widely distributed in this State or through electronic means, or both, as determined by the Secretary to be most advantageous, at least once and at least 10 days prior to the date designated for opening. Except as otherwise provided under this Article, contracts for the purchase of goods and services shall be based on competitive bids and suitable means authorized by the Secretary as provided in G.S. 143-49. The acceptance of bid(s) most advantageous to the State shall be determined upon consideration of the following criteria: prices offered; best value, as the term is defined in G.S. 143-135.9(a)(1); the quality of the articles offered; the general reputation and performance capabilities of the bidders; the substantial conformity with the specifications and other conditions set forth in the request for bids; the suitability of the articles for the intended use; the personal or related services needed; the transportation charges; the date or dates of delivery and performance; and such other factor(s) deemed pertinent or peculiar to the purchase in question, which if controlling shall be made a matter of record. Competitive bids on contracts shall be received in accordance with rules and regulations to be adopted by the Secretary of Administration, which rules and regulations shall prescribe for the manner, time and place for proper advertisement for such bids, the time and place when bids will be received, the articles for which such bids are to be submitted and the specifications prescribed for the articles, the number of the articles desired or the duration of the proposed contract, and the amount, if any, of bonds or certified checks to accompany the bids. Bids shall be publicly opened. Any and all bids received may be rejected. Each and every bid conforming to the terms of the invitation, together with the name of the bidder, shall be tabulated and that tabulation shall become public record in accordance with the rules adopted by the Secretary. All contract information shall be made a matter of public record after the award of contract. Provided, that trade secrets, test data and similar proprietary information may remain confidential. A bond for the faithful performance of any contract may be required of the successful bidder at bidder's expense and in the discretion of the Secretary of Administration. When the dollar value of a contract for the purchase, lease, or lease/purchase of goods exceeds the benchmark established by G.S. 143-53.1, the contract shall be reviewed by the State Purchasing Officer pursuant to G.S. 143-52.1 prior to the contract being awarded. After contracts have been awarded, the Secretary of Administration shall certify to the departments, institutions and agencies of the State government the sources of supply and the contract price of the goods so contracted for.

(b)   Expired.

(c)   Neither the Department of Administration nor any department, agency, or institution of the State may award a cost plus percentage of cost contract for any purpose, except as provided in G.S. 18C-150. (1931, c. 261, s. 5; 1933, c. 441, s. 1; 1957, c. 269, s. 3; 1971, c. 587, s. 1; 1975, c. 879, s. 46; 1981, c. 602, ss. 2, 3; 1983, c. 717, s. 61; 1985 (Reg. Sess., 1986), c. 955, ss. 83-86; 1989 (Reg. Sess., 1990), c. 936, s. 3(a); 1997-412, s. 2; 1999-434, s. 12; 2006-203, s. 83; 2009-475, s. 1; 2010-194, s. 22; 2011-338, s. 3; 2013-234, s. 8.)

§ 143-52.1. Award recommendations; State Purchasing Officer action.

(a)   Award Recommendation. - When the dollar value of a contract to be awarded under Article 3 of Chapter 143 of the General Statutes exceeds the benchmark established pursuant to G.S. 143-53.1, an award recommendation shall be submitted to the State Purchasing Officer for approval or other action. The State Purchasing Officer shall promptly notify the agency or institution making the recommendation, or for which the purchase is to be made, of the action taken.

(b)   through (d) Repealed by Session Laws 2013-234, s. 4, effective July 3, 2013.

(e)   Reporting. - The State Procurement Officer shall provide a monthly report of all contract awards greater than twenty-five thousand dollars ($25,000) approved through the Division of Purchase and Contract to the Cochairs of the Joint Legislative Committee on Governmental Operations. The report shall include the amount of the award, the award recipient, the using agency, and a short description of the nature of the award. (1999-434, s. 13; 2001-487, s. 21(e); 2004-129, s. 41A; 2013-234, s. 4.)

§ 143-52.2. Certain contracts subject to review by Attorney General.

The Secretary of Administration and every department, agency, and institution of the State shall submit all proposed contracts for supplies, materials, printing, equipment, and contractual services that exceed one million dollars ($1,000,000) to the Attorney General or the Attorney General's designee for review as provided in G.S. 114-8.3(a). This section shall not apply to the constituent institutions of The University of North Carolina. (2010-194, s. 23; 2011-326, s. 15(x).)

§ 143-52.3. Multiple award schedule contracts.

(a)   Definitions. - The following definitions apply in this section:

(1)   Communications equipment. - Mobile communications systems, desktop communications systems, base and repeater communications systems, gateway devices, audio switch units, radio routers, microwave radios, microwave antennae, Ethernet switches, wireless access points, or equivalent products and attachments.

(2)   Construction equipment. - Excavators, wheel excavators, track loaders, compact track loaders, wheel loaders, skid steer loaders, backhoe loaders, crawler dozers, crawler loaders, wheel dozers, motor graders, utility cranes, compactors, and appropriate attachments, or equivalent products and attachments.

(3)   Forestry equipment. - Feller bunchers, knuckleboom loaders, forestry swing machines, harvesters, and appropriate attachments, or equivalent products and attachments.

(4) Ground maintenance equipment. - Hand-held equipment, walk-behind products, lawn tractors, lawn and garden tractors, commercial walk-behind mowers, zero turn radius mowers, front mowers, compact utility tractors, utility tractors, utility vehicles, golf and turf equipment, agricultural tractors and implements, and appropriate attachments, or equivalent products and attachments.

(5) Multiple award schedule contract. - A contract that allows multiple vendors to be awarded a State contract for goods or services by providing their total catalogues for lines of equipment and attachments to eligible purchasers, including State agencies, departments, institutions, public school districts, political subdivisions, community colleges, and constituent institutions of The University of North Carolina.

(b) Intent. - The intent of multiple award schedule contracts is to evaluate vendors based upon a variety of factors, including discounts, total lifecycle costs, service, warranty, distribution channel, and past vendor performance. Multiple award schedule contracts allow multiple vendors to compete and be awarded a contract based upon the value of their products or services and result in competitive pricing, transparency, administrative savings, expedited procurement, and flexibility for State purchasers.

(c) Multiple Award Schedule Contracts Required. - The acquisition of ground maintenance equipment, construction equipment, communications equipment, and forestry equipment shall be conducted using multiple award schedule contracts, except as provided in this section. Not later than August 31, 2011, the Department of Administration shall issue requests for proposals for multiple award schedule contracts for all ground maintenance equipment product categories, construction equipment product categories, communications equipment product categories, and forestry equipment product categories. Contracts awarded under this subsection shall be for a term of not less than three years with annual product and pricing update periods.

(d) Limitation. - Any contract awarded under subsection (c) of this section shall be in addition to any existing term contracts for ground maintenance equipment, construction equipment, communications equipment, and forestry equipment. Nothing in this section shall limit the ability of the Department of Administration to issue additional term contracts for the specific purchase of equipment otherwise available through a multiple award schedule contract. The Department of Public Safety shall not be required to purchase from contracts awarded under subsection (c) of this section for communications equipment. (2011-145, s. 19.1(g); 2011-360, s. 1.)

§ 143-53. Rules.

(a) The Secretary of Administration may adopt rules governing the following:

(1) Prescribing the routine and procedures to be followed in canvassing bids and awarding contracts, and for reviewing decisions made pursuant thereto, and the decision of the reviewing body shall be the final administrative review. The Division of Purchase and Contract shall review and decide a protest on a contract valued at twenty-five thousand dollars ($25,000) or more. The Secretary shall adopt rules or criteria governing the review of and decision on a protest on a contract of less than twenty-five thousand dollars ($25,000) by the agency that awarded the contract.

(2) (See Editor's note) Prescribing the routine, including consistent contract language, for securing bids on items that do not exceed the bid value benchmark established under the provisions of G.S. 143-53.1, 115D-58.14, or 116-31.10. The bid value benchmark for securing offers for each State department, institution, and agency established under the provisions of G.S. 143-53.1 shall be determined by the Director of the Division of Purchase and Contract following the Director's consultation with the State Budget Officer and the State Auditor. The Director for the Division of Purchase and Contract may set or lower the benchmark, or raise the benchmark upon written request by the agency, after consideration of their overall capabilities, including staff resources, purchasing compliance reviews, and audit reports of the individual agency. The routine prescribed by the Secretary shall include contract award protest procedures and consistent requirements for advertising of solicitations for securing offers issued by State departments, institutions, universities (including the special responsibility constituent institutions of The University of North Carolina), agencies, community colleges, and the public school administrative units.

(3) Repealed by Session Laws 2011-338, s. 4, effective July 1, 2011.

(4) Prescribing items and quantities, and conditions and procedures, governing the acquisition of goods and services which may be delegated to

departments, institutions and agencies, notwithstanding any other provisions of this Article.

(5) Prescribing conditions under which purchases and contracts for the purchase, installment or lease-purchase, rental or lease of goods and services may be entered into by means other than competitive bidding, including, but not limited to, negotiation, reverse auctions, and acceptance of electronic bids. Notwithstanding the provisions of subsections (a) and (b) of this section, any waiver of competition for the purchase, rental, or lease of goods and services is subject to prior review by the Secretary, if the expenditure exceeds ten thousand dollars ($10,000). The Division may levy a fee, not to exceed one dollar ($1.00), for review of each waiver application.

(6) Prescribing conditions under which partial, progressive and multiple awards may be made.

(7) Prescribing conditions and procedures governing the purchase of used goods.

(8) Providing conditions under which bids may be rejected in whole or in part.

(9) Prescribing conditions under which information submitted by bidders or suppliers may be considered proprietary or confidential.

(10) Prescribing procedures for making purchases under programs involving participation by two or more levels or agencies of government, or otherwise with funds other than State-appropriated.

(11) Prescribing procedures to encourage the purchase of North Carolina farm products, and products of North Carolina manufacturing enterprises.

(12) Repealed by Session Laws 1987, c. 827, s. 216.

(b) In adopting the rules authorized by subsection (a) of this section, the Secretary shall include special provisions for the purchase of goods and services, which provisions are necessary to meet the documented training, work, or independent living needs of persons with disabilities according to the requirements of the Rehabilitation Act of 1973, as amended, and the Americans with Disabilities Act, as amended. The Secretary may consult with other agencies having expertise in meeting the needs of individuals with disabilities in developing these provisions. These special provisions shall establish purchasing procedures that:

(1) Provide for the involvement of the individual in the choice of particular goods, service providers, and in the methods used to provide the goods and services;

(2) Provide the flexibility necessary to meet those varying needs of individuals that are related to their disabilities;

(3) Allow for purchase outside of certified sources of supply and competitive bidding when a single source can provide multiple pieces of equipment, including adaptive equipment, that are more compatible with each other than they would be if they were purchased from multiple vendors;

(4) Permit priority consideration for vendors who have the expertise to provide appropriate and necessary training for the users of the equipment and who will guarantee prompt service, ongoing support, and maintenance of this equipment;

(5) Permit agencies to give priority consideration to suppliers offering the earliest possible delivery date of goods or services especially when a time factor is crucial to the individual's ability to secure a job, meet the probationary training periods of employment, continue to meet job requirements, or avoid residential placement in an institutional setting; and

(6) Allow consideration of the convenience of the provider's location for the individual with the disability.

In developing these purchasing provisions, the Secretary shall also consider the following criteria: (i) cost-effectiveness, (ii) quality, (iii) the provider's general reputation and performance capabilities, (iv) substantial conformity with specifications and other conditions set forth for these purchases, (v) the suitability of the goods or services for the intended use, (vi) the personal or other related services needed, (vii) transportation charges, and (viii) any other factors the Secretary considers pertinent to the purchases in question.

(c) The purpose of rules promulgated hereunder shall be to promote sound purchasing management.

(d) Notwithstanding the provisions of this section or any rule adopted pursuant to this Article, The University of North Carolina may solicit bids for service contracts with a term of 10 years or less, including extensions and renewals, without the prior approval of the State Purchasing Officer.

(e) Expired. (1931, c. 261, s. 5; 1933, c. 441, s. 1; 1957, c. 269, s. 3; 1971, c. 587, s. 1; 1975, c. 879, s. 46; 1981, c. 602, s. 4; 1983, c. 717, ss. 63-64.1; 1985 (Reg. Sess., 1986), c. 955, ss. 87, 88; 1987, c. 827, s. 216; 1989 (Reg. Sess., 1990), c. 936, s. 3(b); 1995, c. 256, s. 1; 1997-412, s. 3; 1998-217, s. 15; 1999-400, ss. 1, 2; 2002-107, s. 2; 2003-147, s. 9; 2004-203, s. 72(b); 2005-125, s. 1; 2006-203, s. 84; 2009-475, s. 2; 2011-338, s. 4; 2013-289, s. 7.)

§ 143-53.1. Setting of benchmarks; increase by Secretary.

(a) On and after July 1, 2014, the procedures prescribed by G.S. 143-52 with respect to competitive bids and the bid value benchmark authorized by G.S. 143-53(a)(2) with respect to rule making by the Secretary of Administration for competitive bidding shall promote compliance with the principles of procurement efficiency, transparency, and fair competition to obtain the State's business. For a special responsibility constituent institution of The University of North Carolina, the benchmark prescribed in this section is as provided in G.S. 116-31.10. For community colleges, the benchmark prescribed in this section is as provided in G.S. 115D-58.14.

(b) The benchmarks set by the Secretary of Administration, The University of North Carolina, and the State Board of Community Colleges in subsection (a) of this section shall be applicable to all contracts for goods, equipment, or services awarded by the Department of Administration, State departments, institutions, agencies, universities, and community colleges using funds from the American Recovery and Reinvestment Act of 2009 (Public Law 111-5). (1989 (Reg. Sess., 1990), c. 936, s. 3(c); 1991, c. 689, s. 206.2(b); 1993 (Reg. Sess., 1994), c. 591, s. 10(a); c. 769, s. 17.6(b); 1997-412, s. 4; 2009-475, s. 5; 2011-326, s. 18(a); 2013-289, s. 8.)

§ 143-54. Certification that bids were submitted without collusion.

(a) The Director of Administration shall require bidders to certify that each bid is submitted competitively and without collusion. False certification is a Class I felony.

(b) Expired. (1961, c. 963; 1971, c. 587, s. 1; 1993, c. 539, s. 1310; 1994, Ex. Sess., c. 24, s. 14(c); 2009-475, s. 6.)

§ 143-55. Requisitioning by agencies; must purchase through sources certified.

(a) Unless otherwise provided by law, where sources of supply have been established by contract and certified by the Secretary of Administration to the said departments, institutions and agencies as herein provided for, it shall be the duty of all departments, institutions and agencies to make requisition or issue orders on forms to be prescribed by the Secretary of Administration, for purchases required by them upon the sources of supply so certified, and, except as herein otherwise provided for, it shall be unlawful for them, or any of them, to purchase from other sources than those certified by the Secretary of Administration. One copy of such requisition or order shall be furnished to and when requested by the Secretary of Administration.

(b) Expired. (1931, c. 261, s. 6; 1957, c. 269, s. 3; 1971, c. 587, s. 1; 1975, c. 879, s. 46; 2006-264, s. 59(c); 2009-475, s. 7; 2011-338, s. 5.)

§ 143-56. Certain purchases excepted from provisions of Article.

Unless as may otherwise be ordered by the Secretary of Administration, the purchase of supplies, materials and equipment through the Secretary of Administration shall be mandatory in the following cases:

(1) Published books, manuscripts, maps, pamphlets and periodicals.

(2) Perishable articles such as fresh vegetables, fresh fish, fresh meat, eggs, and others as may be classified by the Secretary of Administration.

Purchase through the Secretary of Administration shall not be mandatory for information technology purchased in accordance with Article 3D of Chapter 147 of the General Statutes, for a purchase of supplies, materials or equipment for the General Assembly if the total expenditures is less than the expenditure benchmark established under the provisions of G.S. 143-53.1, for group purchases made by hospitals, developmental centers, neuromedical treatment centers, and alcohol and drug abuse treatment centers through a competitive bidding purchasing program, as defined in G.S. 143-129, by the University of North Carolina Health Care System pursuant to G.S. 116-37(h), by the University of North Carolina Hospitals at Chapel Hill pursuant to G.S. 116-37(a)(4), by the University of North Carolina at Chapel Hill on behalf of the clinical patient care programs of the School of Medicine of the University of North Carolina at Chapel Hill pursuant to G.S. 116-37(a)(4), or by East Carolina University on behalf of the Medical Faculty Practice Plan pursuant to G.S. 116-40.6(c).

All purchases of the above articles made directly by the departments, institutions and agencies of the State government shall, whenever possible, be based on competitive bids. Whenever an order is placed or contract awarded for such articles by any of the departments, institutions and agencies of the State government, a copy of such order or contract shall be forwarded to the Secretary of Administration and a record of the competitive bids upon which it was based shall be retained for inspection and review. (1931, c. 261, s. 7; 1957, c. 269, s. 3; 1971, c. 587, s. 1; 1975, c. 879, s. 46; 1981, c. 953; 1983, c. 717, ss. 65, 66; 1985, c. 145, s. 3; 1989 (Reg. Sess., 1990), c. 936, s. 3(e); 1998-212, s. 11.8(c); 1999-434, s. 14; 1999-456, s. 7; 2001-487, s. 21(f); 2009-184, s. 1.)

§ 143-57. Purchases of articles in certain emergencies.

In case of any emergency or pressing need arising from unforeseen causes including but not limited to delay by contractors, delay in transportation, breakdown in machinery, or unanticipated volume of work, the Secretary of Administration shall have power to obtain or authorize obtaining in the open market any necessary supplies, materials, equipment, printing or services for immediate delivery to any department, institution or agency of the State government. A report on the circumstances of such emergency or need and the transactions thereunder shall be made a matter of record promptly thereafter. If the expenditure exceeds ten thousand dollars ($10,000), the report shall also be made promptly thereafter to the Division of Purchase and Contract. (1931, c. 261, s. 8; 1957, c. 269, s. 3; 1971, c. 587, s. 1; 1975, c. 879, s. 46; 1999-400, s. 3.)

§ 143-57.1. Furniture requirements contracts.

(a) State Furniture Requirements Contract. - To ensure agencies access to sufficient sources of furniture supply and service, to provide agencies the necessary flexibility to obtain furniture that is compatible with interior architectural design and needs, to provide small and disadvantaged businesses additional opportunities to participate on State requirements contracts, and to restore the traditional use of multiple award contracts for purchasing furniture requirements, each State furniture requirements contract shall be awarded on a multiple award basis, subject to the following conditions:

(1) Competitive, sealed bids must be solicited for the contract in accordance with Article 3 of Chapter 143 of the General Statutes unless otherwise provided for by the State Purchasing Officer pursuant to that Article. Bids shall be solicited on a historical weighted average of specific contract items and not on a single item within a class of items. Historical weighted average shall be based on information derived from the State's electronic procurement system, when available, or other available data.

(2) Subject to the provisions of this section, bids shall be evaluated and the contract awarded in accordance with Article 3 of Chapter 143 of the General Statutes.

(3) For each category of goods under each State requirements furniture contract, awards shall be made to at least three qualified vendors unless three qualified vendors are not available. Additionally, if the State Purchasing Officer determines that there are no qualified vendors within the three best qualified vendors who offer furniture manufactured or produced in North Carolina or who are incorporated in the State, the State Purchasing Officer shall expand the number of qualified vendors awarded contracts to as many qualified vendors as is necessary to include a qualified vendor who offers furniture manufactured or produced in North Carolina or who is incorporated in the State, but the State Purchasing Officer shall not be required to expand the number of qualified vendors to more than six qualified vendors. A vendor is qualified under this subsection if the vendor's products conform to the term contract specifications, the vendor is listed on the State's qualified products list, and the vendor submits a responsive bid.

(4) Repealed by Session Laws 2013-73, s. 1, effective June 12, 2013.

(a1) GSA Furniture Schedule. - Vendors meeting the following requirements are treated as qualified vendors under any State furniture requirements contract:

(1) The vendor's products are included on a United States General Services Administration (GSA) Furniture Schedule.

(2) The vendor is a federally qualified vendor within the GSA Furniture Schedule.

(3) The vendor offers products on the same pricing and specifications as the vendor's products included on the GSA Furniture Schedule.

(4) The vendor is a resident bidder as defined in G.S. 143-59(c) or the vendor offers products manufactured or produced in North Carolina.

(b) Definition. - For purposes of this section, "furniture requirements contract" means State requirements contracts for casegoods, classroom furniture, bookcases, ergonomic chairs, office swivel and side chairs, computer furniture, mobile and folding furniture, upholstered seating, commercial dining tables, and related items.

(c) Authority to Purchase. - An agency may purchase from any vendor certified on the State furniture requirements contract, including vendors meeting the requirements of subsection (a1) of this section. An agency shall make the most economical purchase that it determines meets its needs, based upon price, compatibility, service, delivery, freight charges, contract terms, and other factors that it considers relevant. (1995, c. 136, ss. 1, 3; 1995 (Reg. Sess., 1996), c. 716, s. 30; 2004-115, s. 1; 2013-73, s. 1.)

§ 143-58. Contracts contrary to provisions of Article made void.

If any department, institution or agency of the State government, required by this Article and the rules adopted pursuant thereto applying to the purchase or lease of supplies, materials, equipment, printing or services through the Secretary of Administration, or any nonstate institution, agency or instrumentality duly authorized or required to make purchases through the Department of Administration, shall contract for the purchase or lease of such supplies, materials, equipment, printing or services contrary to the provisions of this Article or the rules made hereunder, such contract shall be void and of no effect. If any such State or nonstate department, institution, agency or instrumentality purchases any supplies, materials, equipment, printing or services contrary to the provisions of this Article or the rules made hereunder, the executive officer of such department, institution, agency or instrumentality shall be personally liable for the costs thereof. (1931, c. 261, s. 9; 1957, c. 269, s. 3; 1971, c. 587, s. 1; 1975, c. 879, s. 46; 1977, c. 148, s. 3; 1987, c. 827, s. 217.)

§ 143-58.1. Unauthorized use of public purchase or contract procedures for private benefit.

(a)   It shall be unlawful for any person, by the use of the powers, policies or procedures described in this Article or established hereunder, to purchase, attempt to purchase, procure or attempt to procure any property or services for private use or benefit.

(b)   This prohibition shall not apply if:

(1)   The department, institution or agency through which the property or services are procured had theretofore established policies and procedures permitting such purchases or procurement by a class or classes of persons in order to provide for the mutual benefit of such persons and the department, institution or agency involved, or the public benefit or convenience; and

(2)   Such policies and procedures, including any reimbursement policies, are complied with by the person permitted thereunder to use the purchasing or procurement procedures described in this Article or established thereunder.

(c)   A violation of this section is a Class 1 misdemeanor. (1983, c. 409; 1993, c. 539, s. 1004; 1994, Ex. Sess., c. 24, s. 14(c).)

§ 143-58.2. State policy; bid procedures and specifications; identification of products.

(a)   It is the policy of this State to encourage and promote the purchase of products with recycled content. All State departments, institutions, agencies, community colleges, and local school administrative units shall, to the extent economically practicable, purchase and use, or require the purchase and use of, products with recycled content.

(b) No later than January 1, 1995, the Secretary of Administration and each State department, institution, agency, community college, and local school administrative unit authorized to purchase materials and supplies or to contract for services shall review and revise its bid procedures and specifications for the purchase or use of materials and supplies to eliminate any procedures and specifications that explicitly discriminate against materials and supplies with recycled content, except where procedures and specifications are necessary to protect the health, safety, and welfare of the citizens of this State.

(c) The Secretary of Administration and each State department, institution, agency, community college, and local school administrative unit shall review and revise its bid procedures and specifications on a continuing basis to encourage the purchase or use of materials and supplies with recycled content and to the extent economically practicable, the use of materials and supplies with recycled content.

(d) The Department of Administration, in cooperation with the Division of Environmental Assistance and Outreach of the Department of Environment and Natural Resources, shall identify materials and supplies with recycled content that meet appropriate standards for use by State departments, institutions, agencies, community colleges, and local school administrative units.

(e) A list of materials and supplies with recycled content that are identified pursuant to subsection (d) of this section and that are available for purchase under a statewide term contract shall be distributed annually to each State agency authorized to purchase materials and supplies for use by its departments, institutions, agencies, community colleges, or local school administrative units.

(f) Repealed by Session Laws 2009-484, s. 15, effective January 1, 2010.

(g) The Department of Administration and the Department of Environment and Natural Resources shall develop guidelines for minimum content standards for materials and supplies with recycled content and may recommend appropriate goals in addition to those goals set forth in G.S. 143-58.3, for types of materials and supplies with recycled content to be purchased by the State.

(h) The Secretary of Administration may adopt rules to implement the provisions of this section and G.S. 143-58.3. (1993, c. 256, s. 2; 1995 (Reg. Sess., 1996), c. 743, ss. 10, 11; 1997-443, s. 11A.119(a); 2001-452, s. 3.7; 2009-484, s. 15; 2010-31, s. 13.1(f).)

§ 143-58.3. Purchase of recycled paper and paper products; goals.

In furtherance of the State policy, it is the goal of the State that each department, institution, agency, community college, and local school administrative unit purchase paper and paper products with recycled content according to the following schedule:

(1) At least ten percent (10%) by June 30, 1994;

(2) At least twenty percent (20%) by June 30, 1995;

(3) At least thirty-five percent (35%) by June 30, 1996; and

(4) At least fifty percent (50%) by June 30, 1997, and the end of each subsequent fiscal year,

of the total amount spent for the purchase of paper and paper products during that fiscal year. (1993, c. 256, s. 2.)

§ 143-58.4. Energy credit banking and selling program.

(a) The following definitions apply in this section:

(1) AFV. - A hybrid electric vehicle that derives its transportation energy from gasoline and electricity. AFV also means an original equipment manufactured vehicle that operates on compressed natural gas, propane, or electricity.

(2) Alternative fuel. - Biodiesel, biodiesel blend, ethanol, compressed natural gas, propane, and electricity used as a transportation fuel in blends or in a manner as defined by the Energy Policy Act.

(3) B-20. - A blend of twenty percent (20%) by volume biodiesel fuel and eighty percent (80%) by volume petroleum-based diesel fuel.

(3a) Biodiesel. - A fuel comprised of mono-alkyl esters of long fatty acids derived from vegetable oils or animal fats, designated B100 and meeting the requirements of the American Society for Testing and Materials (ASTM) D-6751.

(3b) Biodiesel blend. - A blend of biodiesel fuel with petroleum-based diesel fuel, designated BXX where XX represents the percentage of volume of fuel in the blend meeting the requirements of ASTM D-6751.

(4) Department. - The Department of Environment and Natural Resources.

(5) Energy Policy Act. - The federal Energy Policy Act of 1992, Pub. L. No. 102-486, 106 Stat. 2782, 42 U.S.C. § 13201, et seq.

(6) EPAct credit. - A credit issued pursuant to the Energy Policy Act.

(7) E-85. - A blend of eighty-five percent (85%) by volume ethanol and fifteen percent (15%) by volume gasoline.

(8) Incremental fuel cost. - The difference in cost between an alternative fuel and conventional petroleum fuel at the time the fuel is purchased.

(9) Incremental vehicle cost. - The difference in cost between an AFV and conventional vehicle of the same make and model. For vehicles with no comparable conventional model, incremental vehicle cost means the generally accepted difference in cost between an AFV and a similar conventional model.

(b) Establish Program. - The State Energy Office of the Department, in cooperation with State departments, institutions, and agencies, shall establish and administer an energy credit banking and selling program to allow State departments, institutions, and agencies to use moneys generated by the sale of EPAct credits to purchase alternative fuel, develop alternative fuel refueling infrastructure, and purchase AFVs for use by State departments, institutions, and agencies. Each State department, institution, and agency shall provide the State Energy Office with all vehicle fleet information necessary to determine the number of EPAct credits generated annually by the State. The State Energy Office may sell credits in any manner that is in accordance with the provisions of the Energy Policy Act.

(c) Adopt Rules. - The Secretary of Environment and Natural Resources shall adopt rules as necessary to implement this section. (2005-413, s. 1; 2009-237, s. 1; 2009-446, s. 1(g), (h); 2013-360, s. 15.22(n).)

§ 143-58.5. Alternative Fuel Revolving Fund.

(a) The definitions set out in G.S. 143-58.4 apply to this section.

(b) The Alternative Fuel Revolving Fund is created and shall be held by the State Treasurer. The Fund shall consist of moneys received from the sale of EPAct credits under G.S. 143-58.4, any moneys appropriated to the Fund by the General Assembly, and any moneys obtained or accepted by the Department for deposit into the Fund. The Fund shall be managed to maximize benefits to the State for the purchase of alternative fuel, related refueling infrastructure, and AFV purchases. To the extent possible, benefits from the sale of EPAct credit shall be distributed to State departments, institutions, and agencies in proportion to the number of EPAct credits generated by each. No portion of the Fund shall be transferred to the General Fund, and any appropriation made to the Fund shall not revert. The State Treasurer shall invest moneys in the Fund in the same manner as other funds are invested. Interest and moneys earned on such investments shall be credited to the Fund.

(c) The Fund shall be used to offset the incremental fuel cost of biodiesel and biodiesel blend fuel with a minimum biodiesel concentration of B-20 for use in State vehicles, for the purchase of ethanol fuel with a minimum ethanol concentration of E-85 for use in State vehicles, the incremental vehicle cost of purchasing AFVs, for the development of related refueling infrastructure, for the costs of administering the Fund, and for projects approved by the Energy Policy Council.

(d) The Secretary of Administration shall adopt rules as necessary to implement this section.

(e) The Department shall submit to the Joint Legislative Commission on Governmental Operations and the Fiscal Research Division no later than 1 October of each year a report on the expenditures from the Fund during the preceding fiscal year. (2005-413, s. 1; 2009-237, s. 2.)

§ 143-59. Preference given to North Carolina products and citizens, and articles manufactured by State agencies; reciprocal preferences.

(a) Preference. - The Secretary of Administration and any State agency authorized to purchase foodstuff or other products, shall, in the purchase of or in the contracting for foods, supplies, materials, equipment, printing or services give preference as far as may be practicable to such products or services manufactured or produced in North Carolina or furnished by or through citizens of North Carolina: Provided, however, that in giving such preference no sacrifice or loss in price or quality shall be permitted; and provided further, that preference in all cases shall be given to surplus products or articles produced and manufactured by other State departments, institutions, or agencies which are available for distribution.

(b) Reciprocal Preference. - For the purpose only of determining the low bidder on all contracts for equipment, materials, supplies, and services valued over twenty-five thousand dollars ($25,000), a percent of increase shall be added to a bid of a nonresident bidder that is equal to the percent of increase, if any, that the state in which the bidder is a resident adds to bids from bidders who do not reside in that state. Any amount due under a contract awarded to a nonresident bidder shall not be increased by the amount of the increase added by this subsection. On or before January 1 of each year, the Secretary of Administration shall electronically publish a list of states that give preference to in-State bidders and the amount of the percent increase added to out-of-state bids. All departments, institutions, and agencies of the State shall use this list when evaluating bids. If the reciprocal preference causes the nonresident bidder to no longer be the lowest bidder, the Secretary of Administration may waive the reciprocal preference. In determining whether to waive the reciprocal preference, the Secretary of Administration shall consider factors that include competition, price, product origination, and available resources.

(c) Definitions. - The following definitions apply in this section:

(1) Resident bidder. - A bidder that has paid unemployment taxes or income taxes in this State and whose principal place of business is located in this State.

(2) Nonresident bidder. - A bidder that is not a resident bidder as defined in subdivision (1) of this subsection.

(3) Principal place of business. - The principal place from which the trade or business of the bidder is directed or managed.

(d) Exemptions. - Subsection (b) of this section shall not apply to contracts entered into under G.S. 143-53(a)(5) or G.S. 143-57.

(e) When a contract is awarded by the Secretary using the provisions of subsection (b) of this section, a report of the nature of the contract, the bids received, and the award to the successful bidder shall be posted on the Internet as soon as practicable.

(f) Resident Bidder Notification. - When the Secretary puts a contract up for competitive bidding, the Secretary shall endeavor to provide notice to all resident bidders who have expressed an interest in bidding on contracts of that nature. The Secretary may opt to provide notice under this section by electronic means only. (1931, c. 261, s. 10; 1933, c. 441, s. 2; 1957, c. 269, s. 3; 1971, c. 587, s. 1; 1975, c. 879, s. 46; 2001-240, s. 1; 2005-213, ss. 1, 3; 2013-234, s. 9.)

§ 143-59.1. Contracts with certain foreign vendors.

(a) Ineligible Vendors. - The Secretary of Administration and other entities to which this Article applies shall not contract for goods or services with either of the following:

(1) A vendor if the vendor or an affiliate of the vendor if the Secretary of Revenue has determined that the vendor or affiliate of the vendor meets one or more of the conditions of G.S. 105-164.8(b) but refuses to collect the use tax levied under Article 5 of Chapter 105 of the General Statutes on its sales delivered to North Carolina. The Secretary of Revenue shall provide the Secretary of Administration periodically with a list of vendors to which this section applies.

(2) A vendor if the vendor or an affiliate of the vendor incorporates or reincorporates in a tax haven country after December 31, 2001, but the United States is the principal market for the public trading of the stock of the corporation incorporated in the tax haven country.

(b) Vendor Certification. - The Secretary of Administration shall require each vendor submitting a bid or contract to certify that the vendor is not an ineligible vendor as set forth in subsection (a) of this section. Any person who submits a certification required by this subsection known to be false shall be guilty of a Class I felony.

(c) Definitions. - The following definitions apply in this section:

(1) Affiliate. - As defined in G.S. 105-163.010.

(2) Tax haven country. - Means each of the following: Barbados, Bermuda, British Virgin Islands, Cayman Islands, Commonwealth of the Bahamas, Gibraltar, Isle of Man, the Principality of Monaco, and the Republic of the Seychelles. (1999-341, s. 7; 2002-189, s. 6; 2003-413, s. 28; 2012-79, s. 2.14.)

§ 143-59.1A. Preference given to products made in United States.

If the Secretary of Administration or a State agency cannot give preference to North Carolina products or services as provided in G.S. 143-59, the Secretary or State agency shall give preference, as far as may be practicable and to the extent permitted by State law, federal law, and federal treaty, to products or services manufactured or produced in the United States. Provided, however, that in giving such preference no sacrifice or loss in price or quality shall be permitted; and provided further, that preference in all cases shall be given to surplus products or articles produced and manufactured by other State departments, institutions, or agencies which are available for distribution. (2004-124, s. 6.1.)

§ 143-59.2. Certain vendors prohibited from contracting with State.

(a) Ineligible Vendors. - A vendor is not entitled to enter into a contract for goods or services with any department, institution, or agency of the State government subject to the provisions of this Article if any officer or director of the vendor, or any owner if the vendor is an unincorporated business entity, within 10 years immediately prior to the date of the bid solicitation, has been convicted of any violation of Chapter 78A of the General Statutes or the Securities Act of 1933 or the Securities Exchange Act of 1934.

(b) Vendor Certification. - The Secretary of Administration shall require each vendor submitting a bid or contract to certify that none of its officers, directors, or owners of an unincorporated business entity has been convicted of any violation referenced in subsection (a) of this section within 10 years immediately prior to the date of the bid solicitation. Any person who submits a certification required by this subsection known to be false shall be guilty of a Class I felony.

(c) Void Contracts. - A contract entered into in violation of this section is void. A contract that is void under this section may continue in effect until an alternative can be arranged when: (i) immediate termination would result in harm to the public health or welfare, and (ii) the continuation is approved by the Secretary of Administration. Approval of continuation of contracts under this subsection shall be given for the minimum period necessary to protect the public health or welfare. (2002-189, s. 5.)

§ 143-59.3. Contracts for the purchase of reconstituted or recombined fluid milk products prohibited.

(a) As used in this section, "fluid milk product" has the same meaning as in 7 Code of Federal Regulations § 1000.15 (1 January 2003 Edition).

(b) No department, institution, or agency of the State shall enter into any contract for the purchase of any fluid milk product that is labeled or that is required to be labeled as "reconstituted" or "recombined".

(c) The Secretary of Administration may temporarily suspend the provisions of subsection (b) of this section in case of any emergency or pressing need as provided in G.S. 143-57. (2003-367, s. 1.)

§ 143-59.4. Contracts performed outside the United States.

(a) A vendor submitting a bid shall disclose in a statement, provided contemporaneously with the bid, where services will be performed under the contract sought, including any subcontracts, and whether any services under that contract, including any subcontracts, are anticipated to be performed outside the United States. Nothing in this section is intended to contravene any existing treaty, law, agreement, or regulation of the United States.

(b) The Secretary of Administration shall retain the statements required by subsection (a) of this section regardless of the State entity that awards the contract and shall report annually to the Joint Legislative Commission on Governmental Operations on the number of contracts which are anticipated to be performed outside the United States. (2005-169, s. 1.)

§ 143-60. Rules covering certain purposes.

The Secretary of Administration may adopt, modify, or abrogate rules covering the following purposes, in addition to those authorized elsewhere in this Article:

(1) Requiring reports by State departments, institutions, or agencies of stocks of supplies and materials and equipment on hand and prescribing the form of such reports.

(2) Prescribing the manner in which supplies, materials and equipment shall be delivered, stored and distributed.

(3) Prescribing the manner of inspecting deliveries of supplies, materials and equipment and making chemicals and/or physical tests of samples submitted with bids and samples of deliveries to determine whether deliveries have been made in compliance with specifications. However, the provisions of this subdivision shall not apply to the constituent institutions of The University of North Carolina. The President of The University of North Carolina shall issue regulations or guidelines for the conducting of quality inspections by constituent institutions to ensure that deliveries have been made in compliance with specifications.

(4) Prescribing the manner in which purchases shall be made in emergencies.

(5) Providing for such other matters as may be necessary to give effect to foregoing rules and provisions of this Article.

(6) Prescribing the manner in which passenger vehicles shall be purchased.

Further, the Secretary of Administration may prescribe appropriate procedures necessary to enable the State, its institutions and agencies, to obtain materials surplus or otherwise available from federal, State or local governments or their disposal agencies. (1931, c. 261, s. 11; 1945, c. 145; 1957, c. 269, s. 3; 1961, c. 772; 1971, c. 587, s. 1; 1975, c. 879, s. 46; 1981, c. 268, s. 2; 1983, c. 717, ss. 67, 68; 1985 (Reg. Sess., 1986), c. 955, ss. 89, 90; 1987, c. 282, s. 27; c. 827, s. 217; 2006-203, s. 85; 2011-145, s. 9.6G(a).)

§ 143-61. Repealed by Session Laws 1975, c. 879, s. 45.

§ 143-62. Law applicable to printing Supreme Court Reports not affected.

Nothing in this Article shall be construed as amending or repealing G.S. 7A-6(b), relating to the printing of the Supreme Court Reports, or in any way changing or interfering with the method of printing or contracting for the printing of the Supreme Court Reports as provided for in said section. (1931, c. 261, s. 13; 1969, c. 44, s. 75; 1971, c. 587, s. 1.)

§ 143-63. Financial interest of officers in sources of supply; acceptance of bribes.

Neither the Secretary of Administration, nor any assistant of the Secretary's shall be financially interested, or have any personal beneficial interest, either directly or indirectly, in the purchase of, or contract for, any materials, equipment or supplies, nor in any firm, corporation, partnership or association furnishing any such supplies, materials or equipment to the State government, or any of its departments, institutions or agencies, nor shall such Secretary, assistant, or member of the Commission accept or receive, directly or indirectly, from any person, firm or corporation to whom any contract may be awarded, by rebate, gifts or otherwise, any money or anything of value whatsoever, or any promise, obligation or contract for future reward or compensation. Any violation of this section shall be deemed a Class F felony. Upon conviction thereof, any such Secretary or assistant shall be removed from office. (1931, c. 261, s. 15; 1957, c. 269, s. 3; 1971, c. 587, s. 1; 1975, c. 879, s. 46; 1983, c. 717, s. 81; 1993, c. 539, s. 1311; 1994, Ex. Sess., c. 24, s. 14(c); 2006-203, s. 86.)

§ 143-63.1. Sale, disposal and destruction of firearms.

(a) Except as hereinafter provided, it shall be unlawful for any employee, officer or official of the State in the exercise of his official duty to sell or otherwise dispose of any pistol, revolver, shotgun or rifle to any person, firm, corporation, county or local governmental unit, law-enforcement agency, or other legal entity.

(b) It shall be lawful for the Department of Administration, in the exercise of its official duty, to sell any weapon described in subsection (a) hereof, to any county or local governmental unit, law-enforcement agency in the State; provided, however, that such law-enforcement agency files a written statement, duly notarized, with the seller of said weapon certifying that such weapon is needed in law enforcement by such law-enforcement agency.

(c) All weapons described in subsection (a) hereof which are not sold as herein provided within one year of being declared surplus property shall be destroyed by the Department of Administration.

(d) Notwithstanding the provisions of this section, but subject to the provisions of G.S. 20-187.2, the North Carolina State Highway Patrol, the North Carolina Division of Adult Correction of the Department of Public Safety, and the North Carolina State Bureau of Investigation may sell, trade, or otherwise dispose of any or all surplus weapons they possess to any federally licensed firearm dealers. The sale, trade, or disposal of these weapons shall be in a manner prescribed by the Department of Administration. Any moneys or property obtained from the sale, trade, or disposal shall go to the general fund. (1973, c. 666, ss. 1-3; 1975, c. 879, s. 46; 1981, c. 604; 1981 (Reg. Sess., 1982), c. 1282, s. 52; 2011-145, s. 19.1(h).)

§ 143-63.2. Purchase of tires for State vehicles; repair or refurbishment of tires for State vehicles.

(a) Definitions. - The following terms apply in this section:

(1) Critical tire information. - Tire brand name, tire line name, tire identification numbers, load and pressure markings, tire size designation, service descriptions such as load and speed ratings, and other information and

specifications placed on the original tire sidewall by the original tire manufacturer.

(2) State vehicle. - Any vehicle owned, rented, or leased by the State, or an institution, department, or agency of the State, that is driven on a public road consistently at speeds greater than 30 miles per hour.

(b) Forensic Tire Standards. - In order to preserve critical tire information, the Secretary of Administration and any institution, department, or agency of the State shall only procure and install tires for State vehicles that possess the original, unaltered, and uncovered tire sidewall. Furthermore, neither the Secretary of Administration nor any institution, department, or agency of the State shall execute a contract for the repair or refurbishment of tires for State vehicles that provides for the removal, covering, or other alteration in any manner of the critical tire information contained on the original tire sidewall.

(c) Tire Purchase and Contract Standards Applicability. - All contracts for the purchase, repair, or refurbishment of tires for State vehicles, or contracts for the purchase of products or services related to the repair or refurbishment of tires for State vehicles, executed on or after the date this section becomes effective shall comply with the provisions of this section.

(d) Exemption. - Notwithstanding the provisions of this section, the State or any institution, department, or agency of the State that owns or has a legally binding contract in place for the future purchase of tires having altered or covered sidewalls prior to the date that this section becomes effective shall perform its existing contractual obligations related thereto and may continue to use those tires on State vehicles for the useful life of the retreaded tire. (2011-145, s. 28.36(a).)

§ 143-64: Repealed by Session Laws 2012-89, s. 1, effective June 28, 2012.

Article 3A.

Surplus Property.

Part 1. State Surplus Property Agency.

§ 143-64.01. Department of Administration designated State Surplus Property Agency.

The Department of Administration is designated as the State agency for State surplus property, and with respect to the acquisition of State surplus property the agency shall be subject to the supervision and direction of the Secretary of Administration. (1991, c. 358, s. 2.)

§ 143-64.02. Definitions.

As used in Part 1 of this Article, except where the context clearly requires otherwise:

(1) "Agency" means an existing department, institution, commission, committee, board, division, or bureau of the State.

(2) "Nonprofit tax exempt organizations" means those nonprofit tax exempt medical institutions, hospitals, clinics, health centers, school systems, schools, colleges, universities, schools for the mentally retarded, schools for the physically handicapped, radio and television stations licensed by the Federal Communications Commission as educational radio or educational television stations, public libraries, and civil defense organizations, that have been certified by the Internal Revenue Service as tax-exempt nonprofit organizations under section 501(c)(3) of the United States Internal Revenue Code of 1954.

(3) "Recyclable material" means a recyclable material, as defined in G.S. 130A-290, that the Secretary of Administration determines, consistent with G.S. 130A-309.14, to be a recyclable material. (1991, c. 358, s. 2; 1998-223, s. 1.)

§ 143-64.03. Powers and duties of the State agency for surplus property.

(a) The State Surplus Property Agency is authorized and directed to:

(1) Sell all supplies, materials, and equipment that are surplus, obsolete, or unused;

(2) Warehouse such property; and

(3) Distribute such property to tax-supported or nonprofit tax-exempt organizations.

(b) The State Surplus Property Agency is authorized and empowered to act as a clearinghouse of information for agencies and private nonprofit tax-exempt organizations, to locate property available for acquisition from State agencies, to ascertain the terms and conditions under which the property may be obtained, to receive requests from agencies and private nonprofit tax-exempt organizations, and transmit all available information about the property, and to aid and assist the agencies and private nonprofit tax-exempt organizations in transactions for the acquisition of State surplus property.

(c) The State agency for surplus property, in the administration of Part 1 of this Article, shall cooperate to the fullest extent consistent with the provisions of Part 1 of this Article, with the departments or agencies of the State.

(d) The State agency for surplus property may sell or otherwise dispose of surplus property, including motor vehicles, through an electronic auction service. (1991, c. 358, s. 2; 2003-284, s. 18.6(a).)

§ 143-64.04. Powers of the Secretary to delegate authority.

(a) The Secretary of Administration may delegate to any employees of the State agency for surplus property such power and authority as he or they deem reasonable and proper for the effective administration of Part 1 of this Article. The Secretary of Administration may, in his discretion, bond any person in the employ of the State agency for surplus property, handling moneys, signing checks, or receiving or distributing property from the United States under authority of Part 1 of this Article.

(b) The Secretary of Administration may adopt rules necessary to carry out Part 1 of this Article. (1991, c. 358, s. 2.)

§ 143-64.05. Service charge; receipts.

(a) The State agency for surplus property may assess and collect a service charge for the acquisition, receipt, warehousing, distribution, or transfer of any

State surplus property and for the transfer or sale of recyclable material. The service charge authorized by this subsection does not apply to the transfer or sale of timber on land owned by the Wildlife Resources Commission or the Department of Agriculture and Consumer Services.

(b) All receipts from the transfer or sale of surplus, obsolete, or unused equipment of State departments, institutions, and agencies that are supported by appropriations from the General Fund, except where the receipts have been anticipated for or budgeted against the cost of replacements, shall be credited by the Secretary to the Office of State Treasurer as nontax revenue.

(c) A department, institution, or agency may retain receipts derived from the transfer or sale of recyclable material, less any charge collected pursuant to subsection (a) of this section, and may use the receipts to defray the costs of its recycling activities. A contract for the transfer or sale of recyclable material to which a department, institution, or agency is a party shall not become effective until the contract is approved by the Secretary of Administration. The Secretary of Administration shall adopt rules governing the transfer or sale of recyclable material by a department, institution, or agency and specifying the conditions and procedures under which a department, institution, or agency may retain the receipts derived from the transfer or sale, including the appropriate allocation of receipts when more than one department, institution, or agency is involved in a recycling activity. (1991, c. 358, s. 2; 1991 (Reg. Sess., 1992), c. 900, s. 24; 1998-223, s. 2; 2006-231, s. 3; 2007-323, s. 11.1.)

§ 143-64.06. North Carolina State University may sell timber.

Notwithstanding any provision of this Part or Chapter 146 of the General Statutes, the Board of Trustees of North Carolina State University may cause to be severed and sold or transferred timber from any unimproved timberlands owned by or allocated to the University without involvement by the State Surplus Property Agency and without being required to pay any service charge or surcharge to the State Surplus Property Agency. Any such severance shall be reported to the Council of State through the State Property Office. The Board of Trustees may delegate the authority set out above to responsible University officials. The proceeds of any sales or transfers under this section shall be used to support the management of, and programming costs associated with, forest properties owned, allocated, or managed by North Carolina State University. (2011-145, s. 9.6H.)

Part 2. State Agency for Federal Surplus Property.

§ 143-64.1. Department of Administration designated State agency for federal surplus property.

The Department of Administration is hereby designated as the State agency for federal surplus property, and with respect to the acquisition of federal surplus property said agency shall be subject to the supervision and direction of the Secretary of Administration. (1953, c. 1262, s. 1; 1957, c. 269, s. 3; 1975, c. 879, s. 46; 1991, c. 358, s. 3.)

§ 143-64.2. Authority and duties of the State agency for federal surplus property.

(a) The State agency for federal surplus property is hereby authorized and empowered

(1) To acquire from the United States of America such property, including equipment, materials, books, or other supplies under the control of any department or agency of the United States of America as may be usable and necessary for educational purposes, public health purposes, or civil defense purposes, including research;

(2) To warehouse such property; and

(3) To distribute such property to tax-supported or nonprofit and tax-exempt (under section 501(c)(3) of the United States Internal Revenue Code of 1954) medical institutions, hospitals, clinics, health centers, school systems, schools, colleges, universities, schools for the mentally retarded, schools for the physically handicapped, radio and television stations licensed by the Federal Communications Commission as educational radio or educational television stations, public libraries, civil defense organizations, and such other eligible donees within the State as are permitted to receive surplus property of the United States of America under the Federal Property and Administrative Services Act of 1949, as amended.

(b) The State agency for federal surplus property may adopt rules necessary to carry out Part 2 of this Article.

(c) The State agency for federal surplus property may appoint advisory boards or committees as needed to ensure that Part 2 of this Article and the rules adopted under Part 2 of this Article are consistent with federal law concerning surplus property.

(d) The State agency for surplus property is authorized and empowered to take such action, make such expenditures and enter into such contracts, agreements and undertakings for and in the name of the State, require such reports and make such investigations as may be required by law or regulation of the United States of America in connection with the receipt, warehousing, and distribution of property received by the State agency for federal surplus property from the United States of America.

(e) The State agency for federal surplus property is authorized and empowered to act as clearinghouse of information for the public and private nonprofit institutions and agencies referred to in subsection (a) of this section, to locate property available for acquisition from the United States of America, to ascertain the terms and conditions under which such property may be obtained, to receive requests from the above-mentioned institutions and agencies and to transmit to them all available information in reference to such property, and to aid and assist such institutions and agencies in every way possible in the consummation or acquisition or transactions hereunder.

(f) The State agency for federal surplus property, in the administration of Part 2 of this Article, shall cooperate to the fullest extent consistent with the provisions of Part 2 of this Article, with the departments or agencies of the United States of America and shall make such reports in such form and containing such information as the United States of America or any of its departments or agencies may from time to time require, and it shall comply with the laws of the United States of America and the rules and regulations of any of the departments or agencies of the United States of America governing the allocation, transfer, use, or accounting for, property donable or donated to the State. (1953, c. 1262, s. 2; 1965, c. 1105, ss. 1, 2; 1987, c. 827, s. 218; 1991, c. 358, s. 3.)

§ 143-64.3. Power of Department of Administration and Secretary to delegate authority.

The Department of Administration and/or the Secretary of Administration may delegate to any employees of the State agency for federal surplus property such power and authority as he or they deem reasonable and proper for the effective administration of Part 2 of this Article. The Department of Administration and/or the Secretary of Administration may, in his or their discretion, bond any person in the employ of the State agency for surplus property, handling moneys, signing checks, or receiving or distributing property from the United States under authority of Part 2 of this Article. (1953, c. 1262, s. 3; 1957, c. 269, s. 3; 1975, c. 879, s. 46; 1991, c. 358, s. 3.)

§ 143-64.4. Warehousing, transfer, etc., charges.

The State agency for federal surplus property is hereby authorized and empowered to assess and collect service charges or fees for the acquisition, receipts, warehousing, distribution or transfer of any property acquired by donation from the United States of America for educational purposes, public health purposes, public libraries or civil defense purposes, including research, and any such charges made or fees assessed shall be limited to those reasonably related to the costs of care and handling in respect to the acquisition, receipts, warehousing, distribution or transfer of the property by the State agency for surplus property. (1953, c. 1262, s. 4; 1965, c. 1105, s. 3; 1991, c. 358, s. 3.)

§ 143-64.5. Department of Agriculture and Consumer Services exempted from application of Article.

Notwithstanding any provisions or limitations of Part 2 of this Article, the North Carolina Department of Agriculture and Consumer Services is authorized and empowered to distribute food, surplus commodities and agricultural products under contracts and agreements with the federal government or any of its departments or agencies, and is authorized and empowered to adopt rules in order to conform with federal requirements and standards for such distribution and also for the proper distribution of such food, commodities and agricultural products. To the extent set forth above and in this section, the provisions of Part 2 of this Article shall not apply to the North Carolina Department of Agriculture and Consumer Services. (1953, c. 1262, s. 5; 1987, c. 827, s. 217; 1997-261, s. 89.)

Part 3. Public Agencies.

§ 143-64.6: Repealed by Session Laws 2004-199, s. 36(a), effective August 17, 2004.

§§ 143-64.7 through 143-64.9. Reserved for future codification purposes.

Article 3B.

Conservation of Energy, Water, and Other Utilities in Government Facilities.

Part 1. Energy Policy and Life-Cycle Cost Analysis.

§ 143-64.10. Findings; policy.

(a)   The General Assembly finds all of the following:

(1)   That the State shall take a leadership role in aggressively undertaking the conservation of energy, water, and other utilities in North Carolina.

(2)   That State facilities and facilities of State institutions of higher learning have a significant impact on the State's consumption of energy, water, and other utilities.

(3)   That practices to conserve energy, water, and other utilities that are adopted for the design, construction, operation, maintenance, and renovation of these facilities and for the purchase, operation, and maintenance of equipment for these facilities will have a beneficial effect on the State's overall supply of energy, water, and other utilities.

(4)   That the cost of the energy, water, and other utilities consumed by these facilities and the equipment for these facilities over the life of the facilities shall be considered, in addition to the initial cost.

(5)   That the cost of energy, water, and other utilities is significant and facility designs shall take into consideration the total life-cycle cost, including the initial construction cost, and the cost, over the economic life of the facility, of the energy, water, and other utilities consumed, and of operation and maintenance of the facility as it affects the consumption of energy, water, or other utilities.

(6) That State government shall undertake a program to reduce the use of energy, water, and other utilities in State facilities and facilities of the State institutions of higher learning and equipment in those facilities in order to provide its citizens with an example of energy-use, water-use, and utility-use efficiency.

(b) It is the policy of the State of North Carolina to ensure that practices to conserve energy, water, and other utilities are employed in the design, construction, operation, maintenance, and renovation of State facilities and facilities of the State institutions of higher learning and in the purchase, operation, and maintenance of equipment for these facilities. (1975, c. 434, s. 1; 1993, c. 334, s. 2; 2001-415, s. 1; 2006-190, s. 8; 2007-546, s. 3.1(b).)

§ 143-64.11. Definitions.

For purposes of this Article:

(1) "Economic life" means the projected or anticipated useful life of a facility.

(2) "Energy-consumption analysis" means the evaluation of all energy-consuming systems, including systems that consume water or other utilities, and components of these systems by demand and type of energy or other utility use, including the internal energy load imposed on a facility by its occupants, equipment and components, and the external energy load imposed on the facility by climatic conditions.

(2a) "Energy Office" means the State Energy Office of the Department of Environment and Natural Resources.

(2b) "Energy-consuming system" includes but is not limited to any of the following equipment or measures:

a. Equipment used to heat, cool, or ventilate the facility;

b. Equipment used to heat water in the facility;

c. Lighting systems;

d. On-site equipment used to generate electricity for the facility;

e. On-site equipment that uses the sun, wind, oil, natural gas, liquid propane gas, coal, or electricity as a power source; and

f. Energy conservation measures, as defined in G.S. 143-64.17, in the facility design and construction that decrease the energy, water, or other utility requirements of the facility.

(3) "Facility" means a building or a group of buildings served by a central distribution system for energy, water, or other utility or components of a central distribution system.

(4) "Initial cost" means the required cost necessary to construct or renovate a facility.

(5) "Life-cycle cost analysis" means an analytical technique that considers certain costs of owning, using, and operating a facility over its economic life, including but not limited to:

a. Initial costs;

b. System repair and replacement costs;

c. Maintenance costs;

d. Operating costs, including energy costs; and

e. Salvage value.

(6) Repealed by Session Laws 1993, c. 334, s. 3, effective July 13, 1993.

(7) "State agency" means the State of North Carolina or any board, bureau, commission, department, institution, or agency of the State.

(8) "State-assisted facility" means a facility constructed or renovated in whole or in part with State funds or with funds guaranteed or insured by a State agency.

(9) "State facility" means a facility constructed or renovated, by a State agency.

(10) "State institution of higher learning" means any constituent institution of The University of North Carolina. (1975, c. 434, s. 2; 1989, c. 23, s. 1; 1993, c. 334, s. 3; 2001-415, s. 2; 2006-190, ss. 9, 10, 11; 2007-546, s. 3.1(c); 2009-446, s. 1(f); 2013-360, s. 15.22(o).)

§ 143-64.12. Authority and duties of the Department; State agencies and State institutions of higher learning.

(a) The Department of Environment and Natural Resources through the State Energy Office shall develop a comprehensive program to manage energy, water, and other utility use for State agencies and State institutions of higher learning and shall update this program annually. Each State agency and State institution of higher learning shall develop and implement a management plan that is consistent with the State's comprehensive program under this subsection to manage energy, water, and other utility use, and that addresses any findings or recommendations resulting from the energy audit required by subsection (b1) of this section. The energy consumption per gross square foot for all State buildings in total shall be reduced by twenty percent (20%) by 2010 and thirty percent (30%) by 2015 based on energy consumption for the 2002-2003 fiscal year. Each State agency and State institution of higher learning shall update its management plan annually and include strategies for supporting the energy consumption reduction requirements under this subsection. Each community college shall submit to the State Energy Office an annual written report of utility consumption and costs. Management plans submitted annually by State institutions of higher learning shall include all of the following:

(1) Estimates of all costs associated with implementing energy conservation measures, including pre-installation and post-installation costs.

(2) The cost of analyzing the projected energy savings.

(3) Design costs, engineering costs, pre-installation costs, post-installation costs, debt service, and any costs for converting to an alternative energy source.

(4) An analysis that identifies projected annual energy savings and estimated payback periods.

(a1) State agencies and State institutions of higher learning shall carry out the construction and renovation of facilities in such a manner as to further the policy set forth under this section and to ensure the use of life-cycle cost analyses and practices to conserve energy, water, and other utilities.

(b) The Department of Administration shall develop and implement policies, procedures, and standards to ensure that State purchasing practices improve efficiency regarding energy, water, and other utility use and take the cost of the product over the economic life of the product into consideration. The Department of Administration shall adopt and implement Building Energy Design Guidelines. These guidelines shall include energy-use goals and standards, economic assumptions for life-cycle cost analysis, and other criteria on building systems and technologies. The Department of Administration shall modify the design criteria for construction and renovation of facilities of State buildings and State institutions of higher learning buildings to require that a life-cycle cost analysis be conducted pursuant to G.S. 143-64.15.

(b1) The Department of Administration, as part of the Facilities Condition and Assessment Program, shall identify and recommend energy conservation maintenance and operating procedures that are designed to reduce energy consumption within the facility of a State agency or a State institution of higher learning and that require no significant expenditure of funds. Every State agency or State institution of higher learning shall implement these recommendations. Where energy management equipment is proposed for any facility of a State agency or of a State institution of higher learning, the maximum interchangeability and compatibility of equipment components shall be required. As part of the Facilities Condition and Assessment Program under this section, the Department of Administration, in consultation with the State Energy Office, shall develop an energy audit and a procedure for conducting energy audits. Every five years the Department shall conduct an energy audit for each State agency or State institution of higher learning, and the energy audits conducted shall serve as a preliminary energy survey. The State Energy Office shall be responsible for system-level detailed surveys.

(b2) The Department of Administration shall submit a report of the energy audit required by subsection (b1) of this section to the affected State agency or State institution of higher learning and to the State Energy Office. The State Energy Office shall review each audit and, in consultation with the affected State agency or State institution of higher learning, incorporate the audit findings and recommendations into the management plan required by subsection (a) of this section.

(c) through (g) Repealed by Session Laws 1993, c. 334, s. 4.

(h) When conducting a facilities condition and assessment under this section, the Department of Administration shall identify and recommend to the State Energy Office any facility of a State agency or State institution of higher learning as suitable for building commissioning to reduce energy consumption within the facility or as suitable for installing an energy savings measure pursuant to a guaranteed energy savings contract under Part 2 of this Article.

(i) Consistent with G.S. 150B-2(8a)h., the Department of Administration may adopt architectural and engineering standards to implement this section.

(j) The State Energy Office shall submit a report by December 1 of each year to the Joint Legislative Commission on Governmental Operations describing the comprehensive program to manage energy, water, and other utility use for State agencies and State institutions of higher learning required by subsection (a) of this section. The report shall also contain the following:

(1) A comprehensive overview of how State agencies and State institutions of higher learning are managing energy, water, and other utility use and achieving efficiency gains.

(2) Any new measures that could be taken by State agencies and State institutions of higher learning to achieve greater efficiency gains, including any changes in general law that might be needed.

(3) A summary of the State agency and State institutions of higher learning management plans required by subsection (a) of this section and the energy audits required by subsection (b1) of this section.

(4) A list of the State agencies and State institutions of higher learning that did and did not submit management plans required by subsection (a) of this section and a list of the State agencies and State institutions of higher learning that received an energy audit.

(5) Any recommendations on how management plans can be better managed and implemented. (1975, c. 434, s. 3; 1993, c. 334, s. 4; 2000-140, s. 76(f); 2001-415, s. 3; 2006-190, s. 12; 2007-546, s. 3.1(a); 2008-198, s. 11.1; 2009-446, s. 1(e); 2010-31, s. 14.3; 2010-196, s. 2; 2013-360, s. 15.22(p).)

§ 143-64.13: Repealed by Session Laws 1993, c. 334, s. 5.

§ 143-64.14: Recodified as § 143-64.16 by Session Laws 1993, c. 334, s. 7.

§ 143-64.15. Life-cycle cost analysis.

(a) A life-cycle cost analysis shall be commenced at the schematic design phase of the construction or renovation project, shall be updated or amended as needed at the design development phase, and shall be updated or amended again as needed at the construction document phase. A life-cycle cost analysis shall include, but not be limited to, all of the following elements:

(1) The coordination, orientation, and positioning of the facility on its physical site.

(2) The amount and type of fenestration and the potential for daylighting employed in the facility.

(3) Thermal characteristics of materials and the amount of insulation incorporated into the facility design.

(4) The variable occupancy and operating conditions of the facility, including illumination levels.

(5) Architectural features that affect the consumption of energy, water, and other utilities.

(b) The life-cycle cost analysis performed for any State facility shall, in addition to the requirements set forth in subsection (a) of this section, include, but not be limited to, all of the following:

(1) An energy-consumption analysis of the facility's energy-consuming systems in accordance with the provisions of subsection (g) of this section.

(2) The initial estimated cost of each energy-consuming system being compared and evaluated.

(3) The estimated annual operating cost of all utility requirements.

(4) The estimated annual cost of maintaining each energy-consuming system.

(5) The average estimated replacement cost for each system expressed in annual terms for the economic life of the facility.

(c) Each entity shall conduct a life-cycle cost analysis pursuant to this section for the construction or the renovation of any State facility or State-assisted facility of 20,000 or more gross square feet. For the replacement of heating, ventilation, and air-conditioning equipment in any State facility or State-assisted facility of 20,000 or more gross square feet, the entity shall conduct a life-cycle cost analysis of the replacement equipment pursuant to this section when the replacement is financed under a guaranteed energy savings contract or financed using repair and renovation funds.

(d) The life-cycle cost analysis shall be certified by a registered professional engineer or bear the seal of a North Carolina registered architect, or both. The engineer or architect shall be particularly qualified by training and experience for the type of work involved, but shall not be employed directly or indirectly by a fuel provider, utility company, or group supported by fuel providers or utility funds. Plans and specifications for facilities involving public funds shall be designed in conformance with the provisions of G.S. 133-1.1.

(e) In order to protect the integrity of historic buildings, no provision of this Article shall be interpreted to require the implementation of measures to conserve energy, water, or other utility use that conflict with respect to any property eligible for, nominated to, or entered on the National Register of Historic Places, pursuant to the National Historic Preservation Act of 1966, P.L. 89-665; any historic building located within an historic district as provided in Chapters 160A or 153A of the General Statutes; any historic building listed, owned, or under the jurisdiction of an historic properties commission as provided in Chapter 160A or 153A; nor any historic property owned by the State or assisted by the State.

(f) Each State agency shall use the life-cycle cost analysis over the economic life of the facility in selecting the optimum system or combination of systems to be incorporated into the design of the facility.

(g) The energy-consumption analysis of the operation of energy-consuming systems utilities in a facility shall include, but not be limited to, all of the following:

(1) The comparison of two or more system alternatives.

(2) The simulation or engineering evaluation of each system over the entire range of operation of the facility for a year's operating period.

(3) The engineering evaluation of the consumption of energy, water, and other utilities of component equipment in each system considering the operation of such components at other than full or rated outputs. (1993, c. 334, s. 6; 2001-415, ss. 4, 5; 2006-190, s. 13; 2007-546, s. 4.1.)

§ 143-64.15A. Certification of life-cycle cost analysis.

Each State agency and each State institution of higher learning performing a life-cycle cost analysis for the purpose of constructing or renovating any facility shall, prior to selecting a design option or advertising for bids for construction, submit the life-cycle cost analysis to the Department for certification at the schematic design phase and again when it is updated or amended as needed in accordance with G.S. 143-64.15. The Department shall review the material submitted by the State agency or State institution of higher learning, reserve the right to require an agency or institution to complete additional analysis to comply with certification, perform any additional analysis, as necessary, to comply with G.S. 143-341(11), and require that all construction or renovation conducted by the State agency or State institution of higher learning comply with the certification issued by the Department. (2001-415, s. 6; 2007-546, s. 4.2.)

§ 143-64.16. Application of Part.

The provisions of this Part shall not apply to municipalities or counties, nor to any agency or department of any municipality or county; provided, however, this Part shall apply to any board of a community college. Community college is defined in G.S. 115D-2(2). (1975, c. 434, s. 5; 1989, c. 23, s. 2; 1993, c. 334, s. 7; 1993 (Reg. Sess., 1994), c. 775, s. 2.)

Part 2. Energy Saving Measures for Governmental Units.

§ 143-64.17. Definitions.

As used in this Part:

(1) "Energy conservation measure" means a facility or meter alteration, training, or services related to the operation of the facility or meter, when the alteration, training, or services provide anticipated energy savings or capture lost revenue. Energy conservation measure includes any of the following:

    a.   Insulation of the building structure and systems within the building.

    b.   Storm windows or doors, caulking, weatherstripping, multiglazed windows or doors, heat-absorbing or heat-reflective glazed or coated window or door systems, additional glazing, reductions in glass area, or other window or door system modifications that reduce energy consumption.

    c.   Automatic energy control systems.

    d.   Heating, ventilating, or air-conditioning system modifications or replacements.

    e.   Replacement or modification of lighting fixtures to increase the energy efficiency of a lighting system without increasing the overall illumination of a facility, unless an increase in illumination is necessary to conform to the applicable State or local building code or is required by the light system after the proposed modifications are made.

    f.   Energy recovery systems.

    g.   Cogeneration systems that produce steam or forms of energy such as heat, as well as electricity, for use primarily within a building or complex of buildings.

    h.   Repealed by Session Laws 2006-190, s. 2, effective August 3, 2006, and applicable to contracts entered into or renewed on or after that date.

    i.   Faucets with automatic or metered shut-off valves, leak detection equipment, water meters, water recycling equipment, and wastewater recovery systems.

j. Other energy conservation measures that conserve energy, water, or other utilities.

(2) "Energy savings" means a measured reduction in fuel costs, energy costs, water costs, stormwater fees, other utility costs, or operating costs, including environmental discharge fees, water and sewer maintenance fees, and increased meter accuracy, created from the implementation of one or more energy conservation measures when compared with an established baseline of previous costs, including captured lost revenues, developed by the governmental unit.

(2a) "Governmental unit" means either a local governmental unit or a State governmental unit.

(3) "Guaranteed energy savings contract" means a contract for the evaluation, recommendation, or implementation of energy conservation measures, including the design and installation of equipment or the repair or replacement of existing equipment or meters, in which all payments, except obligations on termination of the contract before its expiration, are to be made over time, and in which energy savings are guaranteed to exceed costs.

(4) "Local governmental unit" means any board or governing body of a political subdivision of the State, including any board of a community college, any school board, or an agency, commission, or authority of a political subdivision of the State.

(5) "Qualified provider" means a person or business experienced in the design, implementation, and installation of energy conservation measures who has been prequalified by the State Energy Office according to the prequalification criteria established by that Office.

(5a) "Qualified reviewer" means an architect or engineer who is (i) licensed in this State and (ii) experienced in the design, implementation, and installation of energy efficiency measures.

(6) "Request for proposals" means a negotiated procurement initiated by a governmental unit by way of a published notice that includes the following:

a. The name and address of the governmental unit.

b. The name, address, title, and telephone number of a contact person in the governmental unit.

c. Notice indicating that the governmental unit is requesting qualified providers to propose energy conservation measures through a guaranteed energy savings contract.

d. The date, time, and place where proposals must be received.

e. The evaluation criteria for assessing the proposals.

f. A statement reserving the right of the governmental unit to reject any or all the proposals.

g. Any other stipulations and clarifications the governmental unit may require.

(7) "State governmental unit" means the State or a department, an agency, a board, or a commission of the State, including the Board of Governors of The University of North Carolina and its constituent institutions. (1993 (Reg. Sess., 1994), c. 775, s. 3; 1995, c. 295, s. 1; 1999-235, ss. 1, 2; 2002-161, s. 2; 2006-190, s. 2; 2013-396, s. 1.)

§ 143-64.17A. Solicitation of guaranteed energy savings contracts.

(a) RFP Issuance. - Before entering into a guaranteed energy savings contract, a governmental unit shall issue a request for proposals. Notice of the request shall be published at least 15 days in advance of the time specified for opening of the proposals in at least one newspaper of general circulation in the geographic area for which the local governmental unit is responsible or, in the case of a State governmental unit, in which the facility or facilities are located. No guaranteed energy savings contract shall be awarded by any governmental unit unless at least two proposals have been received from qualified providers. Provided that if after the publication of the notice of the request for proposals, fewer than two proposals have been received from qualified providers, or fewer than two qualified providers attend the mandatory prebid meeting, the governmental unit may then open the proposals and select a qualified provider even if only one proposal is received.

(b)	Preliminary Proposal Evaluation. - The governmental unit shall evaluate a sealed proposal from any qualified provider. A qualified reviewer shall be required to evaluate the proposals and will provide the governmental unit with a letter report containing both qualitative and quantitative evaluation of the proposals. The report may include a recommendation for selection, but the governmental unit is not obligated to follow it.

(c)	Receipt of Proposals for Unit of Local Government. - In the case of a local governmental unit, proposals received pursuant to this section shall be opened by a member or an employee of the governing body of the local governmental unit at a public opening at which the contents of the proposals shall be announced and recorded in the minutes of the governing body. Proposals shall be evaluated for the local governmental unit by a qualified reviewer on the basis of:

(1)	The information required in subsection (b) of this section; and

(2)	The criteria stated in the request for proposals.

The local governmental unit may require a qualified provider to include in calculating the cost of a proposal for a guaranteed energy savings contract any reasonable fee payable by the local governmental unit for the evaluation of the proposal by a qualified reviewer not employed as a member of the staff of the local governmental unit or the qualified provider.

(c1)	Receipt of Proposals for Unit of State Government. - In the case of a State governmental unit, proposals received pursuant to this section shall be opened by a member or an employee of the State governmental unit at a public opening and the contents of the proposals shall be announced at this opening. Proposals shall be evaluated for the State governmental unit by a qualified reviewer who is either privately retained, employed with the Department of Administration, or employed as a member of the staff of the State governmental unit. The proposal shall be evaluated on the basis of the information and report required in subsection (b) of this section and the criteria stated in the request for proposals.

The State governmental unit shall require a qualified provider to include in calculating the cost of a proposal for a guaranteed energy savings contract any reasonable fee payable by the State governmental unit for evaluation of the proposal by a qualified reviewer not employed as a member of the staff of the State governmental unit or the qualified provider. The Department of

Administration may charge the State governmental unit a reasonable fee for the evaluation of the proposal if the Department's services are used for the evaluation and the cost paid by the State governmental unit to the Department of Administration shall be calculated in the cost of the proposal under this subsection.

(d) Criteria for Selection of Provider. - The governmental unit shall select the qualified provider that it determines to best meet the needs of the governmental unit by evaluating all of the following and following the procedures set forth in subsection (d1) of this section:

(1), (2) Repealed by Session Laws 2013-396, s. 2, effective August 23, 2013.

(3) Quality of the products and energy conservation measures proposed.

(4) Repealed by Session Laws 2013-396, s. 2, effective August 23, 2013.

(5) General reputation and performance capabilities of the qualified providers.

(6) Substantial conformity with the specifications and other conditions set forth in the request for proposals.

(7) Time specified in the proposals for the performance of the contract.

(8) Any other factors the governmental unit deems necessary, which factors shall be made a matter of record.

(d1) Process for Selection of Provider. - The governmental unit shall select a short list of finalists on the basis of its rankings of the written proposals under the criteria set forth in subsection (d) of this section as well as references from past clients. The governmental unit shall have the highest ranked qualified provider prepare a cost-savings analysis for the proposed contract showing at a minimum a comparison of the total estimated project savings to the total estimated project costs for the proposed term. If the governmental unit and the qualified provider cannot negotiate acceptable terms, pricing, and savings estimates, the governmental unit may terminate the process and begin negotiations with the second highest ranked qualified provider. The State Energy Office shall review the selected qualified provider's proposal, cost-benefit analysis, and other relevant documents prior to the governmental unit announcing the award.

(e) Nothing in this section shall limit the authority of governmental units as set forth in Article 3D of this Chapter. (1993 (Reg. Sess., 1994), c. 775, s. 3; 2002-161, s. 3; 2013-396, s. 2.)

§ 143-64.17B. Guaranteed energy savings contracts.

(a) A governmental unit may enter into a guaranteed energy savings contract with a qualified provider if all of the following apply:

(1) The term of the contract does not exceed 20 years from the date of the installation and acceptance by the governmental unit of the energy conservation measures provided for under the contract.

(2) The governmental unit finds that the energy savings resulting from the performance of the contract will equal or exceed the total cost of the contract.

(3) The energy conservation measures to be installed under the contract are for an existing building or utility system.

(b) Before entering into a guaranteed energy savings contract, the governmental unit shall provide published notice of the time and place or of the meeting at which it proposes to award the contract, the names of the parties to the proposed contract, and the contract's purpose. The notice must be published at least 15 days before the date of the proposed award or meeting.

(c) A qualified provider entering into a guaranteed energy savings contract under this Part shall provide security to the governmental unit in the form acceptable to the Office of the State Treasurer and in an amount equal to one hundred percent (100%) of the guaranteed savings for the term of the guaranteed energy savings contract to assure the provider's faithful performance. Any bonds required by this subsection shall be subject to the provisions of Article 3 of Chapter 44A of the General Statutes. If the savings resulting from a guaranteed energy savings contract are not as great as projected under the contract and all required shortfall payments to the governmental unit have not been made, the governmental unit may terminate the contract without incurring any additional obligation to the qualified provider.

(d) As used in this section, "total cost" shall include, but not be limited to, costs of construction, costs of financing, and costs of maintenance and training during the term of the contract. "Total cost" does not include any obligations on termination of the contract before its expiration, provided that those obligations are disclosed when the contract is executed.

(e) A guaranteed energy savings contract may not require the governmental unit to purchase a maintenance contract or other maintenance agreement from the qualified provider who installs energy conservation measures under the contract if the unit of government takes appropriate action to budget for its own forces or another provider to maintain new systems installed and existing systems affected by the guaranteed energy savings contract.

(f) In the case of a State governmental unit, a qualified provider shall, when feasible, after the acceptance of the proposal of the qualified provider by the State governmental unit, conduct an investment grade audit. During this investment grade audit, the qualified provider shall perform in accordance with Part 1 of this Article a life cycle cost analysis of each energy conservation measure in the final proposal. If the results of the audit are not within ten percent (10%) of both the guaranteed savings contained in the proposal and the total proposal amount, either the State governmental unit or the qualified provider may terminate the project without incurring any additional obligation to the other party. However, if the State governmental unit terminates the project after the audit is conducted and the results of the audit are within ten percent (10%) of both the guaranteed savings contained in the proposal and the total proposal amount, the State governmental unit shall reimburse the qualified provider the reasonable cost incurred in conducting the audit, and the results of the audit shall become the property of the State governmental unit.

(g) A qualified provider shall provide an annual reconciliation statement based upon the results of the measurement and verification review. The statement shall disclose any shortfalls or surplus between guaranteed energy and operational savings specified in the guaranteed energy savings contract and actual, not stipulated, energy and operational savings incurred during a given guarantee year. Any guaranteed energy and operational savings shall be determined by using one of the measurement and verification methodologies listed in the United States Department of Energy's Measurement and Verification Guidelines for Energy Savings Performance Contracting, the International Performance Measurement and Verification Protocol (IPMVP) maintained by the Efficiency Valuation Organization, or Guideline 14-2002 of the American Society of Heating, Refrigerating, and Air-Conditioning Engineers. If due to existing data limitations or the nonconformance of specific project characteristics, none of the three methodologies listed in this subsection is sufficient for measuring guaranteed savings, the qualified provider shall develop an alternate method that is compatible with one of the three methodologies and mutually agreeable to the governmental unit. The guarantee year shall consist of a 12-month term commencing from the time that the energy conservation measures become fully operational. A qualified provider shall pay the governmental unit or its assignee any shortfall in the guaranteed energy and operational savings after the total year savings have been determined. In the case of a governmental unit, a surplus in any one year shall not be carried forward or applied to a shortfall in any other year. (1993 (Reg. Sess., 1994), c. 775, s. 3; 1995, c. 295, s. 2; 1999-235, s. 3; 2002-161, s. 4; 2003-138, s. 1; 2006-190, s. 3; 2009-375, s. 2; 2013-396, s. 3.)

§ 143-64.17C: Repealed by Session Laws 2002, ch. 161, s. 5, effective January 1, 2003, and applicable to contracts entered into on or after that date.

§ 143-64.17D. Contract continuance.

A guaranteed energy savings contract may extend beyond the fiscal year in which it becomes effective. Such a contract shall stipulate that it does not constitute a direct or indirect pledge of the taxing power or full faith and credit of any governmental unit. (1993 (Reg. Sess., 1994), c. 775, s. 3; 2002-161, s. 6.)

§ 143-64.17E. Payments under contract.

A local governmental unit may use any funds, whether operating or capital, that are not otherwise restricted by law for the payment of a guaranteed energy savings contract. State appropriations to any local governmental unit shall not be reduced as a result of energy savings occurring as a result of a guaranteed energy savings contract. (1993 (Reg. Sess., 1994), c. 775, s. 3.)

§ 143-64.17F. State agencies to use contracts when feasible; rules; recommendations.

(a) State governmental units shall evaluate the use of guaranteed energy savings contracts in reducing energy costs and may use those contracts when feasible and practical.

(b) The Department of Administration, in consultation with the Department of Environment and Natural Resources, through the State Energy Office, shall adopt rules for: (i) agency evaluation of guaranteed energy savings contracts; (ii) establishing time periods for consideration of guaranteed energy savings contracts by the Office of State Budget and Management, the Office of the State Treasurer, and the Council of State, and (iii) setting measurements and verification criteria, including review, audit, and precertification. Prior to adopting any rules pursuant to this section, the Department shall consult with and obtain approval of those rules from the State Treasurer. The rules adopted pursuant to this subsection shall not apply to energy conservation measures implemented pursuant to G.S. 143-64.17L.

(c) The Department of Administration, and the Department of Environment and Natural Resources through the State Energy Office, may provide to the Council of State its recommendations concerning any energy savings contracts being considered. (2002-161, s. 7; 2003-138, s. 2; 2009-446, s. 1(d); 2011-145, s. 9.6D(d); 2013-360, s. 15.22(d).)

§ 143-64.17G. Report on guaranteed energy savings contracts entered into by local governmental units.

A local governmental unit that enters into a guaranteed energy savings contract must report the contract and the terms of the contract to the Local Government Commission and the State Energy Office of the Department of Environment and Natural Resources. The Commission shall compile the information and report it biennially to the Joint Commission on Governmental Operations. In compiling the information, the Local Government Commission shall include information on the energy savings expected to be realized from a contract and, with the assistance of the Office of State Construction and the State Energy Office, shall evaluate whether expected savings have in fact been realized. (1993 (Reg. Sess., 1994), c. 775, s. 9; 2006-190, s. 4; 2009-375, s. 3; 2013-360, s. 15.22(e).)

§ 143-64.17H. Report on guaranteed energy savings contracts entered into by State governmental units.

A State governmental unit that enters into a guaranteed energy savings contract or implements an energy conservation measure pursuant to G.S. 143-64.17L must report either (i) the contract and the terms of the contract or (ii) the implementation of the measure to the State Energy Office of the Department of Environment and Natural Resources within 30 days of the date the contract is entered into or the measure is implemented. In addition, within 60 days after each annual anniversary date of a guaranteed energy savings contract, the State governmental unit must report the status of the contract to the State Energy Office, including any details required by the State Energy Office. The State Energy Office shall compile the information for each fiscal year and report it to the Joint Legislative Commission on Governmental Operations and to the Local Government Commission annually by December 1. In compiling the information, the State Energy Office shall include information on the energy savings expected to be realized from a contract or implementation and shall evaluate whether expected savings have in fact been realized. (2002-161, s. 8; 2006-190, s. 5; 2009-446, s. 1(c); 2011-145, s. 9.6D(e); 2013-360, s. 15.22(f).)

§ 143-64.17I. Installment and lease purchase contracts.

A local governmental unit may provide for the acquisition, installation, or maintenance of energy conservation measures acquired pursuant to this Part by installment or lease purchase contracts in accordance with and subject to the provisions of G.S. 160A-20 and G.S. 160A-19, as applicable. (2002-161, s. 8.)

§ 143-64.17J. Financing by State governmental units.

State governmental units may finance the acquisition, installation, or maintenance of energy conservation measures acquired pursuant to this Part in the manner and to the extent set forth in Article 8 of Chapter 142 of the General Statutes or as otherwise authorized by law. (2002-161, s. 8.)

§ 143-64.17K. Inspection and compliance certification for State governmental units.

The provisions of G.S. 143-341(3) shall not apply to any energy conservation measure for State governmental units provided pursuant to this Part, except as specifically set forth in this section. Except as otherwise exempt under G.S. 116-31.11, the following shall apply to all energy conservation measures provided to State governmental units pursuant to this Part:

(1)   The provisions of G.S. 133-1.1.

(2)   Inspection and certification by:

a.   The applicable local building inspector under Part 4 of Article 18 of Chapter 153A of the General Statutes or Part 5 of Article 19 of Chapter 160A of the General Statutes; or

b.   At the election of the State governmental unit, the Department of Administration under G.S. 143-341(3)d.

The cost of compliance with this section may be included in the cost of the project in accordance with G.S. 143-64.17A(c1) and may be included in the cost financed under Article 8 of Chapter 142 of the General Statutes. (2002-161, s. 8.)

§ 143-64.17L. Board of Governors may authorize energy conservation measures at constituent institutions.

(a)   Authority. - Notwithstanding the provisions of this Part to the contrary, the Board of Governors of The University of North Carolina may authorize any constituent institution listed in subsection (e) of this section to implement an energy conservation measure without entering into a guaranteed energy savings contract if both of the following conditions are met:

(1)   The Board of Governors finds that the energy savings resulting from the implementation of the energy conservation measure shall, according to the energy savings analysis received pursuant to G.S. 143-64.17M(a), equal or exceed the total cost of implementing the measure. If the proposed implementation will be financed with debt, then the energy savings analysis

must project sufficient energy savings to pay the debt service on any bonds to be issued. As used in this subdivision, the term "total cost' shall have the same meaning as it does in G.S. 143-64.17B(d).

(2) The energy conservation measure is for an existing building or utility system.

(b) Scope of Authority. - In implementing an energy conservation measure pursuant to subsection (a) of this section, the Board of Governors may undertake or authorize any constituent institution listed in subsection (e) of this section to undertake any action that (i) could be required of a qualified provider under a guaranteed energy savings contract or (ii) is otherwise permissible under this Part.

(c) Projects Consisting of Multiple Energy Conservation Measures. - The Board of Governors may authorize the implementation of multiple energy conservation measures simultaneously as part of a single project. When doing so, the findings required by subsection (a) of this section may be made with respect to the project as a whole and need not be made with respect to individual energy conservation measures. Similarly, the analyses required by G.S. 143-64.17M may be conducted for the project as a whole instead of for individual energy conservation measures.

(d) Continuing Applicability of Part to Contracts. - If the Board of Governors or a constituent institution implements an energy conservation measure through a guaranteed energy savings contract, that contract shall accord in all respects with the requirements of this Part.

(e) The Board of Governors may authorize North Carolina State University and the University of North Carolina at Charlotte to implement an energy conservation measure without entering into a guaranteed energy savings contract pursuant to this section. (2011-145, s. 9.6D(a); 2013-396, s. 4(a).)

§ 143-64.17M. Energy savings analysis required prior to implementation; post-implementation analyses required.

(a) Energy Savings Analysis Required Prior to Implementation. - Prior to implementing an energy conservation measure pursuant to G.S. 143-64.17L, an energy savings analysis shall be performed to validate the economic assumptions that purportedly support the implementation of the measure. This analysis shall be performed by a third party selected by the constituent institution and shall include an energy consumption analysis to develop a baseline of previous costs of all utilities' energy consumption for the institution on the assumption that the energy conservation measure was not undertaken. The completed analysis shall be submitted to The University of North Carolina General Administration and to the State Energy Office.

(b) Post-Implementation Analyses Required. - A constituent institution that implements an energy conservation measure pursuant to G.S. 143-64.17L shall retain a third party to perform an annual measurement and verification of energy savings resulting from the energy conservation measure as compared to the baseline of previous costs set forth in the energy savings analysis required by subsection (a) of this section. The third party shall annually provide a reconciliation statement based upon the results of a preagreed upon measurement, monitoring, and verification protocol which shall disclose any shortfall or surplus between the estimated energy usage and operational savings set forth in the energy savings analysis required by subsection (a) of this section and actual, not stipulated, energy usage and operational savings incurred during a given year.

If a reconciliation statement reveals a shortfall in energy savings for a particular year, the constituent institution shall be responsible for and shall pay the shortfall. However, the institution shall not be held responsible for losses due to natural disasters or other emergencies. Any surplus shall be retained by the institution and may be used in the same manner as any other energy savings. (2011-145, s. 9.6D(b).)

§§ 143-64.17L through 143-64.19. Reserved for future codification purposes.

Article 3C.

Contracts to Obtain Consultant Services.

§ 143-64.20. "Agency" defined; Governor's approval required.

(a) For purposes of this Article the term "agency" shall mean every State agency, institution, board, commission, bureau, department, division, council, member of the Council of State, or officer of the State government.

(b) No State agency shall contract to obtain services of a consultant or advisory nature unless the proposed contract has been justified to and approved in writing by the Governor of North Carolina. All written approvals shall be maintained on file as part of the agency's records for not less than five years. (1975, c. 887, s. 1.)

§ 143-64.21. Findings to be made by Governor.

The Governor, before granting written approval of any such contract, must find:

(1) That the contract is reasonably necessary to the proper function of such State agency; and

(2) That such services or advice cannot be performed within the resources of such State agency;

(3) That the estimated cost is reasonable as compared with the likely benefits or results; and

(4) That the General Assembly has appropriated funds for such contract or that such funds are otherwise available; and

(5) That all rules and regulations of the Department of Administration have been or will be complied with. (1975, c. 879, s. 46; c. 887, s. 2.)

§ 143-64.22. Contracts with other State agencies; competitive proposals.

The rules of the Department of Administration shall include provisions to assure that all consultant contracts let by State agencies shall be made with other agencies of the State of North Carolina, if such contract can reasonably be performed by them; or otherwise, that wherever practicable a sufficient number of sources for the performance of such contract are solicited for competitive proposals and that such proposals are properly evaluated for award to the State's best advantage. (1975, c. 879, s. 46; c. 887, s. 3; 1987, c. 827, s. 217.)

§ 143-64.23. Compliance required; penalty for violation of Article.

No disbursement of State funds shall be made and no such contract shall be binding until the provisions of G.S. 143-64.21 and 143-64.22 have been complied with. Any employee or official of the State of North Carolina who violates this Article shall be liable to repay any amount expended in violation of this Article, plus court costs. (1975, c. 887, s. 4.)

§ 143-64.24. Applicability of Article.

This Article shall not apply to the following agencies:

(1)   The General Assembly.

(2)   Special study commissions.

(3)   The Research Triangle Institute.

(4)   The School of Government at the University of North Carolina at Chapel Hill.

(5)   Attorneys employed by the North Carolina Department of Justice.

(6)   Physicians or doctors performing contractual services for any State agency.

(7)   Independent Review Organizations selected by the Commissioner of Insurance pursuant to G.S. 58-50-85.

(8)   The University of North Carolina. The Board of Governors of the University of North Carolina must adopt policies and procedures governing contracts to obtain the services of a consultant by the constituent institutions of the University of North Carolina. (1975, c. 887, s. 5; 1977, c. 802, s. 50.57; 2001-446, s. 4.6A; 2006-95, s. 2.1; 2006-264, s. 29(l).)

§§ 143-64.25 through 143-64.30. Reserved for future codification purposes.

Article 3D.

Procurement of Architectural, Engineering, and Surveying Services.

§ 143-64.31. Declaration of public policy.

(a) It is the public policy of this State and all public subdivisions and Local Governmental Units thereof, except in cases of special emergency involving the health and safety of the people or their property, to announce all requirements for architectural, engineering, surveying, construction management at risk services, design-build services, and public-private partnership construction services to select firms qualified to provide such services on the basis of demonstrated competence and qualification for the type of professional services required without regard to fee other than unit price information at this stage, and thereafter to negotiate a contract for those services at a fair and reasonable fee with the best qualified firm. If a contract cannot be negotiated with the best qualified firm, negotiations with that firm shall be terminated and initiated with the next best qualified firm. Selection of a firm under this Article shall include the use of good faith efforts by the public entity to notify minority firms of the opportunity to submit qualifications for consideration by the public entity.

(a1) A resident firm providing architectural, engineering, surveying, construction management at risk services, design-build services, or public-private partnership construction services shall be granted a preference over a nonresident firm, in the same manner, on the same basis, and to the extent that a preference is granted in awarding contracts for these services by the other state to its resident firms over firms resident in the State of North Carolina. For purposes of this section, a resident firm is a firm that has paid unemployment taxes or income taxes in North Carolina and whose principal place of business is located in this State.

(b) Public entities that contract with a construction manager at risk, design-builder, or private developer under a public-private partnership under this section shall report to the Secretary of Administration the following information on all projects where a construction manager at risk, design-builder, or private developer under a public-private partnership is utilized:

(1)   A detailed explanation of the reason why the particular construction manager at risk, design-builder, or private developer was selected.

(2)   The terms of the contract with the construction manager at risk, design-builder, or private developer.

(3)   A list of all other firms considered but not selected as the construction manager at risk, design-builder, or private developer, and the amount of their proposed fees for services.

(4)   A report on the form of bidding utilized by the construction manager at risk, design-builder, or private developer on the project.

(5)   A detailed explanation of why the particular delivery method was used in lieu of the delivery methods identified in G.S. 143-128(a1) subdivisions (1) through (3) and the anticipated benefits to the public entity from using the particular delivery method.

(c)   The Secretary of Administration shall adopt rules to implement the provisions of this subsection including the format and frequency of reporting.

(d)   A public body letting a contract pursuant to any of the delivery methods identified in subdivisions (a1)(4), (a1)(6), (a1)(7), or (a1)(8) of G.S. 143-128 shall submit the report required by G.S. 143-64.31(b) no later than 12 months from the date the public body takes beneficial occupancy of the project. In the event that the public body fails to do so, the public body shall be prohibited from utilizing subdivisions (a1)(4), (a1)(6), (a1)(7), or (a1)(8) of G.S. 143-128 until such time as the public body completes the reporting requirement under this this section. Contracts entered into in violation of this prohibition shall not be deemed ultra vires and shall remain valid and fully enforceable. Any person, corporation or entity, however, which has submitted a bid or response to a request for proposals on any construction project previously advertised by the public body shall be entitled to obtain an injunction against the public body compelling the public body to comply with the reporting requirements of this section and from commencing or continuing a project let in violation of this subdivision until such time as the public body has complied with the reporting requirements of this section. The plaintiff in such cases shall not be entitled to recover monetary damages caused by the public body's failure to comply with this reporting requirements section, and neither the plaintiff nor the defendant shall be allowed to recover attorneys fees except as otherwise allowed by G.S. 1A-11 or G.S. 6-21.5. An action seeking the injunctive relief allowed by this subdivision must be filed within four years from the date that the owner took beneficial occupancy of the project for which the report remains due.

(e)   For purposes of this Article, the definition in G.S. 143-128.1B and G.S. 143-128.1C shall apply. (1987, c. 102, s. 1; 1989, c. 230, s. 2; 2001-496, s. 1; 2006-210, s. 1; 2013-401, s. 1.)

§ 143-64.32. Written exemption of particular contracts.

Units of local government or the North Carolina Department of Transportation may in writing exempt particular projects from the provisions of this Article in the case of proposed projects where an estimated professional fee is in an amount less than fifty thousand dollars ($50,000). (1987, c. 102, s. 2; 2013-401, s. 2.)

§ 143-64.33. Advice in selecting consultants or negotiating consultant contracts.

On architectural, engineering, or surveying contracts, the Department of Transportation or the Department of Administration may provide, upon request by a county, city, town or other subdivision of the State, advice in the process of selecting consultants or in negotiating consultant contracts with architects, engineers, or surveyors or any or all. (1987, c. 102, s. 3; 1989, c. 230, s. 3, c. 770, s. 44.)

§ 143-64.34. Exemption of certain projects.

State capital improvement projects under the jurisdiction of the State Building Commission, capital improvement projects of The University of North Carolina, and community college capital improvement projects, where the estimated expenditure of public money is less than five hundred thousand dollars ($500,000), are exempt from the provisions of this Article. (1987, c. 102, s. 3.1; c. 830, s. 78(a); 1997-314, s. 1; 1997-412, s. 5; 2001-496, ss. 8(b), 8(c); 2005-300, s. 1; 2005-370, s. 1; 2007-322, s. 2; 2007-446, s. 7.)

§§ 143-64.35 through 143-64.49. Reserved for future codification purposes.

Article 3E.

State/Public School Child Care Contracts.

§ 143-64.50. State/public school-contracted on-, near-site child care facilities; location authorization; contract for program services authorization.

State agencies and local boards of education may contract with any city, county, or other political subdivision of the State, governmental or private agency, person, association, or corporation to establish child care services in State buildings and public schools. If the child care program is located in a State building that is not used for legislative activity, the procedure for approving the location of the program shall be pursuant to G.S. 143-341(4). If the child care program is located in a State building used for legislative activity, the procedure for approving the location of the program shall be pursuant to G.S. 120-32.1. If the child care program is located in any other State building, the procedure for contracting for child care services shall be pursuant to G.S. 143-49(3). If the child care program is located in a State building used for legislative activity, the procedure for contracting for child care services shall be pursuant to G.S. 120-32(4).

Contracts for services awarded pursuant to this section are exempt from the provisions of G.S. 66-58(a) and the contract may provide for payment of rent by the lessee or the operator of the facility. (1991, c. 345, s. 1; 1997-506, s. 49.)

§ 143-64.51. State/public school-contracted child care facilities; licensing requirements.

All child care facilities established pursuant to this Article shall be licensed and regulated under the provisions of Article 7 of Chapter 110 of the General Statutes, entitled "Child Care Facilities." (1991, c. 345, s. 1; 1997-506, s. 50.)

§ 143-64.52. State/public school-contracted child care facilities; limitation of State/local board liability.

The operators of the child care facilities established pursuant to this Article shall assume all financial and legal responsibility for the operation of the programs and shall maintain adequate insurance coverage for the operations taking place in the facilities. Neither the operator or any of the staff of the facilities are considered State employees or local board of education employees by virtue of this Article alone. The State or the local boards of education are financially and legally responsible only for the maintenance of the building. (1991, c. 345, s. 1; 1997-506, s. 51.)

Article 3F.

State Privacy Act.

§ 143-64.60. State Privacy Act.

(a) It is unlawful for any State or local government agency to deny to any individual any right, benefit, or privilege provided by law because of such individual's refusal to disclose his social security account number.

The provisions of this subsection shall not apply with respect to:

(1) Any disclosure which is required or permitted by federal statute, or

(2) The disclosure of a social security number to any State or local agency maintaining a system of records in existence and operating before January 1, 1975, if such disclosure was required under statute or regulation adopted prior to such date to verify the identity of an individual.

(b) Any State or local government agency which requests an individual to disclose his social security account number shall inform that individual whether that disclosure is mandatory or voluntary, by what statutory or other authority such number is solicited, and what uses will be made of it. (2001-256, s. 1; 2001-487, s. 87.)

§§ 143-64.61 through 143-64.69. Reserved for future codification purposes.

Article 3G.

Personal Service Contracts.

§ 143-64.70. Personal service contracts - reporting requirements.

(a) By January 1 of each year, each State department, agency, and institution shall make a detailed written report to the Office of State Budget and Management and the Office of State Human Resources on its utilization of personal services contracts that have an annual expenditure greater than twenty-five thousand dollars ($25,000). The report by each State department, agency, and institution shall include the following:

(1) Identification of the department and employee responsible for oversight of the performance of the contract.

(2) Vendor or contractor name, object of expenditure description, contract award amount, purchase order or contract number, purchase order start and end date, source of funds, and amount disbursed during the fiscal year.

(3) through (7) Repealed by Session Laws 2007-322, s. 7, effective July 30, 2007.

(b) By March 15 of each year, the Office of State Budget and Management and the Office of State Human Resources shall compile and analyze the information required under subsection (a) of this section and shall submit to the Joint Legislative Commission on Governmental Operations a detailed report on the type, number, duration, cost and effectiveness of State personal services contracts throughout State government.

(c) Repealed by Session Laws 2013-410, s. 38.5, effective August 23, 2013. (2001-424, ss. 6.19(a), (b); 2005-276, s. 6.38; 2007-322, s. 7; 2013-375, s. 1; 2013-382, s. 9.1(c); 2013-410, s. 38.5.)

§§ 143-64.71 through 143-64.79: Reserved for future codification purposes.

Article 3H.

Overpayments of State Funds.

§ 143-64.80. Overpayments of State funds to persons in State-supported positions; recoupment required.

(a) An overpayment of State funds to any person in a State-funded position, whether in the form of salary or otherwise, shall be recouped by the entity that made the overpayment and, to the extent allowed by law, the amount of the overpayment may be offset against the net wages of the person receiving the overpayment.

(b) No State department, agency, or institution, or other State-funded entity may forgive repayment of an overpayment of State funds, but shall have a duty to pursue the repayment of State funds by all lawful means available, including the filing of a civil action in the General Court of Justice. (2003-263, s. 1.)

§§ 143-64.81 through 143-64.85: Reserved for future codification purposes.

Article 4.

World War Veterans Loan Administration.

§§ 143-65 through 143-105: Deleted by Session Laws 1951, c. 349.

Article 5.

Check on License Forms, Tags and Certificates Used or Issued.

§ 143-106: Repealed by Session Laws 1983, c. 913, s. 33.

§ 143-107. Transferred to § 143-106 by Session Laws 1951, c. 1010, s. 2.

Article 6.

Officers of State Institutions.

§ 143-108. Secretary to be elected from directors.

The board of directors of the various State institutions shall elect one of their number as secretary, who shall act as such at all regular or special meetings of such boards. (1907, c. 883, s. 1; C.S., s. 7517.)

§ 143-109. Directors to elect officers and employees.

All officers and employees of the various State institutions who hold elective positions shall be nominated and elected by the board of directors of the respective institutions. (1907, c. 883, s. 3; C.S., s. 7518.)

§ 143-110. Places vacated for failure to attend meetings.

Unless otherwise specially provided by law, whenever a trustee or director of any institution supported in whole or in part by State appropriation shall fail to be present for two successive years at the regular meetings of the board, his place as trustee or director shall be deemed vacant and shall be filled as provided by law for other vacancies on such boards.

This section shall not apply to any trustee or director who holds office as such by virtue of another public office held by him and shall not apply to any trustee or director chosen by any agency or authority other than the State of North Carolina. (1927, c. 225.)

§ 143-111. Director not to be elected to position under board.

It shall be unlawful for any board of directors, board of trustees or other governing body of any of the various State institutions (penal, charitable, or otherwise) to appoint or elect any person who may be or has been at any time within six months a member of such board of directors, board of trustees, or other governing body, to any position in the institution, which position may be under the control of such board of directors, board of trustees, or other governing body. (1909, c. 831; C.S., s. 7519.)

§ 143-112. Superintendents to be within call of board meetings.

The superintendent of each of the various State institutions shall be present on the premises of his institution and within the call of the board of directors during all regular or special meetings of the board, and shall respond to all calls of the board for any information which it may wish at his hands. (1907, c. 883, s. 1; C.S., s. 7520.)

§ 143-113. Trading by interested officials forbidden.

The directors, stewards, and superintendents of the State institutions shall not trade directly or indirectly with or among themselves, or with any concern in which they are interested, for any supplies needed by any such institutions. (1907, c. 883, s. 2; C.S., s. 7521.)

§ 143-114. Diversion of appropriations to State institutions.

It shall be unlawful for the board of trustees, board of directors, or other body controlling any State institution, to divert, use, or expend any moneys appropriated for the use of said institutions for its permanent improvement and enlargement to the payment of any of the current expenses of said institution or for the payment of the cost of the maintenance thereof; it shall likewise be unlawful for any board of trustees, board of directors, or other controlling body of any State institution to which money is appropriated for its maintenance by the State to divert, use or expend any money so appropriated for maintenance, for the permanent enlargement or permanent equipment, or the purchase of land for said institution. (1921, c. 232, s. 1; C.S., s. 7521 (a).)

§ 143-115. Trustee, director, officer or employee violating law guilty of misdemeanor.

Any member or members of any board of trustees, board of directors, or other controlling body governing any of the institutions of the State, or any officer, employee of, or person holding any position with any of the institutions of the State, violating any of the provisions of G.S. 143-114, shall be guilty of a Class 1 misdemeanor, and upon conviction in any court of competent jurisdiction judgment shall be rendered by such court removing such member, officer, employee, or person holding any position from his place, office or position. (1921, c. 232, s. 2; C.S., s. 7521 (b); 1993, c. 539, s. 1005; 1994, Ex. Sess., c. 24, s. 14(c).)

§ 143-116. Venue for trial of offenses.

All offenses against G.S. 143-114 and 143-115 shall be held to have been committed in the County of Wake and shall be tried and disposed of by the courts of said county having jurisdiction thereof. (1921, c. 232, s. 3; C.S., s. 7521 (c).)

§§ 143-116.1 through 143-116.5. Reserved for future codification purposes.

Article 6A.

Rules of Conduct; Traffic Laws for Institutions.

§ 143-116.6. Rules concerning conduct; violation.

(a)   The Secretary of Health and Human Services may adopt rules for State-owned institutions under the jurisdiction of the Department of Health and Human Services for the regulation and deportment of persons in the buildings and grounds of the institutions, and for the suppression of nuisances and disorder. Rules adopted under this section shall be consistent with G.S. 14-132. Copies of the rules shall be posted at the entrance to the grounds and at different places on the grounds.

(b) Any person violating such rules shall, upon conviction, be guilty of a Class 2 misdemeanor. (1981, c. 614, s. 5; 1987, c. 827, s. 255; 1993, c. 539, s. 1006; 1994, Ex. Sess., c. 24, s. 14(c); 1997-443, s. 11A.118(a).)

§ 143-116.7. Motor vehicle laws applicable to streets, alleys and driveways on the grounds of Department of Health and Human Services institutions; traffic regulations; registration and regulation of motor vehicles.

(a) Except as otherwise provided in this section, all the provisions of Chapter 20 of the General Statutes relating to the use of the highways of the State and the operation of motor vehicles thereon are made applicable to the streets, alleys, roads and driveways on the grounds of all State institutions under the jurisdiction of the Department of Health and Human Services. Any person violating any of the provisions of the Chapter in or on such streets, alleys, roads or driveways shall, upon conviction be punished as prescribed in this section. Nothing herein contained shall be construed as in any way interfering with the ownership and control of the streets, alleys, roads and driveways on the grounds of the State institutions operated by the Department of Health and Human Services.

(b) The Secretary of Health and Human Services may adopt rules consistent with the provisions of Chapter 20 of the General Statutes, with respect to the use of the streets, alleys, and driveways of institutions of the Department of Health and Human Services. Based upon a traffic and engineering investigation, the Secretary of Health and Human Services may also determine and establish speed limits on streets lower than those provided in G.S. 20-141.

(c) The Secretary may, by rule, regulate parking and establish parking areas on the grounds of institutions of the Department of Health and Human Services.

(d) The Secretary may, by rule, provide for the registration and parking of motor vehicles maintained and operated by employees of the institution, and may fix fees, not to exceed ten dollars ($10.00) per year, for such registration.

(e) Rules adopted under this section may provide that violation subjects the offender to a civil penalty, not to exceed fifty dollars ($50.00). Penalties may be graduated according to the seriousness of the offense or the number of prior offenses by the person charged but shall not exceed fifty dollars ($50.00). The Secretary may establish procedures for the collection of penalties, and they may be enforced by civil action in the nature of debt.

(f)   A rule adopted under this section may provide for the removal of illegally parked motor vehicles. Any such removal must be in compliance with Article 7A of Chapter 20 of the General Statutes.

(g)   Any violation under this section or of a provision of Chapter 20 of the General Statutes made applicable to the grounds of State institutions solely by operation of this section shall be considered an infraction and shall be subject to an infraction penalty not to exceed fifty dollars ($50.00). A rule adopted under this section may provide that a violation shall not be an infraction, but shall be enforced by other methods available, including the methods authorized by subsection (e).

(h)   Any fees or civil penalties collected pursuant to this section shall be deposited in the General Fund Budget Code of the institution where the fees or civil penalties are collected and shall only be used to support the cost of administration of this section. Infraction penalties shall be disbursed as provided in G.S. 14-3.1(a). (1981, c. 614, s. 5; 1985, c. 672; c. 764, s. 39; 1985 (Reg. Sess., 1986), c. 852, ss. 13, 14; 1987, c. 827, s. 256; 1997-443, s. 11A.118(a).)

§ 143-116.8. Motor vehicle laws applicable to State parks and forests road system.

(a)   Except as otherwise provided in this section, all the provisions of Chapter 20 of the General Statutes relating to the use of highways and public vehicular areas of the State and the operation of vehicles thereon are made applicable to the State parks and forests road system. For the purposes of this section, the term "State parks and forests road system" shall mean the streets, alleys, roads, public vehicular areas and driveways of the State parks, State forests, State recreation areas, State lakes, and all other lands administered by the Department of Environment and Natural Resources or the Department of Agriculture and Consumer Services. This term shall not be construed, however, to include streets that are a part of the State highway system. Any person violating any of the provisions of Chapter 20 of the General Statutes hereby made applicable in the State parks and forests road system shall, upon conviction, be punished in accordance with Chapter 20 of the General Statutes.

Nothing herein contained shall be construed as in any way interfering with the ownership and control of the State parks road system by the Department of Environment and Natural Resources and the forests road system by the Department of Agriculture and Consumer Services.

(b) (1) It shall be unlawful for a person to operate a vehicle in the State parks road system at a speed in excess of twenty-five miles per hour (25 mph). When the Secretary of Environment and Natural Resources determines that this speed is greater than reasonable and safe under the conditions found to exist in the State parks road system, the Secretary may establish a lower reasonable and safe speed limit. No speed limit established by the Secretary pursuant to this provision shall be effective until posted in the part of the system where the limit is intended to apply.

(1a) It shall be unlawful for a person to operate a vehicle in the State forests road system at a speed in excess of 25 miles per hour. When the Commissioner of Agriculture determines that this speed is greater than reasonable and safe under the conditions found to exist in the State forests road system, the Commissioner may establish a lower reasonable and safe speed limit. No speed limit established by the Commissioner pursuant to this provision shall be effective until posted in the part of the system where the limit is intended to apply.

(2) Any person convicted of violating this subsection by operating a vehicle on the State parks and forests road system while fleeing or attempting to elude arrest or apprehension by a law enforcement officer with authority to enforce the motor vehicle laws, shall be punished as provided in G.S. 20-141.5.

(3) For the purposes of enforcement and administration of Chapter 20, the speed limits stated and authorized to be adopted by this section are speed limits under Chapter 20.

(4) The Secretary may designate any part of the State parks road system and the Commissioner may designate any part of the State forests road system for one-way traffic and shall erect appropriate signs giving notice thereof. It shall be a violation of G.S. 20-165.1 for any person to willfully drive or operate any vehicle on any part of the State parks and forests road system so designated except in the direction indicated.

(5) The Secretary shall have power, equal to the power of local authorities under G.S. 20-158 and G.S. 20-158.1, to place vehicle control signs and signals

and yield-right-of-way signs in the State parks road system; the Secretary also shall have power to post such other signs and markers and mark the roads in accordance with Chapter 20 of the General Statutes as the Secretary may determine appropriate for highway safety and traffic control. The failure of any vehicle driver to obey any vehicle control sign or signal, or any yield-right-of-way sign placed under the authority of this section in the State parks road system shall be an infraction and shall be punished as provided in G.S. 20-176.

(5a)   The Commissioner shall have power, equal to the power of local authorities under G.S. 20-158 and G.S. 20-158.1, to place vehicle control signs and signals and yield right-of-way signs in the State forests road system. The Commissioner also shall have power to post such other signs and markers and mark the roads in accordance with Chapter 20 of the General Statutes as the Commissioner may determine appropriate for highway safety and traffic control. The failure of any vehicle driver to obey any vehicle control sign or signal or any yield right-of-way sign placed under the authority of this section in the State forests road system shall be an infraction and shall be punished as provided in G.S. 20-176.

(c)   The Secretary of Environment and Natural Resources may, by rule, regulate parking and establish parking areas, and provide for the removal of illegally parked motor vehicles on the State parks road system, and the Commissioner of Agriculture may, by rule, regulate and establish parking areas and provide for the removal of illegally parked motor vehicles on the State forests road system. Any rule of the Secretary or the Commissioner shall be consistent with the provisions of G.S. 20-161, 20-161.1, and 20-162. Any removal of illegally parked motor vehicles shall be in compliance with Article 7A of Chapter 20 of the General Statutes.

(d)   A violation of the rules issued by the Secretary of Environment and Natural Resources or the Commissioner of Agriculture under subsection (c) of this section is an infraction pursuant to G.S. 20-162.1, and shall be punished as therein provided. These rules may be enforced by the Commissioner of Motor Vehicles, the Highway Patrol, forest law enforcement officers, or other law enforcement officers of the State, counties, cities or other municipalities having authority under Chapter 20 of the General Statutes to enforce laws or rules on travel or use or operation of vehicles or the use or protection of the highways of the State.

(e)   The provisions of Chapter 20 of the General Statutes are applicable at all times to the State parks and forests road system, including closing hours, regardless of the fact that during closing hours the State parks and forests road system is not open to the public as a matter of right. (1987, c. 474, s. 1; 1989, c. 727, s. 218(96); 1997-443, ss. 11A.119(a), 19.26(e); 2013-155, s. 19.)

§ 143-676. Powers and duties of the Commission.

(a) Powers and Duties. - The Commission shall have the following powers and duties:

(1) To advise the Secretary of Cultural Resources on the collection, preservation, cataloging, publication, and exhibition of materials associated with North Carolina's postal history in cooperation with the North Carolina Museum of History.

(2) To adopt bylaws by a majority vote of the Commission.

(3) To accept grants, contributions, devises, gifts, and services for the purpose of providing support to the Commission. The funds and property shall be retained by the Commission, and the Commission shall prescribe rules under which the Commission may accept donations of money, property, or personal services, and determine the value of donations of property or personal services.

(b) Contract Authority. - The Commission may procure supplies, services, and property as appropriate and may enter into contracts, leases, or other legal agreements within funds available to carry out the purposes of this Article. All contracts, leases, or legal agreements entered into by the Commission shall terminate on the date of termination of the Commission. Termination shall not affect any disputed or causes of action of the Commission that arise before the date of termination, and the Department of Cultural Resources may prosecute or defend any causes of action arising before the date of termination. All property acquired by the commission that remains in the possession of the Commission on the date of termination shall become the property of the Department of Cultural Resources. (1997-443, s. 30.5; 2011-284, s. 96.)

Article 7A.

Damage of Personal Property in State Institutions.

§ 143-127.2. Repair or replacement of personal property.

The Secretary of Health and Human Services may adopt rules governing repair or replacement of personal property items excluding private passenger vehicles that belong to employees, volunteers, or clients of State facilities within the Department of Health and Human Services and that are damaged or stolen by clients of the State facilities provided that the item is determined by the Secretary to be:

(1) Damaged or stolen on or off facility grounds during the performance of employment or volunteer duty and necessary for the employee or volunteer to have in his possession to perform his assigned duty; or

(2) Damaged or stolen on or off the facility grounds while the client is under the supervision of the facility and necessary for the client to have in his possession as part of his treatment environment. (1985, c. 393, s. 1; 1987, c. 264, s. 4; 1989, c. 189, s. 1; 1997-443, s. 11A.118(a).)

§ 143-127.3. Negligence.

Reimbursement for items damaged or stolen shall not be granted in instances in which the employee, volunteer, or client, if competent, is determined to be negligent or otherwise at fault for the damage or loss of the property. Negligence shall be determined by the director of the facility. (1985, c. 393, s. 1; 1987, c. 264, s. 4; 1989, c. 189, s. 1.)

§ 143-127.4. Other remedies.

The director of the facility shall determine if the person seeking reimbursement has made a good faith effort to recover the loss from all other non-State sources and has failed before reimbursement is granted. (1985, c. 393, s. 1; 1987, c. 264, s. 4; 1989, c. 189, s. 1.)

§ 143-127.5. Limitations.

Reimbursement shall be limited to the amount specified in the rules and shall not exceed a maximum of two hundred dollars ($200.00) per incident. No employee, volunteer, or client shall receive more than five hundred dollars ($500.00) per year in reimbursement. Reimbursement is subject to the availability of funds. (1985, c. 393, s. 1; 1987, c. 264, s. 1; 1989, c. 189, s. 1.)

§ 143-127.6. Administrative and judicial review.

Chapter 150B of the General Statutes governs administrative and judicial review of a decision under this Article by the director of a facility. (1985, c. 393, s. 1; 1987, c. 264, ss. 2, 4, c. 827, s. 257; 1989, c. 189, s. 1.)

Article 8.

Public Contracts.

§ 143-128. Requirements for certain building contracts.

(a) Preparation of specifications. - Every officer, board, department, commission or commissions charged with responsibility of preparation of specifications or awarding or entering into contracts for the erection, construction, alteration or repair of any buildings for the State, or for any county, municipality, or other public body, shall have prepared separate specifications for each of the following subdivisions or branches of work to be performed:

(1) Heating, ventilating, air conditioning and accessories (separately or combined into one conductive system), refrigeration for cold storage (where the cold storage cooling load is 15 tons or more of refrigeration), and all related work.

(2) Plumbing and gas fittings and accessories, and all related work.

(3) Electrical wiring and installations, and all related work.

(4) General work not included in subdivisions (1), (2), and (3) of this subsection relating to the erection, construction, alteration, or repair of any building.

Specifications for contracts that will be bid under the separate-prime system or dual bidding system shall be drawn as to permit separate and independent bidding upon each of the subdivisions of work enumerated in this subsection. The above enumeration of subdivisions or branches of work shall not be construed to prevent any officer, board, department, commission or commissions from preparing additional separate specifications for any other category of work.

(a1) Construction methods. - The State, a county, municipality, or other public body shall award contracts to erect, construct, alter, or repair buildings pursuant to any of the following methods:

(1) Separate-prime bidding.

(2) Single-prime bidding.

(3) Dual bidding pursuant to subsection (d1) of this section.

(4) Construction management at risk contracts pursuant to G.S. 143-128.1.

(5) Alternative contracting methods authorized pursuant to G.S. 143-135.26(9).

(6) Design-build contracts pursuant to G.S. 143-128.1A.

(7) Design-build bridging contracts pursuant to G.S. 143-128.1B.

(8) Public-private partnership construction contracts pursuant to G.S. 143-128.1C.

(a2) Repealed by Session Laws 2012-142, s. 9.4(g), effective July 1, 2012.

(b) Separate-prime contracts. - When the State, county, municipality, or other public body uses the separate-prime contract system, it shall accept bids for each subdivision of work for which specifications are required to be prepared under subsection (a) of this section and shall award the respective work specified separately to responsible and reliable persons, firms or corporations regularly engaged in their respective lines of work. When the estimated cost of work to be performed in any single subdivision or branch for which separate bids are required by this subsection is less than twenty-five thousand dollars ($25,000), the same may be included in the contract for one of the other subdivisions or branches of the work, irrespective of total project cost. The contracts shall be awarded to the lowest responsible, responsive bidders, taking into consideration quality, performance, the time specified in the bids for performance of the contract, and compliance with G.S. 143-128.2. Bids may also be accepted from and awards made to separate contractors for other categories of work.

Each separate contractor shall be directly liable to the State of North Carolina, or to the county, municipality, or other public body and to the other separate contractors for the full performance of all duties and obligations due respectively under the terms of the separate contracts and in accordance with the plans and specifications, which shall specifically set forth the duties and obligations of each separate contractor. For the purpose of this section, "separate contractor" means any person, firm or corporation who shall enter into a contract with the State, or with any county, municipality, or other public entity to erect, construct, alter or repair any building or buildings, or parts of any building or buildings.

(c)   Repealed by Session Laws 2001-496, s. 3, effective January 1, 2001.

(d)   Single-prime contracts. - All bidders in a single-prime project shall identify on their bid the contractors they have selected for the subdivisions or branches of work for:

(1)   Heating, ventilating, and air conditioning;

(2)   Plumbing;

(3)   Electrical; and

(4)   General.

The contract shall be awarded to the lowest responsible, responsive bidder, taking into consideration quality, performance, the time specified in the bids for performance of the contract, and compliance with G.S. 143-128.2. A contractor whose bid is accepted shall not substitute any person as subcontractor in the place of the subcontractor listed in the original bid, except (i) if the listed subcontractor's bid is later determined by the contractor to be nonresponsible or nonresponsive or the listed subcontractor refuses to enter into a contract for the complete performance of the bid work, or (ii) with the approval of the awarding authority for good cause shown by the contractor. The terms, conditions, and requirements of each contract between the contractor and a subcontractor performing work under a subdivision or branch of work listed in this subsection shall incorporate by reference the terms, conditions, and requirements of the contract between the contractor and the State, county, municipality, or other public body.

When contracts are awarded pursuant to this section, the public body shall make available to subcontractors the dispute resolution process as provided for in subsection (f1) of this section.

(d1) Dual bidding. - The State, a county, municipality, or other public entity may accept bids to erect, construct, alter, or repair a building under both the single-prime and separate-prime contracting systems and shall award the contract to the lowest responsible, responsive bidder under the single-prime system or to the lowest responsible, responsive bidder under the separate-prime system, taking into consideration quality, performance, compliance with G.S. 143-128.2, and time specified in the bids to perform the contract. In determining the system under which the contract will be awarded to the lowest responsible, responsive bidder, the public entity may consider cost of construction oversight, time for completion, and other factors it considers appropriate. The bids received as separate-prime bids shall be received, but not opened, one hour prior to the deadline for the submission of single-prime bids. The amount of a bid submitted by a subcontractor to the general contractor under the single-prime system shall not exceed the amount bid, if any, for the same work by that subcontractor to the public entity under the separate-prime system. The provisions of subsection (b) of this section shall apply to separate-prime contracts awarded pursuant to this section and the provisions of subsection (d) of this section shall apply to single-prime contracts awarded pursuant to this section.

(e) Project expediter; scheduling; public body to resolve project disputes. - The State, county, municipality, or other public body may, if specified in the bid documents, provide for assignment of responsibility for expediting the work on a project to a single responsible and reliable person, firm or corporation, which may be a prime contractor. In executing this responsibility, the designated project expediter may recommend to the State, county, municipality, or other public body whether payment to a contractor should be approved. The project expediter, if required by the contract documents, shall be responsible for preparing the project schedule and shall allow all contractors and subcontractors performing any of the branches of work listed in subsection (d) of this section equal input into the preparation of the initial schedule. Whenever separate contracts are awarded and separate contractors engaged for a project pursuant to this section, the public body may provide in the contract documents for resolution of project disputes through alternative dispute resolution processes as provided for in subsection (f1) of this section.

(f) Repealed by Session Laws 2001-496, s. 3, effective January 1, 2001.

(f1) Dispute resolution. - A public entity shall use the dispute resolution process adopted by the State Building Commission pursuant to G.S. 143-135.26(11), or shall adopt another dispute resolution process, which shall include mediation, to be used as an alterative to the dispute resolution process adopted by the State Building Commission. This dispute resolution process will be available to all the parties involved in the public entity's construction project including the public entity, the architect, the construction manager, the contractors, and the first-tier and lower-tier subcontractors and shall be available for any issues arising out of the contract or construction process. The public entity may set a reasonable threshold, not to exceed fifteen thousand dollars ($15,000), concerning the amount in controversy that must be at issue before a party may require other parties to participate in the dispute resolution process. The public entity may require that the costs of the process be divided between the parties to the dispute with at least one-third of the cost to be paid by the public entity, if the public entity is a party to the dispute. The public entity may require in its contracts that a party participate in mediation concerning a dispute as a precondition to initiating litigation concerning the dispute.

(g) Exceptions. - This section shall not apply to:

(1) The purchase and erection of prefabricated or relocatable buildings or portions thereof, except that portion of the work which must be performed at the construction site.

(2) The erection, construction, alteration, or repair of a building when the cost thereof is three hundred thousand dollars ($300,000) or less.

(3) The erection, construction, alteration, or repair of a building by The University of North Carolina or its constituent institutions when the cost thereof is five hundred thousand dollars ($500,000) or less.

Notwithstanding the other provisions of this subsection, subsection (f1) of this section shall apply to any erection, construction, alteration, or repair of a building by a public entity. (1925, c. 141, s. 2; 1929, c. 339, s. 2; 1931, c. 46; 1943, c. 387; 1945, c. 851; 1949, c. 1137, s. 1; 1963, c. 406, ss. 2-7; 1967, c.

860; 1973, c. 1419; 1977, c. 620; 1987 (Reg. Sess., 1988), c. 1108, ss. 4, 5; 1989, c. 480, s. 1; 1995, c. 358, s. 4; c. 367, ss. 1, 4, 5; c. 509, s. 79; 1998-137, s. 1; 1998-193, s. 1; 2001-496, ss. 3, 13; 2002-159, s. 42; 2007-322, s. 3; 2012-142, s. 9.4(g); 2013-401, s. 3.)

§ 143-128.1. Construction management at risk contracts.

(a) For purposes of this section and G.S. 143-64.31:

(1) "Construction management services" means services provided by a construction manager, which may include preparation and coordination of bid packages, scheduling, cost control, value engineering, evaluation, preconstruction services, and construction administration.

(2) "Construction management at risk services" means services provided by a person, corporation, or entity that (i) provides construction management services for a project throughout the preconstruction and construction phases, (ii) who is licensed as a general contractor, and (iii) who guarantees the cost of the project.

(3) "Construction manager at risk" means a person, corporation, or entity that provides construction management at risk services.

(4) "First-tier subcontractor" means a subcontractor who contracts directly with the construction manager at risk.

(b) The construction manager at risk shall be selected in accordance with Article 3D of this Chapter. Design services for a project shall be performed by a licensed architect or engineer. The public owner shall contract directly with the architect or engineer. The public owner shall make a good-faith effort to comply with G.S. 143-128.2, G.S. 143-128.4, and to recruit and select small business entities when selecting a construction manager at risk.

(c) The construction manager at risk shall contract directly with the public entity for all construction; shall publicly advertise as prescribed in G.S. 143-129; and shall prequalify and accept bids from first-tier subcontractors for all construction work under this section. The prequalification criteria shall be determined by the public entity and the construction manager at risk to address quality, performance, the time specified in the bids for performance of the contract, the cost of construction oversight, time for completion, capacity to perform, and other factors deemed appropriate by the public entity. The public entity shall require the construction manager at risk to submit its plan for compliance with G.S. 143-128.2 for approval by the public entity prior to soliciting bids for the project's first-tier subcontractors. A construction manager at risk and first-tier subcontractors shall make a good faith effort to comply with G.S. 143-128.2, G.S. 143-128.4, and to recruit and select small business entities. A construction manager at risk may perform a portion of the work only if (i) bidding produces no responsible, responsive bidder for that portion of the work, the lowest responsible, responsive bidder will not execute a contract for the bid portion of the work, or the subcontractor defaults and a prequalified replacement cannot be obtained in a timely manner, and (ii) the public entity approves of the construction manager at risk's performance of the work. All bids shall be opened publicly, and once they are opened, shall be public records under Chapter 132 of the General Statutes. The construction manager at risk shall act as the fiduciary of the public entity in handling and opening bids. The construction manager at risk shall award the contract to the lowest responsible, responsive bidder, taking into consideration quality, performance, the time specified in the bids for performance of the contract, the cost of construction oversight, time for completion, compliance with G.S. 143-128.2, and other factors deemed appropriate by the public entity and advertised as part of the bid solicitation. The public entity may require the selection of a different first-tier subcontractor for any portion of the work, consistent with this section, provided that the construction manager at risk is compensated for any additional cost incurred.

When contracts are awarded pursuant to this section, the public entity shall provide for a dispute resolution procedure as provided in G.S. 143-128(f1).

(d)   The construction manager at risk shall provide a performance and payment bond to the public entity in accordance with the provisions of Article 3 of Chapter 44A of the General Statutes. (2001-496, s. 2; 2013-401, s. 5.)

§ 143-128.1A. Design-build contracts.

(a)   Definitions for purposes of this section:

(1)   Design-builder. - As defined in G.S. 143-128.1B.

(2) Governmental entity. - As defined in G.S. 143-128.1B.

(b) A governmental entity shall establish in writing the criteria used for determining the circumstances under which the design-build method is appropriate for a project, and such criteria shall, at a minimum, address all of the following:

(1) The extent to which the governmental entity can adequately and thoroughly define the project requirements prior to the issuance of the request for qualifications for a design-builder.

(2) The time constraints for the delivery of the project.

(3) The ability to ensure that a quality project can be delivered.

(4) The capability of the governmental entity to manage and oversee the project, including the availability of experienced staff or outside consultants who are experienced with the design-build method of project delivery.

(5) A good-faith effort to comply with G.S. 143-128.2, G.S. 143-128.4, and to recruit and select small business entities. The governmental entity shall not limit or otherwise preclude any respondent from submitting a response so long as the respondent, itself or through its proposed team, is properly licensed and qualified to perform the work defined by the public notice issued under subsection (c) of this section.

(6) The criteria utilized by the governmental entity, including a comparison of the costs and benefits of using the design-build delivery method for a given project in lieu of the delivery methods identified in subdivisions (1), (2), and (4) of G.S. 143-128(a1).

(c) A governmental entity shall issue a public notice of the request for qualifications that includes, at a minimum, general information on each of the following:

(1) The project site.

(2) The project scope.

(3) The anticipated project budget.

(4) The project schedule.

(5) The criteria to be considered for selection and the weighting of the qualifications criteria.

(6) Notice of any rules, ordinances, or goals established by the governmental entity, including goals for minority- and women-owned business participation and small business participation.

(7) Other information provided by the owner to potential design-builders in submitting qualifications for the project.

(8) A statement providing that each design-builder shall submit in its response to the request for qualifications an explanation of its project team selection, which shall consist of either of the following:

a. A list of the licensed contractors, licensed subcontractors, and licensed design professionals whom the design-builder proposes to use for the project's design and construction.

b. An outline of the strategy the design-builder plans to use for open contractor and subcontractor selection based upon the provisions of Article 8 of Chapter 143 of the General Statutes.

(d) Following evaluation of the qualifications of the design-builders, the three most highly qualified design-builders shall be ranked. If after the solicitation for design-builders not as many as three responses have been received from qualified design-builders, the governmental entity shall again solicit for design-builders. If as a result of such second solicitation not as many as three responses are received, the governmental entity may then begin negotiations with the highest-ranked design-builder under G.S. 143-64.31 even though fewer than three responses were received. If the governmental entity deems it appropriate, the governmental entity may invite some or all responders to interview with the governmental entity.

(e) The design-builder shall be selected in accordance with Article 3D of this Chapter. Each design-builder shall certify to the governmental entity that each licensed design professional who is a member of the design-build team, including subconsultants, was selected based upon demonstrated competence and qualifications in the manner provided by G.S. 143-64.31.

(f)   The design-builder shall provide a performance and payment bond to the governmental entity in accordance with the provisions of Article 3 of Chapter 44A of the General Statutes. The design-builder shall obtain written approval from the governmental entity prior to changing key personnel as listed in sub-subdivision (c)(8)a. of this section after the contract has been awarded. (2013-401, s. 4.)

§ 143-128.1B. Design-build bridging contracts.

(a)   Definitions for purposes of this section:

(1)   Design-build bridging. - A design and construction delivery process whereby a governmental entity contracts for design criteria services under a separate agreement from the construction phase services of the design-builder.

(2)   Design-builder. - An appropriately licensed person, corporation, or entity that, under a single contract, offers to provide or provides design services and general contracting services where services within the scope of the practice of professional engineering or architecture are performed respectively by a licensed engineer or licensed architect and where services within the scope of the practice of general contracting are performed by a licensed general contractor.

(3)   Design criteria. - The requirements for a public project expressed in drawings and specifications sufficient to allow the design-builder to make a responsive bid proposal.

(4)   Design professional. - Any professional licensed under Chapters 83A, 89A, or 89C of the General Statutes.

(5)   First-tier subcontractor. - A subcontractor who contracts directly with the design-builder, excluding design professionals.

(6)   Governmental entity. - Every officer, board, department, commission, or commissions charged with responsibility of preparation of specifications or awarding or entering into contracts for the erection, construction, alteration, or repair of any buildings for the State or for any county, municipality, or other public body.

(b) A governmental entity shall establish in writing the criteria used for determining the circumstances under which engaging a design criteria design professional is appropriate for a project, and such criteria shall, at a minimum, address all of the following:

(1) The extent to which the governmental entity can adequately and thoroughly define the project requirements prior to the issuance of the request for proposals for a design-builder.

(2) The time constraints for the delivery of the project.

(3) The ability to ensure that a quality project can be delivered.

(4) The capability of the governmental entity to manage and oversee the project, including the availability of experienced staff or outside consultants who are experienced with the design-build method of project delivery.

(5) A good-faith effort to comply with G.S. 143-128.2, G.S. 143-128.4, and to recruit and select small business entities. The governmental entity shall not limit or otherwise preclude any respondent from submitting a response so long as the respondent, itself or through its proposed team, is properly licensed and qualified to perform the work defined by the public notice issued under subsection (d) of this section.

(6) The criteria utilized by the governmental entity, including a comparison of the cost and benefit of using the design-build delivery method for a given project in lieu of the delivery methods identified in subdivisions (1), (2), and (4) of G.S. 143-128(a1).

(c) On or before entering into a contract for design-build services under this section, the governmental entity shall select or designate a staff design professional, or a design professional who is independent of the design-builder, to act as its design criteria design professional as its representative for the procurement process and for the duration of the design and construction. If the design professional is not a full-time employee of the governmental entity, the governmental entity shall select the design professional on the basis of demonstrated competence and qualifications as provided by G.S. 143-64.31. The design criteria design professional shall develop design criteria in consultation with the governmental entity. The design criteria design professional shall not be eligible to submit a response to the request for proposals nor provide design input to a design-build response to the request for proposals. The design criteria design professional shall prepare a design criteria package equal to thirty-five percent (35%) of the completed design documentation for the entire construction project. The design criteria package shall include all of the following:

(1) Programmatic needs, interior space requirements, intended space utilization, and other capacity requirements.

(2) Information on the physical characteristics of the site, such as a topographic survey.

(3) Material quality standards or performance criteria.

(4) Special material requirements.

(5) Provisions for utilities.

(6) Parking requirements.

(7) The type, size, and location of adjacent structures.

(8) Preliminary or conceptual drawings and specifications sufficient in detail to allow the design-builder to make a proposal which is responsive to the request for proposals.

(9) Notice of any ordinances, rules, or goals adopted by the governmental entity.

(d) A governmental entity shall issue a public notice of the request for proposals that includes, at a minimum, general information on each of the following:

(1) The project site.

(2) The project scope.

(3) The anticipated project budget.

(4) The project schedule.

(5) The criteria to be considered for selection and the weighting of the selection criteria.

(6) Notice of any rules, ordinances, or goals established by the governmental entity, including goals for minority- and women-owned business participation and small business entities.

(7) The thirty-five percent (35%) design criteria package prepared by the design criteria design professional.

(8) Other information provided by the owner to design-builders in submitting responses to the request for proposals for the project.

(9) A statement providing that each design-builder shall submit in its request for proposal response an explanation of its project team selection, which shall consist of a list of the licensed contractor and licensed design professionals whom the design-builder proposes to use for the project's design and construction.

(10) A statement providing that each design-builder shall submit in its request for proposal a sealed envelope with all of the following:

a. The design-builder's price for providing the general conditions of the contract.

b. The design-builder's proposed fee for general construction services.

c. The design-builder's fee for design services.

(e) Following evaluation of the qualifications of the design-builders, the governmental entity shall rank the design-builders who have provided responses, grouping the top three without ordinal ranking. If after the solicitation for design-builders not as many as three responses have been received from qualified design-builders, the governmental entity shall again solicit for design-builders. If as a result of such second solicitation not as many as three responses are received, the governmental entity may then make its selection. From the grouping of the top three design-builders, the governmental entity shall select the design-builder who is the lowest responsive, responsible bidder based on the cumulative amount of fees provided in accordance with subdivision (d)(10) of this section and taking into consideration quality, performance, and the time specified in the proposals for the performance of the contract. Each design-builder shall certify to the governmental entity that each licensed design professional who is a member of the design-build team, including subconsultants, was selected based upon demonstrated competence and qualifications in the manner provided by G.S. 143-64.31.

(f) The design-builder shall accept bids based upon the provisions of this Article from first-tier subcontractors for all construction work under this section.

(g) The design-builder shall provide a performance and payment bond to the governmental entity in accordance with the provisions of Article 3 of Chapter 44A of the General Statutes. The design-builder shall obtain written approval from the governmental entity prior to changing key personnel, as listed under subdivision (d)(9) of this section, after the contract has been awarded. (2013-401, s. 4.)

§ 143-128.1C. Public-private partnership construction contracts.

(a) Definitions for purposes of this section:

(1) Construction contract. - Any contract entered into between a private developer and a contractor for the design, construction, reconstruction, alteration, or repair of any building or other work or improvement required for a private developer to satisfy its obligations under a development contract.

(2) Contractor. - Any person who has entered into a construction contract with a private developer under this section.

(3) Design-builder. - Defined in G.S. 143-128.1B.

(4) Development contract. - Any contract between a governmental entity and a private developer under this section and, as part of the contract, the private developer is required to provide at least fifty percent (50%) of the financing for the total cost necessary to deliver the capital improvement project, whether through lease or ownership, for the governmental entity.

(5) Governmental entity. - Defined in G.S. 143-128.1B.

(6) Labor or materials. - Includes all materials furnished or labor performed in the performance of the work required by a construction contract whether or

not the labor or materials enter into or become a component part of the improvement and shall include gas, power, light, heat, oil, gasoline, telephone services, and rental of equipment or the reasonable value of the use of equipment directly utilized in the performance of the work required by a construction contract.

(7)   Private developer. - Any person who has entered into a development contract with a governmental entity under this section.

(8)   Public-private project. - A capital improvement project undertaken for the benefit of a governmental entity and a private developer pursuant to a development contract that includes construction of a public facility or other improvements, including paving, grading, utilities, infrastructure, reconstruction, or repair, and may include both public and private facilities.

(9)   State entity. - The State and every agency, authority, institution, board, commission, bureau, council, department, division, officer, or employee of the State. The term does not include a unit of local government as defined in G.S. 159-7.

(10)   State-supported financing arrangement. - Any installment financing arrangement, lease-purchase arrangement, arrangement under which funds are to be paid in the future based upon the availability of an asset or funds for payment, or any similar arrangement in the nature of a financing, under which a State entity agrees to make payments to acquire or obtain a capital asset for the State entity or any other State entity for a term, including renewal options, of greater than one year. Any arrangement that results in the identification of a portion of a lease payment, installment payment, or similar scheduled payment thereunder by a State entity as "interest" for purposes of federal income taxation shall automatically be a State-supported financing arrangement for purposes of this section.

(11)   Subcontractor. - Any person who has contracted to furnish labor, services, or materials to, or who has performed labor or services for, a contractor or another subcontractor in connection with a development contract.

(b)   If the governmental entity determines in writing that it has a critical need for a capital improvement project, the governmental entity may acquire, construct, own, lease as lessor or lessee, and operate or participate in the acquisition, construction, ownership, leasing, and operation of a public-private project, or of specific facilities within such a project, including the making of loans and grants from funds available to the governmental entity for these purposes. If the governmental entity is a public body under Article 33C of this Chapter, the determination shall occur during an open meeting of that public body. The governmental entity may enter into development contracts with private developers with respect to acquiring, constructing, owning, leasing, or operating a project under this section. The development contract shall specify the following:

(1) The property interest of the governmental entity and all other participants in the development of the project.

(2) The responsibilities of the governmental entity and all other participants in the development of the project.

(3) The responsibilities of the governmental entity and all other participants with respect to financing of the project.

(4) The responsibilities to put forth a good-faith effort to comply with G.S. 143-128.2, G.S. 143-128.4, and to recruit and select small business entities.

(c) The development contract may provide that the private developer shall be responsible for any or all of the following:

(1) Construction of the entire public-private project.

(2) Reconstruction or repair of the public-private project or any part thereof subsequent to construction of the project.

(3) Construction of any addition to the public-private project.

(4) Renovation of the public-private project or any part thereof.

(5) Purchase of apparatus, supplies, materials, or equipment for the public-private project whether during or subsequent to the initial equipping of the project.

(6) A good-faith effort to comply with G.S. 143-128.2, G.S. 143-128.4, and to recruit and select small business entities.

(d) The development contract may also provide that the governmental entity and private developer shall use the same contractor or contractors in constructing a portion of or the entire public-private project. If the development contract provides that the governmental entity and private developer shall use the same contractor, the development contract shall include provisions deemed appropriate by the governmental entity to assure that the public facility or facilities included in or added to the public-private project are constructed, reconstructed, repaired, or renovated at a reasonable price and that the apparatus, supplies, materials, and equipment purchased for the public facility or facilities included in the public-private project are purchased at a reasonable price. For public-private partnerships using the design-build project delivery method, the provisions of G.S. 143-128.1A shall apply.

(e)   A private developer and its contractors shall make a good-faith effort to comply with G.S. 143-128.2, G.S. 143-128.4, and to recruit and select small business entities.

(f)   A private developer may perform a portion of the construction or design work only if both of the following criteria apply:

(1)   A previously engaged contractor defaults, and a qualified replacement cannot be obtained after a good-faith effort has been made in a timely manner.

(2)   The governmental entity approves the private developer to perform the work.

(g)   The following bonding provisions apply to any development contract entered into under this section:

(1)   A payment bond shall be required for any development contract as follows: A payment bond in the amount of one hundred percent (100%) of the total anticipated amount of the construction contracts to be entered into between the private developer and the contractors to design or construct the improvements required by the development contract. The payment bond shall be conditioned upon the prompt payment for all labor or materials for which the private developer or one or more of its contractors or those contractors' subcontractors are liable. The payment bond shall be solely for the protection of the persons furnishing materials or performing labor or services for which the private developer or its contractors or subcontractors are liable. The total anticipated amount of the construction contracts shall be stated in the development contract and certified by the private developer as being a good-faith projection of its total costs for designing and constructing the improvements required by the development contract. The payment bond shall be executed by

one or more surety companies legally authorized to do business in the State of North Carolina and shall become effective upon the awarding of the development contract. The development contract may provide for the requirement of a performance bond.

(2) a. Subject to the provisions of this subsection, any claimant who has performed labor or furnished materials in the prosecution of the work required by any contract for which a payment bond has been given pursuant to the provisions of this subsection, and who has not been paid in full therefor before the expiration of 90 days after the day on which the claimant performed the last labor or furnished the last materials for which that claimant claims payment, may bring an action on the payment bond in that claimant's own name to recover any amount due to that claimant for the labor or materials and may prosecute the action to final judgment and have execution on the judgment.

b. Any claimant who has a direct contractual relationship with any contractor or any subcontractor but has no contractual relationship, express or implied, with the private developer may bring an action on the payment bond only if that claimant has given written notice of claim on the payment bond to the private developer within 120 days from the date on which the claimant performed the last of the labor or furnished the last of the materials for which that claimant claims payment, in which that claimant states with substantial accuracy the amount claimed and the name of the person for whom the work was performed or to whom the material was furnished.

c. The notice required by sub-subdivision b. of this subdivision shall be served by certified mail or by signature confirmation as provided by the United States Postal Service, postage prepaid, in an envelope addressed to the private developer at any place where that private developer's office is regularly maintained for the transaction of business or in any manner provided by law for the service of summons. The claimants' service of a claim of lien on real property or a claim of lien on funds as funds as allowed by Article 2 of Chapter 44A of the General Statutes on the private developer shall be deemed, nonexclusively, as adequate notice under this section.

(3) Every action on a payment bond as provided in this subsection shall be brought in a court of appropriate jurisdiction in a county where the development contract or any part thereof is to be or has been performed. Except as provided in G.S. 44A-16(c), no action on a payment bond shall be commenced after one year from the day on which the last of the labor was performed or material was furnished by the claimant.

(4) No surety shall be liable under a payment bond for a total amount greater than the face amount of the payment bond. A judgment against any surety may be reduced or set aside upon motion by the surety and a showing that the total amount of claims paid and judgments previously rendered under the payment bond, together with the amount of the judgment to be reduced or set aside, exceeds the face amount of the bond.

(5) No act of or agreement between the governmental entity, a private developer, or a surety shall reduce the period of time for giving notice under sub-subdivision (2)b. of this subsection or commencing action under subdivision (3) of this subsection or otherwise reduce or limit the liability of the private developer or surety as prescribed in this subsection. Every bond given by a private developer pursuant to this subsection shall be conclusively presumed to have been given in accordance with the provisions of this subsection, whether or not the bond is drawn as to conform to this subsection. The provisions of this subsection shall be conclusively presumed to have been written into every bond given pursuant to this subsection.

(6) Any person entitled to bring an action or any defendant in an action on a payment bond shall have a right to require the governmental entity or the private developer to certify and furnish a copy of the payment bond, the development contract, and any construction contracts covered by the bond. It shall be the duty of the private developer or the governmental entity to give any such person a certified copy of the payment bond and the construction contract upon not less than 10 days' notice and request. The governmental entity or private developer may require a reasonable payment for the actual cost of furnishing the certified copy. A copy of any payment bond, development contract, and any construction contracts covered by the bond certified by the governmental entity or private developer shall constitute prima facie evidence of the contents, execution, and delivery of the bond, development contract, and construction contracts.

(7) A payment bond form containing the following provisions shall comply with this subsection:

a. The date the bond is executed.

b. The name of the principal.

c. The name of the surety.

d. The governmental entity.

e. The development contract number.

f. All of the following:

1. "KNOW ALL MEN BY THESE PRESENTS, That we, the PRINCIPAL and SURETY above named, are held and firmly bound unto the above named [governmental entity], hereinafter called [governmental entity], in the penal sum of the amount stated above, for the payment of which sum well and truly to be made, we bind ourselves, our heirs, executors, administrators, and successors, jointly and severally, firmly by these presents."

2. "THE CONDITION OF THIS OBLIGATION IS SUCH, that whereas the Principal entered into a certain development contract with [governmental entity], numbered as shown above and hereto attached."

3. "NOW THEREFORE, if the Principal shall promptly make payment to all persons supplying labor and material in the prosecution of the construction or design work provided for in the development contract, and any and all duly authorized modifications of the contract that may hereafter be made, notice of which modifications to the surety being hereby waived, then this obligation to be void; otherwise to remain in full force and virtue."

4. "IN WITNESS WHEREOF, the above bounden parties have executed this instrument under their several seals on the date indicated above, the name and corporate seal of each corporate party being hereto affixed and these presents duly signed by its undersigned representative, pursuant to authority of its governing body." Appropriate places for execution by the surety and principal shall be provided.

(8) In any suit brought or defended under the provisions of this subsection, the presiding judge may allow reasonable attorneys' fees to the attorney representing the prevailing party. Attorneys' fees under this subdivision are to be taxed as part of the court costs and shall be payable by the losing party upon a finding that there was an unreasonable refusal by the losing party to fully resolve the matter which constituted the basis of the suit or the basis of the defense. For purposes of this subdivision, the term "prevailing party" means a party plaintiff or third-party plaintiff who obtains a judgment of at least fifty percent (50%) of the monetary amount sought in a claim or a party defendant or third-party defendant against whom a claim is asserted which results in a judgment of less than fifty percent (50%) of the amount sought in the claim defended. Notwithstanding the provisions of this subdivision, if an offer of

judgment is served in accordance with G.S. 1A-1, Rule 68, a "prevailing party" is an offeree who obtains judgment in an amount more favorable than the last offer or is an offeror against whom judgment is rendered in an amount less favorable than the last offer.

(9) The obligations and lien rights set forth in Article 2 of Chapter 44A of the General Statutes shall apply to a project awarded under this section to the extent of any property interests held by the private developer in the project. For purposes of applying the provisions of Article 2 of Chapter 44A of the General Statutes, the private developer shall be deemed the owner to the extent of that private developer's ownership interest. This subdivision shall not be construed as making the provisions of Article 2 of Chapter 44A of the General Statutes apply to governmental entities or public buildings to the extent of any property interest held by the governmental entity in the building.

(h) The governmental entity shall determine its programming requirements for facilities to be constructed under this section and shall determine the form in which private developers may submit their qualifications. The governmental entity shall advertise a notice for interested private developers to submit qualifications in a newspaper having general circulation within the county in which the governmental entity is located. Prior to the submission of qualifications, the governmental entity shall make available, in whatever form it deems appropriate, the programming requirements for facilities included in the public-private project. Any private developer submitting qualifications shall include the following:

(1) Evidence of financial stability. However, "trade secrets" as that term is defined in G.S. 66-152(3) shall be exempt from disclosure under Chapter 132 of the General Statutes.

(2) Experience with similar projects.

(3) Explanation of project team selection by either listing of licensed contractors, licensed subcontractors, and licensed design professionals whom the private developer proposes to use for the project's design and construction or a statement outlining a strategy for open contractor and subcontractor selection based upon the provisions of this Article.

(4) Statement of availability to undertake the public-private project and projected time line for project completion.

(5) Any other information required by the governmental entity.

(i) Based upon the qualifications package submitted by the private developers and any other information required by the governmental entity, the governmental entity may select one or more private developers with whom to negotiate the terms and conditions of a contract to perform the public-private project. The governmental entity shall advertise the terms of the proposed contract to be entered into by the governmental entity in a newspaper having general circulation within the county in which the governmental entity is located at least 30 days prior to entering into the development contract. If the governmental entity is a public body under Article 33C of this Chapter, the development contract shall be considered in an open meeting of that public body following a public hearing on the proposed development contract. Notice of the public hearing shall be published in the same notice as the advertisement of the terms under this subsection.

(j) The governmental entity shall make available a summary of the development contract terms which shall include a statement of how to obtain a copy of the complete development contract.

(k) Leases entered into under this section are subject to approval as follows:

(1) If a capital lease or operating lease is entered into by a unit of local government as defined in G.S. 159-7, that capital lease or operating lease is subject to approval by the local government commission under Article 8 of Chapter 159 of the General Statutes if it meets the standards set out in G.S. 159-148(a)(1), 159-148(a)(2), and 159-148(a)(3), 159-148(a)(4) or 159-153. For purposes of determining whether the standards set out in G.S. 159-148(a)(3) have been met, only the five hundred thousand dollar ($500,000) threshold applies.

(2) If a capital lease is entered into by a State entity that constitutes a State-supported financing arrangement and requires payments thereunder that are payable, whether directly or indirectly, and whether or not subject to the appropriation of funds for such payment, by payments from the General Fund of the State or other funds and accounts of the State that are funded from the general revenues and other taxes and fees of the State or State entities, not including taxes and fees that are required to be deposited to the Highway Fund or Highway Trust Fund, that capital lease shall be subject to the approval procedures required for special indebtedness by G.S. 142-83 and G.S. 142-84.

This requirement shall not apply to any arrangement where bonds or other obligations are issued or incurred by a State entity to carry out a financing program authorized by the General Assembly under which such bonds or other obligations are payable from monies derived from specified, limited, nontax sources, so long as the payments under that arrangement by a State entity are limited to the sources authorized by the General Assembly.

(l) A capital lease or operating lease entered into under this section may not contain any provision with respect to the assignment of specific students or students from a specific area to any specific school.

(m) This section shall not apply to any contract or other agreement between or among The University of North Carolina or one of its constituent institutions, a private, nonprofit corporation established under Part 2B of Article 1 of Chapter 116 of the General Statutes, or any private foundation, private association, or private club created for the primary purpose of financial support to The University of North Carolina or one of its constituent institutions. (2013-401, s. 4.)

§ 143-128.2. Minority business participation goals.

(a) The State shall have a verifiable ten percent (10%) goal for participation by minority businesses in the total value of work for each State building project, including building projects done by a private entity on a facility to be leased or purchased by the State. A local government unit or other public or private entity that receives State appropriations for a building project or other State grant funds for a building project, including a building project done by a private entity on a facility to be leased or purchased by the local government unit, where the project cost is one hundred thousand dollars ($100,000) or more, shall have a verifiable ten percent (10%) goal for participation by minority businesses in the total value of the work; provided, however, a local government unit may apply a different verifiable goal that was adopted prior to December 1, 2001, if the local government unit had and continues to have a sufficiently strong basis in evidence to justify the use of that goal. On State building projects and building projects subject to the State goal requirement, the Secretary shall identify the appropriate percentage goal, based on adequate data, for each category of minority business as defined in G.S. 143-128.2(g)(1) based on the specific contract type.

Except as otherwise provided for in this subsection, each city, county, or other local public entity shall adopt, after a notice and public hearing, an appropriate verifiable percentage goal for participation by minority businesses in the total value of work for building projects.

Each entity required to have verifiable percentage goals under this subsection shall make a good faith effort to recruit minority participation in accordance with this section or G.S. 143-131(b), as applicable.

(b) A public entity shall establish prior to solicitation of bids the good faith efforts that it will take to make it feasible for minority businesses to submit successful bids or proposals for the contracts for building projects. Public entities shall make good faith efforts as set forth in subsection (e) of this section. Public entities shall require contractors to make good faith efforts pursuant to subsection (f) of this section. Each first-tier subcontractor on a construction management at risk project shall comply with the requirements applicable to contractors under this subsection.

(c) Each bidder, which shall mean first-tier subcontractor for construction manager at risk projects for purposes of this subsection, on a project bid under any of the methods authorized under G.S. 143-128(a1) shall identify on its bid the minority businesses that it will use on the project and an affidavit listing the good faith efforts it has made pursuant to subsection (f) of this section and the total dollar value of the bid that will be performed by the minority businesses. A contractor, including a first-tier subcontractor on a construction manager at risk project, that performs all of the work under a contract with its own workforce may submit an affidavit to that effect in lieu of the affidavit otherwise required under this subsection. The apparent lowest responsible, responsive bidder shall also file the following:

(1) Within the time specified in the bid documents, either:

a. An affidavit that includes a description of the portion of work to be executed by minority businesses, expressed as a percentage of the total contract price, which is equal to or more than the applicable goal. An affidavit under this sub-subdivision shall give rise to a presumption that the bidder has made the required good faith or effort; or

b. Documentation of its good faith effort to meet the goal. The documentation must include evidence of all good faith efforts that were implemented, including any advertisements, solicitations, and evidence of other specific actions demonstrating recruitment and selection of minority businesses for participation in the contract.

(2)   Within 30 days after award of the contract, a list of all identified subcontractors that the contractor will use on the project.

Failure to file a required affidavit or documentation that demonstrates that the contractor made the required good faith effort is grounds for rejection of the bid.

(d)   No subcontractor who is identified and listed pursuant to subsection (c) of this section may be replaced with a different subcontractor except:

(1)   If the subcontractor's bid is later determined by the contractor or construction manager at risk to be nonresponsible or nonresponsive, or the listed subcontractor refuses to enter into a contract for the complete performance of the bid work, or

(2)   With the approval of the public entity for good cause.

Good faith efforts as set forth in G.S. 143-131(b) shall apply to the selection of a substitute subcontractor. Prior to substituting a subcontractor, the contractor shall identify the substitute subcontractor and inform the public entity of its good faith efforts pursuant to G.S. 143-131(b).

(e)   Before awarding a contract, a public entity shall do the following:

(1)   Develop and implement a minority business participation outreach plan to identify minority businesses that can perform public building projects and to implement outreach efforts to encourage minority business participation in these projects to include education, recruitment, and interaction between minority businesses and nonminority businesses.

(2)   Attend the scheduled prebid conference.

(3)   At least 10 days prior to the scheduled day of bid opening, notify minority businesses that have requested notices from the public entity for public construction or repair work and minority businesses that otherwise indicated to the Office of Historically Underutilized Businesses an interest in the type of work being bid or the potential contracting opportunities listed in the proposal. The notification shall include the following:

a. A description of the work for which the bid is being solicited.

b. The date, time, and location where bids are to be submitted.

c. The name of the individual within the public entity who will be available to answer questions about the project.

d. Where bid documents may be reviewed.

e. Any special requirements that may exist.

(4) Utilize other media, as appropriate, likely to inform potential minority businesses of the bid being sought.

(f) A public entity shall require bidders to undertake the following good faith efforts to the extent required by the Secretary on projects subject to this section. The Secretary shall adopt rules establishing points to be awarded for taking each effort and the minimum number of points required, depending on project size, cost, type, and other factors considered relevant by the Secretary. In establishing the point system, the Secretary may not require a contractor to earn more than fifty (50) points, and the Secretary must assign each of the efforts listed in subdivisions (1) through (10) of this subsection at least 10 points. The public entity may require that additional good faith efforts be taken, as indicated in its bid specifications. Good faith efforts include:

(1) Contacting minority businesses that reasonably could have been expected to submit a quote and that were known to the contractor or available on State or local government maintained lists at least 10 days before the bid or proposal date and notifying them of the nature and scope of the work to be performed.

(2) Making the construction plans, specifications and requirements available for review by prospective minority businesses, or providing these documents to them at least 10 days before the bid or proposals are due.

(3) Breaking down or combining elements of work into economically feasible units to facilitate minority participation.

(4) Working with minority trade, community, or contractor organizations identified by the Office of Historically Underutilized Businesses and included in the bid documents that provide assistance in recruitment of minority businesses.

(5)   Attending any prebid meetings scheduled by the public owner.

(6)   Providing assistance in getting required bonding or insurance or providing alternatives to bonding or insurance for subcontractors.

(7)   Negotiating in good faith with interested minority businesses and not rejecting them as unqualified without sound reasons based on their capabilities. Any rejection of a minority business based on lack of qualification should have the reasons documented in writing.

(8)   Providing assistance to an otherwise qualified minority business in need of equipment, loan capital, lines of credit, or joint pay agreements to secure loans, supplies, or letters of credit, including waiving credit that is ordinarily required. Assisting minority businesses in obtaining the same unit pricing with the bidder's suppliers in order to help minority businesses in establishing credit.

(9)   Negotiating joint venture and partnership arrangements with minority businesses in order to increase opportunities for minority business participation on a public construction or repair project when possible.

(10)   Providing quick pay agreements and policies to enable minority contractors and suppliers to meet cash-flow demands.

(g)   As used in this section:

(1)   The term "minority business" means a business:

a.   In which at least fifty-one percent (51%) is owned by one or more minority persons or socially and economically disadvantaged individuals, or in the case of a corporation, in which at least fifty-one percent (51%) of the stock is owned by one or more minority persons or socially and economically disadvantaged individuals; and

b.   Of which the management and daily business operations are controlled by one or more of the minority persons or socially and economically disadvantaged individuals who own it.

(2)   The term "minority person" means a person who is a citizen or lawful permanent resident of the United States and who is:

a. Black, that is, a person having origins in any of the black racial groups in Africa;

b. Hispanic, that is, a person of Spanish or Portuguese culture with origins in Mexico, South or Central America, or the Caribbean Islands, regardless of race;

c. Asian American, that is, a person having origins in any of the original peoples of the Far East, Southeast Asia and Asia, the Indian subcontinent, or the Pacific Islands;

d. American Indian, that is, a person having origins in any of the original Indian peoples of North America; or

e. Female.

(3) The term "socially and economically disadvantaged individual" means the same as defined in 15 U.S.C. 637.

(h) The State, counties, municipalities, and all other public bodies shall award public building contracts, including those awarded under G.S. 143-128.1, 143-129, and 143-131, without regard to race, religion, color, creed, national origin, sex, age, or handicapping condition, as defined in G.S. 168A-3. Nothing in this section shall be construed to require contractors or awarding authorities to award contracts or subcontracts to or to make purchases of materials or equipment from minority-business contractors or minority-business subcontractors who do not submit the lowest responsible, responsive bid or bids.

(i) Notwithstanding G.S. 132-3 and G.S. 121-5, all public records created pursuant to this section shall be maintained by the public entity for a period of not less than three years from the date of the completion of the building project.

(j) Except as provided in subsections (a), (g), (h) and (i) of this section, this section shall only apply to building projects costing three hundred thousand dollars ($300,000) or more. This section shall not apply to the purchase and erection of prefabricated or relocatable buildings or portions thereof, except that portion of the work which must be performed at the construction site. (2001-496, s. 3.1.)

§ 143-128.3. Minority business participation administration.

(a) All public entities subject to G.S. 143-128.2 shall report to the Department of Administration, Office of Historically Underutilized Business, the following with respect to each building project:

(1) The verifiable percentage goal.

(2) The type and total dollar value of the project, minority business utilization by minority business category, trade, total dollar value of contracts awarded to each minority group for each project, the applicable good faith effort guidelines or rules used to recruit minority business participation, and good faith documentation accepted by the public entity from the successful bidder.

(3) The utilization of minority businesses under the various construction methods under G.S. 143-128(a1).

The reports shall be in the format and contain the data prescribed by the Secretary of Administration. The University of North Carolina and the State Board of Community Colleges shall report quarterly and all other public entities shall report semiannually. The Secretary of the Department of Administration shall make reports every six months to the Joint Legislative Committee on Governmental Operations on information reported pursuant to this subsection.

(b) A public entity that has been notified by the Secretary of its failure to comply with G.S. 143-128.2 on a project shall develop a plan of compliance that addresses the deficiencies identified by the Secretary. The corrective plan shall apply to the current project or to subsequent projects under G.S. 143-128, as appropriate, provided that the plan must be implemented, at a minimum, on the current project to the extent feasible. If the public entity, after notification from the Secretary, fails to file a corrective plan, or if the public entity does not implement the corrective plan in accordance with its terms, the Secretary shall require one or both of the following:

(1) That the public entity consult with the Department of Administration, Office of Historically Underutilized Businesses on the development of a new corrective plan, subject to the approval of the Department and the Attorney General. The public entity may designate a representative to appear on its behalf, provided that the representative has managerial responsibility for the construction project.

(2) That the public entity not bid another contract under G.S. 143-128 without prior review by the Department and the Attorney General of a good faith compliance plan developed pursuant to subdivision (1) of this subsection. The public entity shall be subject to the review and approval of its good faith compliance plan under this subdivision with respect to any projects bid pursuant to G.S. 143-128 during a period of time determined by the Secretary, not to exceed one year.

A public entity aggrieved by the decision of the Secretary may file a contested case proceeding under Chapter 150B of the General Statutes.

(c) The Secretary shall study and recommend to the General Assembly and other State agencies ways to improve the effectiveness and efficiency of the State capital facilities development, minority business participation program and good faith efforts in utilizing minority businesses as set forth in G.S. 143-128.2, and other appropriate good faith efforts that may result in the increased utilization of minority businesses.

(d) The Secretary shall appoint an advisory board to develop recommendations to improve the recruitment and utilization of minority businesses. The Secretary, with the input of its advisory board, shall review the State's programs for promoting the recruitment and utilization of minority businesses involved in State capital projects and shall recommend to the General Assembly, the State Construction Office, The University of North Carolina, and the community colleges system changes in the terms and conditions of State laws, rules, and policies that will enhance opportunities for utilization of minority businesses on these projects. The Secretary shall provide guidance to these agencies on identifying types of projects likely to attract increased participation by minority businesses and breaking down or combining elements of work into economically feasible units to facilitate minority business participation.

(e) The Secretary shall adopt rules for State entities, The University of North Carolina, and community colleges and shall adopt guidelines for local government units to implement the provisions of G.S. 143-128.2.

(e1) Repealed by Session Laws 2007-392, s. 3, effective October 1, 2007.

(f) The Secretary shall provide the following information to the Attorney General:

(1) Failure by a public entity to report data to the Secretary in accordance with this section.

(2) Upon the request of the Attorney General, any data or other information collected under this section.

(3) False statements knowingly provided in any affidavit or documentation under G.S. 143-128.2 to the State or other public entity. Public entities shall provide to the Secretary information concerning any false information knowingly provided to the public entity pursuant to G.S. 143-128.2.

(g) The Secretary shall report findings and recommendations as required under this section to the Joint Legislative Committee on Governmental Operations annually on or before June 1, beginning June 1, 2002. (2001-496, s. 3.6; 2005-270, s. 2; 2007-392, s. 3.)

§ 143-128.4. Historically underutilized business defined; statewide uniform certification.

(a) As used in this Chapter, the term "historically underutilized business" means a business that meets all of the following conditions:

(1) At least fifty-one percent (51%) of the business is owned by one or more persons who are members of at least one of the groups set forth in subsection (b) of this section, or in the case of a corporation, at least fifty-one percent (51%) of the stock is owned by one or more persons who are members of at least one of the groups set forth in subsection (b) of this section.

(2) The management and daily business operations are controlled by one or more owners of the business who are members of at least one of the groups set forth in subsection (b) of this section.

(a1) As used in this Chapter, the term "minority business" means a historically underutilized business.

(b) To qualify as a historically underutilized business under this section, a business must be owned and controlled as set forth in subsection (a) of this section by one or more citizens or lawful permanent residents of the United States who are members of one or more of the following groups:

(1) Black. - A person having origins in any of the black racial groups of Africa.

(2) Hispanic. - A person of Spanish or Portuguese culture having origins in Mexico, South or Central America, or the Caribbean islands, regardless of race.

(3) Asian American. - A person having origins in any of the original peoples of the Far East, Southeast Asia, Asia, Indian continent, or Pacific islands.

(4) American Indian. - A person having origins in any of the original Indian peoples of North America.

(5) Female.

(6) Disabled. - A person with a disability as defined in G.S. 168-1 or G.S. 168A-3.

(7) Disadvantaged. - A person who is socially and economically disadvantaged as defined in 15 U.S.C. § 637.

(c) In addition to the powers and duties provided in G.S. 143-49, the Secretary of Administration shall have the power, authority, and duty to:

(1) Develop and administer a statewide uniform program for: (i) the certification of a historically underutilized business, as defined in this section, for use by State departments, agencies, and institutions, and political subdivisions of the State; and (ii) the creation and maintenance of a database of the businesses certified as historically underutilized businesses.

(2) Adopt rules and procedures for the statewide uniform certification of historically underutilized businesses.

(3) Provide for the certification of all businesses designated as historically underutilized businesses to be used by State departments, agencies, and institutions, and political subdivisions of the State.

(d) The Secretary of Administration shall seek input from State departments, agencies, and institutions, political subdivisions of the State, and any other entity deemed appropriate to determine the qualifications and criteria for statewide uniform certification of historically underutilized businesses.

(e) Only businesses certified in accordance with this section shall be considered by State departments, agencies, and institutions, and political subdivisions of the State as historically underutilized businesses for minority business participation purposes under this Chapter. (2005-270, s. 3; 2007-392, s. 4; 2009-243, s. 3.)

§ 143-129. Procedure for letting of public contracts.

(a) Bidding Required. - No construction or repair work requiring the estimated expenditure of public money in an amount equal to or more than five hundred thousand dollars ($500,000) or purchase of apparatus, supplies, materials, or equipment requiring an estimated expenditure of public money in an amount equal to or more than ninety thousand dollars ($90,000) may be performed, nor may any contract be awarded therefor, by any board or governing body of the State, or of any institution of the State government, or of any political subdivision of the State, unless the provisions of this section are complied with; provided that The University of North Carolina and its constituent institutions may award contracts for construction or repair work that requires an estimated expenditure of less than five hundred thousand dollars ($500,000) without complying with the provisions of this section.

For purchases of apparatus, supplies, materials, or equipment, the governing body of any political subdivision of the State may, subject to any restriction as to dollar amount, or other conditions that the governing body elects to impose, delegate to the manager, school superintendent, chief purchasing official, or other employee the authority to award contracts, reject bids, or readvertise to receive bids on behalf of the unit. Any person to whom authority is delegated under this subsection shall comply with the requirements of this Article that would otherwise apply to the governing body.

(b) Advertisement and Letting of Contracts. - Where the contract is to be let by a board or governing body of the State government or of a State institution, proposals shall be invited by advertisement in a newspaper having general circulation in the State of North Carolina. Where the contract is to be let by a political subdivision of the State, proposals shall be invited by advertisement in a newspaper having general circulation in the political subdivision or by electronic means, or both. A decision to advertise solely by electronic means, whether for particular contracts or generally for all contracts that are subject to this Article, shall be approved by the governing board of the political subdivision of the State at a regular meeting of the board.

The advertisements for bidders required by this section shall appear at a time where at least seven full days shall lapse between the date on which the notice appears and the date of the opening of bids. The advertisement shall: (i) state the time and place where plans and specifications of proposed work or a complete description of the apparatus, supplies, materials, or equipment may be had; (ii) state the time and place for opening of the proposals; and (iii) reserve to the board or governing body the right to reject any or all proposals.

Proposals may be rejected for any reason determined by the board or governing body to be in the best interest of the unit. However, the proposal shall not be rejected for the purpose of evading the provisions of this Article. No board or governing body of the State or political subdivision thereof may assume responsibility for construction or purchase contracts, or guarantee the payments of labor or materials therefor except under provisions of this Article.

All proposals shall be opened in public and the board or governing body shall award the contract to the lowest responsible bidder or bidders, taking into consideration quality, performance and the time specified in the proposals for the performance of the contract.

In the event the lowest responsible bids are in excess of the funds available for the project or purchase, the responsible board or governing body is authorized to enter into negotiations with the lowest responsible bidder above mentioned, making reasonable changes in the plans and specifications as may be necessary to bring the contract price within the funds available, and may award a contract to such bidder upon recommendation of the Department of Administration in the case of the State government or of a State institution or agency, or upon recommendation of the responsible commission, council or board in the case of a subdivision of the State, if such bidder will agree to perform the work or provide the apparatus, supplies, materials, or equipment at the negotiated price within the funds available therefor. If a contract cannot be let under the above conditions, the board or governing body is authorized to readvertise, as herein provided, after having made such changes in plans and specifications as may be necessary to bring the cost of the project or purchase within the funds available therefor. The procedure above specified may be repeated if necessary in order to secure an acceptable contract within the funds available therefor.

No proposal for construction or repair work may be considered or accepted by said board or governing body unless at the time of its filing the same shall be accompanied by a deposit with said board or governing body of cash, or a cashier's check, or a certified check on some bank or trust company insured by the Federal Deposit Insurance Corporation in an amount equal to not less than five percent (5%) of the proposal. In lieu of making the cash deposit as above provided, such bidder may file a bid bond executed by a corporate surety licensed under the laws of North Carolina to execute such bonds, conditioned that the surety will upon demand forthwith make payment to the obligee upon said bond if the bidder fails to execute the contract in accordance with the bid bond. This deposit shall be retained if the successful bidder fails to execute the contract within 10 days after the award or fails to give satisfactory surety as required herein.

Bids shall be sealed and the opening of an envelope or package with knowledge that it contains a bid or the disclosure or exhibition of the contents of any bid by anyone without the permission of the bidder prior to the time set for opening in the invitation to bid shall constitute a Class 1 misdemeanor.

(c) Contract Execution and Security. - All contracts to which this section applies shall be executed in writing. The board or governing body shall require the person to whom the award of a contract for construction or repair work is made to furnish bond as required by Article 3 of Chapter 44A; or require a deposit of money, certified check or government securities for the full amount of said contract to secure the faithful performance of the terms of said contract and the payment of all sums due for labor and materials in a manner consistent with Article 3 of Chapter 44A; and the contract shall not be altered except by written agreement of the contractor and the board or governing body. The surety bond or deposit required herein shall be deposited with the board or governing body for which the work is to be performed. When a deposit, other than a surety bond, is made with the board or governing body, the board or governing body assumes all the liabilities, obligations and duties of a surety as provided in Article 3 of Chapter 44A to the extent of said deposit.

The owning agency or the Department of Administration, in contracts involving a State agency, and the owning agency or the governing board, in contracts involving a political subdivision of the State, may reject the bonds of any surety company against which there is pending any unsettled claim or complaint made by a State agency or the owning agency or governing board of any political subdivision of the State arising out of any contract under which State funds, in contracts with the State, or funds of political subdivisions of the State, in contracts with such political subdivision, were expended, provided such claim or complaint has been pending more than 180 days.

(d) Use of Unemployment Relief Labor. - Nothing in this section shall operate so as to require any public agency to enter into a contract which will prevent the use of unemployment relief labor paid for in whole or in part by appropriations or funds furnished by the State or federal government.

(e) Exceptions. - The requirements of this Article do not apply to:

(1) The purchase, lease, or other acquisition of any apparatus, supplies, materials, or equipment from: (i) the United States of America or any agency thereof; or (ii) any other government unit or agency thereof within the United States. The Secretary of Administration or the governing board of any political subdivision of the State may designate any officer or employee of the State or political subdivision to enter a bid or bids in its behalf at any sale of apparatus, supplies, materials, equipment, or other property owned by: (i) the United States of America or any agency thereof; or (ii) any other governmental unit or agency thereof within the United States. The Secretary of Administration or the governing board of any political subdivision of the State may authorize the officer or employee to make any partial or down payment or payment in full that may be required by regulations of the governmental unit or agency disposing of the property.

(2) Cases of special emergency involving the health and safety of the people or their property.

(3) Purchases made through a competitive bidding group purchasing program, which is a formally organized program that offers competitively obtained purchasing services at discount prices to two or more public agencies.

(4) Construction or repair work undertaken during the progress of a construction or repair project initially begun pursuant to this section.

(5) Purchase of gasoline, diesel fuel, alcohol fuel, motor oil, fuel oil, or natural gas. These purchases are subject to G.S. 143-131.

(6) Purchases of apparatus, supplies, materials, or equipment when: (i) performance or price competition for a product are not available; (ii) a needed product is available from only one source of supply; or (iii) standardization or compatibility is the overriding consideration. Notwithstanding any other provision

of this section, the governing board of a political subdivision of the State shall approve the purchases listed in the preceding sentence prior to the award of the contract.

In the case of purchases by hospitals, in addition to the other exceptions in this subsection, the provisions of this Article shall not apply when: (i) a particular medical item or prosthetic appliance is needed; (ii) a particular product is ordered by an attending physician for his patients; (iii) additional products are needed to complete an ongoing job or task; (iv) products are purchased for "over-the-counter" resale; (v) a particular product is needed or desired for experimental, developmental, or research work; or (vi) equipment is already installed, connected, and in service under a lease or other agreement and the governing body of the hospital determines that the equipment should be purchased. The governing body of a hospital shall keep a record of all purchases made pursuant to this subdivision. These records are subject to public inspection.

(7)   Purchases of information technology through contracts established by the State Office of Information Technology Services as provided in G.S. 147-33.82(b) and G.S. 147-33.92(b).

(8)   Guaranteed energy savings contracts, which are governed by Article 3B of Chapter 143 of the General Statutes.

(9)   Purchases from contracts established by the State or any agency of the State, if the contractor is willing to extend to a political subdivision of the State the same or more favorable prices, terms, and conditions as established in the State contract.

(9a)   Purchases of apparatus, supplies, materials, or equipment from contracts established by the United States of America or any federal agency, if the contractor is willing to extend to a political subdivision of the State the same or more favorable prices, terms, and conditions as established in the federal contract.

(10)   Purchase of used apparatus, supplies, materials, or equipment. For purposes of this subdivision, remanufactured, refabricated or demo apparatus, supplies, materials, or equipment are not included in the exception. A demo item is one that is used for demonstration and is sold by the manufacturer or retailer at a discount.

(11)	Contracts by a public entity with a construction manager at risk executed pursuant to G.S. 143-128.1.

(12)	(Repealed effective July 1, 2015) Build-to-suit capital leases with a private developer under G.S. 115C-532.

(f)	Repealed by Session Laws 2001-328, s. 1, effective August 2, 2001.

(g)	Waiver of Bidding for Previously Bid Contracts. - When the governing board of any political subdivision of the State, or the person to whom authority has been delegated under subsection (a) of this section, determines that it is in the best interest of the unit, the requirements of this section may be waived for the purchase of apparatus, supplies, materials, or equipment from any person or entity that has, within the previous 12 months, after having completed a public, formal bid process substantially similar to that required by this Article, contracted to furnish the apparatus, supplies, materials, or equipment to:

(1)	The United States of America or any federal agency;

(2)	The State of North Carolina or any agency or political subdivision of the State; or

(3)	Any other state or any agency or political subdivision of that state, if the person or entity is willing to furnish the items at the same or more favorable prices, terms, and conditions as those provided under the contract with the other unit or agency. Notwithstanding any other provision of this section, any purchase made under this subsection shall be approved by the governing body of the purchasing political subdivision of the State at a regularly scheduled meeting of the governing body no fewer than 10 days after publication of notice that a waiver of the bid procedure will be considered in order to contract with a qualified supplier pursuant to this section. Notice may be published in a newspaper having general circulation in the political subdivision or by electronic means, or both. A decision to publish notice solely by electronic means for a particular contract or for all contracts under this subsection shall be approved by the governing board of the political subdivision. Rules issued by the Secretary of Administration pursuant to G.S. 143-49(6) shall apply with respect to participation in State term contracts.

(h)	Transportation Authority Purchases. - Notwithstanding any other provision of this section, any board or governing body of any regional public transportation authority, hereafter referred to as a "RPTA," created pursuant to

Article 26 of Chapter 160A of the General Statutes, or a regional transportation authority, hereafter referred to as a "RTA," created pursuant to Article 27 of Chapter 160A of the General Statutes, may approve the entering into of any contract for the purchase, lease, or other acquisition of any apparatus, supplies, materials, or equipment without competitive bidding and without meeting the requirements of subsection (b) of this section if the following procurement by competitive proposal (Request for Proposal) method is followed.

The competitive proposal method of procurement is normally conducted with more than one source submitting an offer or proposal. Either a fixed price or cost reimbursement type contract is awarded. This method of procurement is generally used when conditions are not appropriate for the use of sealed bids. If this procurement method is used, all of the following requirements apply:

(1) Requests for proposals shall be publicized. All evaluation factors shall be identified along with their relative importance.

(2) Proposals shall be solicited from an adequate number of qualified sources.

(3) RPTAs or RTAs shall have a method in place for conducting technical evaluations of proposals received and selecting awardees, with the goal of promoting fairness and competition without requiring strict adherence to specifications or price in determining the most advantageous proposal.

(4) The award may be based upon initial proposals without further discussion or negotiation or, in the discretion of the evaluators, discussions or negotiations may be conducted either with all offerors or with those offerors determined to be within the competitive range, and one or more revised proposals or a best and final offer may be requested of all remaining offerors. The details and deficiencies of an offeror's proposal may not be disclosed to other offerors during any period of negotiation or discussion.

(5) The award shall be made to the responsible firm whose proposal is most advantageous to the RPTA's or the RTA's program with price and other factors considered.

The contents of the proposals shall not be public records until 14 days before the award of the contract.

The board or governing body of the RPTA or the RTA shall, at the regularly scheduled meeting, by formal motion make findings of fact that the procurement by competitive proposal (Request for Proposals) method of procuring the particular apparatus, supplies, materials, or equipment is the most appropriate acquisition method prior to the issuance of the requests for proposals and shall by formal motion certify that the requirements of this subsection have been followed before approving the contract.

Nothing in this subsection subjects a procurement by competitive proposal under this subsection to G.S. 143-49, 143-52, or 143-53.

RPTAs and RTAs may adopt regulations to implement this subsection.

(i) Procedure for Letting of Public Contracts. - The Department of Transportation ("DOT"), The University of North Carolina and its constituent institutions ("UNC"), and the Department of Administration ("DOA") shall monitor all projects in those agencies and institutions that are let without a performance or payment bond to determine the number of defaults on those projects, the cost to complete each defaulted project, and each project's contract price. Beginning March 1, 2011, and annually thereafter, DOT, UNC, and DOA shall report this information to the Joint Legislative Committee on Governmental Operations.

(j) [Use of E-Verify Required. -] No contract subject to this section may be awarded by any board or governing body of the State, institution of State government, or any political subdivision of the State unless the contractor and the contractor's subcontractors comply with the requirements of Article 2 of Chapter 64 of the General Statutes. (1931, c. 338, s. 1; 1933, c. 50; c. 400, s. 1; 1937, c. 355; 1945, c. 144; 1949, c. 257; 1951, c. 1104, ss. 1, 2; 1953, c. 1268; 1955, c. 1049; 1957, c. 269, s. 3; c. 391; c. 862, ss. 1-4; 1959, c. 392, s. 1; c. 910, s. 1; 1961, c. 1226; 1965, c. 841, s. 2; 1967, c. 860; 1971, c. 847; 1973, c. 1194, s. 2; 1975, c. 879, s. 46; 1977, c. 619, ss. 1, 2; 1979, c. 182, s. 1; 1979, 2nd Sess., c. 1081; 1981, c. 346, s. 1; c. 754, s. 1; 1985, c. 145, ss. 1, 2; 1987, c. 590; 1987 (Reg. Sess., 1988), c. 1108, ss. 7, 8; 1989, c. 350; 1993, c. 539, s. 1007; 1994, Ex. Sess., c. 24, s. 14(c); 1995, c. 367, s. 6; 1997-174, ss. 1-4; 1998-185, s. 1; 1998-217, s. 16; 2001-328, s. 1; 2001-487, s. 88; 2001-496, ss. 4, 5; 2005-227, s. 1; 2006-232, s. 2; 2007-94, s. 1; 2007-322, s. 4; 2007-446, s. 6; 2010-148, s. 1.2; 2011-234, s. 1; 2013-418, s. 2(c).)

§ 143-129.1. Withdrawal of bid.

A public agency may allow a bidder submitting a bid pursuant to G.S. 143-129 for construction or repair work or for the purchase of apparatus, supplies, materials, or equipment to withdraw his bid from consideration after the bid opening without forfeiture of his bid security if the price bid was based upon a mistake, which constituted a substantial error, provided the bid was submitted in good faith, and the bidder submits credible evidence that the mistake was clerical in nature as opposed to a judgment error, and was actually due to an unintentional and substantial arithmetic error or an unintentional omission of a substantial quantity of work, labor, apparatus, supplies, materials, equipment, or services made directly in the compilation of the bid, which unintentional arithmetic error or unintentional omission can be clearly shown by objective evidence drawn from inspection of the original work papers, documents or materials used in the preparation of the bid sought to be withdrawn. A request to withdraw a bid must be made in writing to the public agency which invited the proposals for the work prior to the award of the contract, but not later than 72 hours after the opening of bids, or for a longer period as may be specified in the instructions to bidders provided prior to the opening of bids.

If a request to withdraw a bid has been made in accordance with the provisions of this section, action on the remaining bids shall be considered, in accordance with North Carolina G.S. 143-129, as though said bid had not been received. Notwithstanding the foregoing, such bid shall be deemed to have been received for the purpose of complying with the requirements of G.S. 143-132. If the work or purchase is relet for bids, under no circumstances may the bidder who has filed a request to withdraw be permitted to rebid the work or purchase.

If a bidder files a request to withdraw his bid, the agency shall promptly hold a hearing thereon. The agency shall give to the withdrawing bidder reasonable notice of the time and place of any such hearing. The bidder, either in person or through counsel, may appear at the hearing and present any additional facts and arguments in support of his request to withdraw his bid. The agency shall issue a written ruling allowing or denying the request to withdraw within five days after the hearing. If the agency finds that the price bid was based upon a mistake of the type described in the first paragraph of this section, then the agency shall issue a ruling permitting the bidder to withdraw without forfeiture of the bidder's security. If the agency finds that the price bid was based upon a mistake not of the type described in the first paragraph of this section, then the agency shall issue a ruling denying the request to withdraw and requiring the forfeiture of the bidder's security. A denial by the agency of the request to withdraw a bid shall have the same effect as if an award had been made to the bidder and a refusal by the bidder to accept had been made, or as if there had been a refusal to enter into the contract, and the bidder's bid deposit or bid bond shall be forfeited.

In the event said ruling denies the request to withdraw the bid, the bidder shall have the right, within 20 days after receipt of said ruling, to contest the matter by the filing of a civil action in any court of competent jurisdiction of the State of North Carolina. The procedure shall be the same as in all civil actions except all issues of law and fact and every other issue shall be tried de novo by the judge without jury; provided that the matter may be referred in the instances and in the manner provided for by North Carolina G.S. 1A-1, Rule 53, as amended. Notwithstanding the foregoing, if the public agency involved is the Department of Administration, it may follow its normal rules and regulations with respect to contested matters, as opposed to following the administrative procedures set forth herein. If it is finally determined that the bidder did not have the right to withdraw his bid pursuant to the provisions of this section, the bidder's security shall be forfeited. Every bid bond or bid deposit given by a bidder to a public agency pursuant to G.S. 143-129 shall be conclusively presumed to have been given in accordance with this section, whether or not it be so drawn as to conform to this section. This section shall be conclusively presumed to have been written into every bid bond given pursuant to G.S. 143-129.

Neither the agency nor any elected or appointed official, employee, representative or agent of such agency shall incur any liability or surcharge, in the absence of fraud or collusion, by permitting the withdrawal of a bid pursuant to the provisions of this section.

No withdrawal of the bid which would result in the award of the contract on another bid of the same bidder, his partner, or to a corporation or business venture owned by or in which he has an interest shall be permitted. No bidder who is permitted to withdraw a bid shall supply any material or labor to, or perform any subcontract or work agreement for, any person to whom a contract or subcontract is awarded in the performance of the contract for which the withdrawn bid was submitted, without the prior written approval of the agency. Whoever violates the provisions of the foregoing sentence shall be guilty of a Class 1 misdemeanor. (1977, c. 617, s. 1; 1993, c. 539, s. 1008; 1994, Ex. Sess., c. 24, s. 14(c); 2001-328, s. 2.)

§ 143-129.2. Construction, design, and operation of solid waste management and sludge management facilities.

(a) All terms relating to solid waste management and disposal as used in this section shall be defined as set forth in G.S. 130A-290, except that the term "unit of local government" also includes a sanitary district created under Part 2 of Article 2 of Chapter 130A of the General Statutes, an authority created under Article 1 of Chapter 162A of the General Statutes, a metropolitan sewerage district created under Article 5 of Chapter 162A of the General Statutes, and a county water and sewer district created under Article 6 of Chapter 162A of the General Statutes. As used in this section, the term "sludge management facility" means a facility that processes sludge that has been generated by a municipal wastewater treatment plant for final end use or disposal but does not include any component of a wastewater treatment process or facility that generates sludge.

(b) To acknowledge the highly complex and innovative nature of solid waste and sludge management technologies for processing mixed solid waste and sludge generated by water and wastewater treatment facilities, the relatively limited availability of existing and proven proprietary technology involving solid waste and sludge management facilities, the desirability of a single point of responsibility for the development of facilities and the economic and technical utility of contracts for solid waste and sludge management which include in their scope combinations of design, construction, operation, management and maintenance responsibilities over prolonged periods of time and that in some instances it may be beneficial to a unit of local government to award a contract on the basis of factors other than cost alone, including but not limited to facility design, operational experience, system reliability, energy production efficiency, long-term operational costs, compatibility with source separation and other recycling systems, environmental impact and operational guarantees. Accordingly, and notwithstanding other provisions of this Article or any local law, a contract entered into between a unit of local government and any person pursuant to this section may be awarded in accordance with the following provisions for the award of a contract based upon an evaluation of proposals submitted in response to a request for proposals prepared by or for a unit of local government.

(c) The unit of local government shall require in its request for proposals that each proposal to be submitted shall include all of the following:

(1) Information relating to the experience of the proposer on the basis of which said proposer purports to be qualified to carry out all work required by a proposed contract; the ability of the proposer to secure adequate financing; and

proposals for project staffing, implementation of work tasks, and the carrying out of all responsibilities required by a proposed contract.

(2)   A proposal clearly identifying and specifying all elements of cost which would become charges to the unit of local government, in whatever form, in return for the fulfillment by the proposer of all tasks and responsibilities established by the request for the proposal for the full lifetime of a proposed contract, including, as appropriate, but not limited to, the cost of planning, design, construction, operation, management and/or maintenance of any facility; provided, that the unit of local government may prescribe the form and content of the proposal and that, in any event, the proposer must submit sufficiently detailed information to permit a fair and equitable evaluation of the proposal.

(3)   Any other information as the unit of local government may determine to have a material bearing on its ability to evaluate any proposal in accordance with this section.

(d)   Proposals received in response to a request for proposals may be evaluated on the basis of a technical analysis of facility design, operational experience of the technology to be utilized in the proposed facility, system reliability and availability, energy production balance and efficiency, environmental impact and protection, recovery of materials, required staffing level during operation, projection of anticipated revenues from the sale of energy and materials recovered by the facility, net cost to the unit of local government for operation and maintenance of the facility for the duration of time to be established in the request for proposals and upon any other factors and information that the unit of local government determined to have a material bearing on its ability to evaluate any proposal, which factors were set forth in said request for proposal.

(e)   The unit of local government may make a contract award to any responsible proposer selected pursuant to this section based upon a determination that the selected proposal is more responsive to the request for proposals and may thereupon negotiate a contract with said proposer for the performance of the services set forth in the request for proposals and the response thereto, the determination shall be deemed to be conclusive. Notwithstanding other provisions of this Article or any local law, a contract may be negotiated and entered into between a unit of local government and any person selected as a responsible proposer hereunder which may provide for, but not be limited to, the following:

(1) A contract, lease, rental, license, permit or other authorization to design, construct, operate and maintain a solid waste or sludge management facility upon such terms and conditions, for such consideration, and for such duration, not to exceed 40 years, as may be agreed upon by the unit of local government and the person.

(2) Payment by the unit of local government of a fee or other charge to the person for acceptance, processing, recycling, management and disposal of solid waste or sludge.

(3) An obligation on the part of a unit of local government to deliver or cause to be delivered to a solid waste or sludge management facility guaranteed quantities of solid wastes or sludge.

(4) The sale, utilization or disposal of any form of energy, recovered material or residue resulting from the operation of any solid waste or sludge management facility.

(f) Except for authorities created pursuant to Article 22 of Chapter 153A of the General Statutes, the construction work for any facility or structure that is ancillary to a solid waste or sludge management facility and that does not involve storage and processing of solid waste or sludge or the separation, extraction, and recovery of useful or marketable forms of energy and materials from solid waste at a solid waste management facility shall be procured through competitive bidding procedures described by G.S. 143-128 through 143-129.1. Ancillary facilities include but are not limited to roads, water and sewer lines to the facility limits, transfer stations, scale houses, administration buildings, and residue and bypass disposal sites. (1983, c. 795, ss. 4, 8.1; 2005-176, s. 1; 2007-131, s. 3.)

§ 143-129.3. Exemption of General Assembly from certain purchasing requirements.

(a) The Legislative Services Commission may provide that the provisions of G.S. 143-129 and Article 3 of this Chapter do not apply to purchases by the General Assembly of data processing and data communications equipment, supplies, and services. Such exemption may vary according to the type or amount of purchase, and may vary as to whether the exemption is from some or all of those statutory provisions.

(b) The Legislative Services Commission must give specific approval to any purchase in excess of five thousand dollars ($5,000) made under an exemption provided by subsection (a) of this section. (1989, c. 82.)

§ 143-129.4. Guaranteed energy savings contracts.

The solicitation and evaluation of proposals for guaranteed energy savings contracts, as defined in Part 2 of Article 3B of this Chapter, and the letting of contracts for these proposals are not governed by this Article but instead are governed by the provisions of that Part; except that guaranteed energy savings contracts are subject to the requirements of G.S. 143-128.2 and G.S. 143-135.3. (1993 (Reg. Sess., 1994), c. 775, s. 4; 1995, c. 509, s. 135.2(k); 2001-496, s. 3.3; 2002-161, s. 11.)

§ 143-129.5. Purchases from nonprofit work centers for the blind and severely disabled.

Notwithstanding G.S. 143-129, a city, county, or other governmental entity subject to this Article may purchase goods and services directly from a nonprofit work center for the blind and severely disabled, as defined in G.S. 143-48.

The Department of Administration shall report annually to the Joint Legislative Commission on Governmental Operations on its administration of this program. (1995, c. 265, s. 4; 1999-20, s. 1.)

§ 143-129.6. Reserved for future codification purposes.

§ 143-129.7. Purchase with trade-in of apparatus, supplies, materials, and equipment.

Notwithstanding the provisions of Article 12 of Chapter 160A of the General Statutes, municipalities, counties, and other political subdivisions of the State may include in specifications for the purchase of apparatus, supplies, materials, or equipment an opportunity for bidders to purchase as "trade-in" specified personal property owned by the municipality, county, or other political subdivision, and the awarding authority may award a contract for both the purchase of the apparatus, supplies, materials, or equipment and the sale of trade-in property, taking into consideration the amount offered on the trade-in when applying the criteria for award established in this Article. (1997-174, s. 7.)

§ 143-129.8. Purchase of information technology goods and services.

(a)   In recognition of the complex and innovative nature of information technology goods and services and of the desirability of a single point of responsibility for contracts that include combinations of purchase of goods, design, installation, training, operation, maintenance, and related services, a political subdivision of the State may contract for information technology, as defined in G.S. 147-33.81(2), using the procedure set forth in this section, in addition to or instead of any other procedure available under North Carolina law.

(b)   Contracts for information technology may be entered into under a request for proposals procedure that satisfies the following minimum requirements:

(1)   Notice of the request for proposals shall be given in accordance with G.S. 143-129(b).

(2)   Contracts shall be awarded to the person or entity that submits the best overall proposal as determined by the awarding authority. Factors to be considered in awarding contracts shall be identified in the request for proposals.

(c)   The awarding authority may use procurement methods set forth in G.S. 143-135.9 in developing and evaluating requests for proposals under this section. The awarding authority may negotiate with any proposer in order to obtain a final contract that best meets the needs of the awarding authority. Negotiations allowed under this section shall not alter the contract beyond the scope of the original request for proposals in a manner that: (i) deprives the proposers or potential proposers of a fair opportunity to compete for the contract; and (ii) would have resulted in the award of the contract to a different person or entity if the alterations had been included in the request for proposals.

(d) Proposals submitted under this section shall not be subject to public inspection until a contract is awarded. (2001-328, s. 3; 2004-199, s. 36(b); 2004-203, s. 10.)

§ 143-129.8A. Purchase of certain goods and services for the North Carolina Zoological Park.

(a) Exemption. - The North Carolina Zoological Park is a State entity whose primary purpose is the attraction of, interaction with, and education of the public regarding issues of global conservation, ecological preservation, and scientific exploration, and that purpose presents unique challenges requiring greater flexibility and faster responsiveness in meeting the needs of and creating the attractions for the Park. Accordingly, the Department of Environment and Natural Resources may use the procedure set forth in this section, in addition to or instead of any other procedure available under North Carolina law, to contract with a non-State entity on behalf of the Park for the acquisition of goods and services where: (i) the contract directly results in the generation of revenue for the State of North Carolina or (ii) the use of the acquired goods and services by the Park results in increased revenue or decreased expenditures for the State of North Carolina.

(b) Limitation. - Contracts executed pursuant to the exemption of subsection (a) of this section may be entered into under a request for proposals procedure that satisfies the following minimum requirements:

(1) Notice of the request for proposals shall be given in accordance with G.S. 143-129(b).

(2) Contracts shall be awarded to the person or entity that submits the best overall proposal as determined by the awarding authority. Factors to be considered in awarding contracts shall be identified in the request for proposals.

(c) Procurement Methods. - The Department may use procurement methods set forth in G.S. 143-135.9 in developing and evaluating requests for proposals under this section. The Department may negotiate with any proposer in order to obtain a final contract that best meets the needs of the awarding authority. Negotiations allowed under this section shall not alter the contract beyond the scope of the original request for proposals in a manner that: (i) deprives the proposers or potential proposers of a fair opportunity to compete for the contract; and (ii) would have resulted in the award of the contract to a different person or entity if the alterations had been included in the request for proposals.

(d) Promotional Rights. - Subject to the approval of the Department, a non-State entity awarded a contract that results in increased revenue or decreased expenditures for the Park may advertise, announce, or otherwise publicize the provision of services pursuant to award of the contract. (2009-329, s. 1.1.)

§ 143-129.9. Alternative competitive bidding methods.

(a) A political subdivision of the State may use any of the following methods to obtain competitive bids for the purchase of apparatus, supplies, materials, or equipment as an alternative to the otherwise applicable requirements in this Article:

(1) Reverse auction. - For purposes of this section, "reverse auction" means a real-time purchasing process in which bidders compete to provide goods at the lowest selling price in an open and interactive environment. The bidders' prices may be revealed during the reverse auction. A reverse auction may be conducted by the political subdivision or by a third party under contract with the political subdivision. A political subdivision may also conduct a reverse auction through the State electronic procurement system, and compliance with the procedures and requirements of the State's reverse auction process satisfies the political subdivision's obligations under this Article.

(2) Electronic bidding. - A political subdivision may receive bids electronically in addition to or instead of paper bids. Procedures for receipt of electronic bids for contracts that are subject to the requirements of G.S. 143-129 shall be designed to ensure the security, authenticity, and confidentiality of the bids to at least the same extent as is provided for with sealed paper bids.

(b) The requirements for advertisement of bidding opportunities, timeliness of the receipt of bids, the standard for the award of contracts, and all other requirements in this Article that are not inconsistent with the methods authorized in this section shall apply to contracts awarded under this section.

(c) Reverse auctions shall not be utilized for the purchase or acquisition of construction aggregates, including, but not limited to, crushed stone, sand, and gravel. (2002-107, s. 1.)

§ 143-130. Allowance for convict labor must be specified.

In cases where the board or governing body of a State agency or of any political subdivision of the State may furnish convict or other labor to the contractor, manufacturer, or others entering into contracts for the performance of construction work, installation of apparatus, supplies, materials or equipment, the specifications covering such projects shall carry full information as to what wages shall be paid for such labor or the amount of allowance for same. (1933, c. 400, s. 2; 1967, c. 860.)

§ 143-131. When counties, cities, towns and other subdivisions may let contracts on informal bids.

(a) All contracts for construction or repair work or for the purchase of apparatus, supplies, materials, or equipment, involving the expenditure of public money in the amount of thirty thousand dollars ($30,000) or more, but less than the limits prescribed in G.S. 143-129, made by any officer, department, board, local school administrative unit, or commission of any county, city, town, or other subdivision of this State shall be made after informal bids have been secured. All such contracts shall be awarded to the lowest responsible, responsive bidder, taking into consideration quality, performance, and the time specified in the bids for the performance of the contract. It shall be the duty of any officer, department, board, local school administrative unit, or commission entering into such contract to keep a record of all bids submitted, and such record shall not be subject to public inspection until the contract has been awarded.

(b) All public entities shall solicit minority participation in contracts for the erection, construction, alteration or repair of any building awarded pursuant to this section. The public entity shall maintain a record of contractors solicited and shall document efforts to recruit minority business participation in those contracts. Nothing in this section shall be construed to require formal advertisement of bids. All data, including the type of project, total dollar value of the project, dollar value of minority business participation on each project, and documentation of efforts to recruit minority participation shall be reported to the Department of Administration, Office for Historically Underutilized Business, upon the completion of the project. (1931, c. 338, s. 2; 1957, c. 862, s. 5; 1959, c. 406; 1963, c. 172; 1967, c. 860; 1971, c. 593; 1981, c. 719, s. 1; 1987 (Reg. Sess., 1988), c. 1108, s. 6; 1997-174, s. 5; 2001-496, s. 5.1; 2005-227, s. 2.)

§ 143-132. Minimum number of bids for public contracts.

(a)   No contract to which G.S. 143-129 applies for construction or repairs shall be awarded by any board or governing body of the State, or any subdivision thereof, unless at least three competitive bids have been received from reputable and qualified contractors regularly engaged in their respective lines of endeavor; however, this section shall not apply to contracts which are negotiated as provided for in G.S. 143-129. Provided that if after advertisement for bids as required by G.S. 143-129, not as many as three competitive bids have been received from reputable and qualified contractors regularly engaged in their respective lines of endeavor, said board or governing body of the State agency or of a county, city, town or other subdivision of the State shall again advertise for bids; and if as a result of such second advertisement, not as many as three competitive bids from reputable and qualified contractors are received, such board or governing body may then let the contract to the lowest responsible bidder submitting a bid for such project, even though only one bid is received.

(b)   For purposes of contracts bid in the alternative between the separate-prime and single-prime contracts, pursuant to G.S. 143-128(d1) each single-prime bid shall constitute a competitive bid in each of the four subdivisions or branches of work listed in G.S. 143-128(a), and each full set of separate-prime bids shall constitute a competitive single-prime bid in meeting the requirements of subsection (a) of this section. If there are at least three single-prime bids but there is not at least one full set of separate-prime bids, no separate-prime bids shall be opened.

(c)   The State Building Commission shall develop guidelines no later than January 1, 1991, governing the opening of bids pursuant to this Article. These guidelines shall be distributed to all public bodies subject to this Article. The guidelines shall not be subject to the provisions of Chapter 150B of the General Statutes. (1931, c. 291, s. 3; 1951, c. 1104, s. 3; 1959, c. 392, s. 2; 1963, c. 289; 1967, c. 860; 1977, c. 644; 1979, c. 182, s. 2; 1989, c. 480, s. 2; 1989

(Reg. Sess., 1990), c. 1051, s. 4; 1991 (Reg. Sess., 1992), c. 985, s. 1; 1995, c. 358, s. 4; c. 367, ss. 1, 7; 2001-496, s. 9.)

§ 143-133. No evasion permitted.

No bill or contract shall be divided for the purpose of evading the provisions of this Article. (1933, c. 400, s. 3; 1967, c. 860.)

§ 143-133.1: Reserved for future codification purposes.

§ 143-133.2: Reserved for future codification purposes.

§ 143-133.3: Reserved for future codification purposes.

§ 143-133.4: Reserved for future codification purposes.

§ 143-133.5. Public contracts; labor organizations.

(a) It is the intent of the General Assembly that the provisions of this section will provide for more economical, nondiscriminatory, neutral, and efficient procurement of construction-related services by the State and political subdivisions of the State as market participants. The General Assembly finds that providing for fair and open competition best effectuates this intent.

(b) Every officer, board, department, commission, or commissions charged with the responsibility of preparation of specifications or awarding or entering into contracts for the erection, construction, alteration, or repair of any buildings for the State, or for any county, municipality, or other public body subject to this Article shall not in any bid specifications, project agreements, or other controlling documents:

(1) Require or prohibit a bidder, offeror, contractor, or subcontractor from adhering to an agreement with one or more labor organizations in regard to that project or a related construction project.

(2) Otherwise discriminate against a bidder, offeror, contractor, or subcontractor for becoming, remaining, refusing to become or remain a

signatory to, or for adhering or refusing to adhere to an agreement with one or more labor organizations in regard to that project or a related construction project.

(c)   No officer, board, department, commission, or commissions charged with the responsibility of awarding grants or tax incentives, or any county, municipality, or other public body in the award of grants or tax incentives, may award a grant or tax incentive that is conditioned upon a requirement that the awardee include a term described in subsection (b) of this section in a contract document for any construction, improvement, maintenance, or renovation to real property or fixtures that are the subject of the grant or tax incentive.

(d)   This section does not prohibit any officer, board, department, commission, or commissions or any county, municipality, or other public body from awarding a contract, grant, or tax incentive to a private owner, bidder, contractor, or subcontractor who enters into or who is party to an agreement with a labor organization if being or becoming a party or adhering to an agreement with a labor organization is not a condition for award of the contract, grant, or tax incentive, and if the State agent, employee, or board or the political subdivision does not discriminate against a private owner, bidder, contractor, or subcontractor in the awarding of that contract, grant, or tax incentive based upon the person's status as being or becoming, or the willingness or refusal to become, a party to an agreement with a labor organization.

(e)   This section does not prohibit a contractor or subcontractor from voluntarily entering into or complying with an agreement entered into with one or more labor organizations in regard to a contract with the State or a political subdivision of the State or funded in whole or in part from a grant or tax incentive from the State or political subdivision.

(f)   The State or the governing body of a political subdivision may exempt a particular project, contract, subcontract, grant, or tax incentive from the requirements of any or all of the provisions of subsection (b) or (c) of this section if the State or governing body of the political subdivision finds, after public notice and a hearing, that special circumstances require an exemption to avert a significant, documentable threat to public health or safety. A finding of special circumstances under this section shall not be based on the possibility or presence of a labor dispute concerning the use of contractors or subcontractors who are nonsignatories to, or otherwise do not adhere to, agreements with one or more labor organizations, or concerning employees on the project who are not members of or affiliated with a labor organization.

(g)   This section does not do either of the following:

(1)   Prohibit employers or other parties from entering into agreements or engaging in any other activity protected by the National Labor Relations Act, 29 U.S.C. §§ 151 to 169.

(2)   Interfere with labor relations of parties that are left unregulated under the National Labor Relations Act, 29 U.S.C. §§ 151 to 169. (2013-267, s. 1.)

§ 143-134. Applicable to Department of Transportation and Department of Public Safety; exceptions; all contracts subject to review by Attorney General and State Auditor.

(a)   This Article applies to the Department of Transportation and the Department of Public Safety except in the construction of roads, bridges and their approaches; provided however, that whenever the Director of the Budget determines that the repair or construction of a building by the Department of Transportation or by the Department of Public Safety can be done more economically through use of employees of the Department of Transportation and/or prison inmates than by letting the repair or building construction to contract, the provisions of this Article shall not apply to the repair or construction.

(b)   Notwithstanding subsection (a) of this section, the Department of Transportation and the Department of Public Safety shall: (i) submit all proposed contracts for supplies, materials, printing, equipment, and contractual services that exceed one million dollars ($1,000,000) to the Attorney General or the Attorney General's designee for review as provided in G.S. 114-8.3; and (ii) include in all contracts to be awarded by the Department of Transportation or the Department of Public Safety a standard clause providing that the State Auditor and internal auditors of the Department of Transportation or the Department of Public Safety may audit the records of the contractor during and after the term of the contract to verify accounts and data affecting fees and performance. Neither the Department of Transportation nor the Department of Public Safety shall award a cost plus percentage of cost agreement or contract for any purpose. (1933, c. 400, s. 3-A; 1955, c. 572; 1957, c. 65, s. 11; 1967, c. 860; c. 996, s. 13; 1973, c. 507, s. 5; 1977, c. 464, s. 34; 2010-194, s. 24; 2011-145, s. 19.1(h); 2011-326, s. 15(y); 2012-83, s. 45; 2013-289, s. 1.)

§ 143-134.1. Interest on final payments due to prime contractors; payments to subcontractors.

(a) On all public construction contracts which are let by a board or governing body of the State government or any political subdivision thereof, except contracts let by the Department of Transportation pursuant to G.S. 136-28.1, the balance due prime contractors shall be paid in full within 45 days after respective prime contracts of the project have been accepted by the owner, certified by the architect, engineer or designer to be completed in accordance with terms of the plans and specifications, or occupied by the owner and used for the purpose for which the project was constructed, whichever occurs first. However, when the architect or consulting engineer in charge of the project determines that delay in completion of the project in accordance with terms of the plans and specifications is the fault of the contractor, the project may be occupied and used for the purposes for which it was constructed without payment of any interest on amounts withheld past the 45 day limit.

No payment shall be delayed because of the failure of another prime contractor on the project to complete his contract. Should final payment to any prime contractor beyond the date the contracts have been certified to be completed by the designer or architect, accepted by the owner, or occupied by the owner and used for the purposes for which the project was constructed, be delayed by more than 45 days, the prime contractor shall be paid interest, beginning on the 46th day, at the rate of one percent (1%) per month or fraction thereof unless a lower rate is agreed upon on the unpaid balance as may be due. In addition to the above final payment provisions, periodic payments due a prime contractor during construction shall be paid in accordance with the provisions of this section and the payment provisions of the contract documents that do not conflict with this section, or the prime contractor shall be paid interest on any unpaid amount at the rate stipulated above for delayed final payments. The interest shall begin on the date the payment is due and continue until the date on which payment is made. The due date may be established by the terms of the contract. Funds for payment of the interest on state-owned projects shall be obtained from the current budget of the owning department, institution, or agency. Where a conditional acceptance of a contract exists, and where the owner is retaining a reasonable sum pending correction of the conditions, interest on the reasonable sum shall not apply.

(b) Within seven days of receipt by the prime contractor of each periodic or final payment, the prime contractor shall pay the subcontractor based on work completed or service provided under the subcontract. If any periodic or final payment to the subcontractor is delayed by more than seven days after receipt of periodic or final payment by the prime contractor, the prime contractor shall pay the subcontractor interest, beginning on the eighth day, at the rate of one percent (1%) per month or fraction thereof on the unpaid balance as may be due.

(b1)   No retainage on periodic or final payments made by the owner or prime contractor shall be allowed on public construction contracts in which the total project costs are less than one hundred thousand dollars ($100,000). Retainage on periodic or final payments on public construction contracts in which the total project costs are equal to or greater than one hundred thousand dollars ($100,000) is allowed as follows:

(1)   The owner shall not retain more than five percent (5%) of any periodic payment due a prime contractor.

(2)   When the project is fifty percent (50%) complete, the owner, with written consent of the surety, shall not retain any further retainage from periodic payments due the contractor if the contractor continues to perform satisfactorily and any nonconforming work identified in writing prior to that time by the architect, engineer, or owner has been corrected by the contractor and accepted by the architect, engineer, or owner. If the owner determines the contractor's performance is unsatisfactory, the owner may reinstate retainage for each subsequent periodic payment application as authorized in this subsection up to the maximum amount of five percent (5%). The project shall be deemed fifty percent (50%) complete when the contractor's gross project invoices, excluding the value of materials stored off-site, equal or exceed fifty percent (50%) of the value of the contract, except the value of materials stored on-site shall not exceed twenty percent (20%) of the contractor's gross project invoices for the purpose of determining whether the project is fifty percent (50%) complete.

(3)   A subcontract on a contract governed by this section may include a provision for the retainage on periodic payments made by the prime contractor to the subcontractor. However, the percentage of the payment retained: (i) shall be paid to the subcontractor under the same terms and conditions as provided in subdivision (2) of this subsection and (ii) subject to subsection (b3) of this section, shall not exceed the percentage of retainage on payments made by the owner to the prime contractor. Subject to subsection (b3) of this section, any percentage of retainage on payments made by the prime contractor to the subcontractor that exceeds the percentage of retainage on payments made by the owner to the prime contractor shall be subject to interest to be paid by the

prime contractor to the subcontractor at the rate of one percent (1%) per month or fraction thereof.

(4)   Within 60 days after the submission of a pay request and one of the following occurs, as specified in the contract documents, the owner with written consent of the surety shall release to the contractor all retainage on payments held by the owner: (i) the owner receives a certificate of substantial completion from the architect, engineer, or designer in charge of the project; or (ii) the owner receives beneficial occupancy or use of the project. However, the owner may retain sufficient funds to secure completion of the project or corrections on any work. If the owner retains funds, the amount retained shall not exceed two and one-half times the estimated value of the work to be completed or corrected. Any reduction in the amount of the retainage on payments shall be with the consent of the contractor's surety.

(5)   The existence of any third-party claims against the contractor or any additive change orders to the construction contract shall not be a basis for delaying the release of any retainage on payments.

(b2)   Full payment, less authorized deductions, shall also be made for those trades that have reached one hundred percent (100%) completion of their contract by or before the project is fifty percent (50%) complete if the contractor has performed satisfactorily. However, payment to the early finishing trades is contingent upon the owner's receipt of an approval or certification from the architect of record or applicable engineer that the work performed by the subcontractor is acceptable and in accordance with the contract documents. At that time, the owner shall reduce the retainage for such trades to five-tenths percent (0.5%) of the contract. Payments under this subsection shall be made no later than 60 days following receipt of the subcontractor's request or immediately upon receipt of the surety's consent, whichever occurs later. Early finishing trades under this subsection shall include structural steel, piling, caisson, and demolition. The early finishing trades for which line-item release of retained funds is required shall not be construed to prevent an owner or an owner's representative from identifying any other trades not listed in this subsection that are also allowed line-item release of retained funds. Should the owner or owner's representative identify any other trades to be afforded line-item release of retainage, the trade shall be listed in the original bid documents. Each bid document shall list the inspections required by the owner before accepting the work, and any financial information required by the owner to release payment to the trades, except the failure of the bid documents to contain this information shall not obligate the owner to release the retainage if it has not received the required certification from the architect of record or applicable engineer.

(b3) Notwithstanding subdivisions (2) and (3) of subsection (b1) of this section, and subsection (b2) of this section, following fifty percent (50%) completion of the project, the owner shall be authorized to withhold additional retainage from a subsequent periodic payment, not to exceed five percent (5%) as set forth in subdivision (1) of subsection (b1) of this section, in order to allow the owner to retain two and one-half percent (2.5%) total retainage through the completion of the project. In the event that the owner elects to withhold additional retainage on any periodic payment subsequent to release of retainage pursuant to subsection (b2) of this section, the general contractor may also withhold from the subcontractors remaining on the project sufficient retainage to offset the additional retainage held by the owner, notwithstanding the actual percentage of retainage withheld by the owner of the project as a whole.

(b4) Neither the owner's nor contractor's release of retainage on payments as part of a payment in full on a line-item of work under subsection (b2) of this section shall affect any applicable warranties on work done by the contractor or subcontractor, and the warranties shall not begin to run any earlier than either the owner's receipt of a certificate of substantial completion from the architect, engineer, or designer in charge of the project or the owner receives beneficial occupancy.

(b5) The State or any political subdivision of the State may allow contractors to bid on bonded projects with and without retainage on payments.

(b6) Nothing in subsections (b1), (b2), (b3), and (b4) of this section shall operate to prevent any agency or any political subdivision of the State from complying with the requirements of a federal contract or grant when the requirements of the federal contract or grant conflict with subsections (b1), (b2), (b3), or (b4) of this section. Each bid document must specify when federal preemption of this section shall apply.

(c) Repealed by Session Laws 2007-365, s. 1, effective January 1, 2008.

(d) Nothing in this section shall prevent the prime contractor at the time of application and certification to the owner from withholding application and certification to the owner for payment to the subcontractor for unsatisfactory job progress; defective construction not remedied; disputed work; third party claims filed or reasonable evidence that claim will be filed; failure of subcontractor to make timely payments for labor, equipment, and materials; damage to prime contractor or another subcontractor; reasonable evidence that subcontract cannot be completed for the unpaid balance of the subcontract sum; or a reasonable amount for retainage not to exceed the initial percentage retained by the owner.

(e)   Nothing in this section shall prevent the owner from withholding payment to the contractor in addition to the amounts authorized by this section for unsatisfactory job progress, defective construction not remedied, disputed work, or third-party claims filed against the owner or reasonable evidence that a third-party claim will be filed. (1959, c. 1328; 1967, c. 860; 1979, c. 778; 1983, c. 804, ss. 1, 2; 2007-365, s. 1.)

§ 143-134.2. Actions by contractor on behalf of subcontractor.

(a)   A contractor may, on behalf of a subcontractor of any tier under the contractor, file an action against an owner regarding a claim arising out of or relating to labor, materials, or services furnished by the subcontractor to the contractor pursuant to a contract between the subcontractor and the contractor for the same project that is the subject of the contract between the contractor and the owner.

(b)   In any action filed by a contractor against an owner under subsection (a) of this section, it shall not be a defense that the costs and damages at issue were incurred by a subcontractor and that subcontractor has not been paid for these costs and damages. The owner shall not be required to pay the contractor for the costs and damages incurred by a subcontractor, unless the subcontractor submits proof to the court that the contractor has paid these costs and damages to the subcontractor. (1997-489, s. 1.)

§ 143-134.3. No damage for delay clause.

No contractual language forbidding or limiting compensable damages for delays caused solely by the owner or its agent may be enforced in any construction contract let by any board or governing body of the State, or of any institution of State government, or of any county, city, town, or other political subdivision thereof. For purposes of this section, the phrase "owner or its agent" does not include prime contractors or their subcontractors. (1997-489, s. 1.)

§ 143-135. Limitation of application of Article.

Except for the provisions of G.S. 143-129 requiring bids for the purchase of apparatus, supplies, materials or equipment, this Article shall not apply to construction or repair work undertaken by the State or by subdivisions of the State of North Carolina (i) when the work is performed by duly elected officers or agents using force account qualified labor on the permanent payroll of the agency concerned and (ii) when either the total cost of the project, including without limitation all direct and indirect costs of labor, services, materials, supplies and equipment, does not exceed one hundred twenty-five thousand dollars ($125,000) or the total cost of labor on the project does not exceed fifty thousand dollars ($50,000); provided that, for The University of North Carolina and its constituent institutions, force account qualified labor may be used (i) when the work is performed by duly elected officers or agents using force account qualified labor on the permanent payroll of the university and (ii) when either the total cost of the project, including, without limitation, all direct and indirect costs of labor, services, materials, supplies, and equipment, does not exceed two hundred thousand dollars ($200,000) or the total cost of labor on the project does not exceed one hundred thousand dollars ($100,000). This force account work shall be subject to the approval of the Director of the Budget in the case of State agencies, of the responsible commission, council, or board in the case of subdivisions of the State. Complete and accurate records of the entire cost of such work, including without limitation, all direct and indirect costs of labor, services, materials, supplies and equipment performed and furnished in the prosecution and completion thereof, shall be maintained by such agency, commission, council or board for the inspection by the general public. Construction or repair work undertaken pursuant to this section shall not be divided for the purposes of evading the provisions of this Article. (1933, c. 552, ss. 1, 2; 1949, c. 1137, s. 2; 1951, c. 1104, s. 6; 1967, c. 860; 1975, c. 292, ss. 1, 2; c. 879, s. 46; 1979, 2nd Sess., c. 1248; 1981, c. 860, s. 13; 1995, c. 274, s. 1; 2007-322, s. 5.)

§ 143-135.1. State buildings exempt from county and municipal building requirements; consideration of recommendations by counties and municipalities.

(a) Buildings constructed by the State of North Carolina or by any agency or institution of the State in accordance with plans and specifications approved by the Department of Administration or by The University of North Carolina or one of its affiliated or constituent institutions pursuant to G.S. 116-31.11 shall not be subject to inspection by any county or municipal authorities and shall not be subject to county or municipal building codes and requirements.

(b) Inspection fees fixed by counties and municipalities shall not be applicable to such construction by the State of North Carolina. County and municipal authorities may inspect any plans or specifications upon their request to the Department of Administration or, with respect to projects under G.S. 116-31.11, The University of North Carolina, and any and all recommendations made by them shall be given consideration. Requests by county and municipal authorities to inspect plans and specifications for State projects shall be on the basis of a specific project. Should any agency or institution of the State require the services of county or municipal authorities, notice shall be given for the need of such services, and appropriate fees for such services shall be paid to the county or municipality; provided, however, that the application for such services to be rendered by any county or municipality shall have prior written approval of the Department of Administration, or with respect to projects under G.S. 116-31.11, The University of North Carolina.

(c) Notwithstanding any law to the contrary, including any local act, no county or municipality may impose requirements that exceed the North Carolina State Building Code regarding the design or construction of buildings constructed by the State of North Carolina. (1951, c. 1104, s. 4; 1967, c. 860; 1971, c. 563; 1985, c. 757, s. 170(a); 1997-412, s. 10; 2001-496, s. 8(c); 2005-300, s. 1.)

§ 143-135.2. Contracts for restoration of historic buildings with private donations.

This Article shall not apply to building contracts let by a State agency for restoration of a historic building or structure where the funds for the restoration of such building or structure are provided entirely by funds donated from private sources. (1955, c. 27; 1967, c. 860.)

§ 143-135.3. Adjustment and resolution of State board construction contract claim.

(a) The word "board" as used in this section shall mean the State of North Carolina or any board, bureau, commission, institution, or other agency of the State, as distinguished from a board or governing body of a subdivision of the State. "A contract for construction or repair work," as used in this section, is defined as any contract for the construction of buildings and appurtenances thereto, including, but not by way of limitation, utilities, plumbing, heating, electrical, air conditioning, elevator, excavation, grading, paving, roofing, masonry work, tile work and painting, and repair work as well as any contract for the construction of airport runways, taxiways and parking aprons, sewer and water mains, power lines, docks, wharves, dams, drainage canals, telephone lines, streets, site preparation, parking areas and other types of construction on which the Department of Administration or The University of North Carolina enters into contracts.

"Contractor" as used in this section includes any person, firm, association or corporation which has contracted with a State board for architectural, engineering or other professional services in connection with construction or repair work as well as those persons who have contracted to perform such construction or repair work.

(b) A contractor who has not completed a contract with a board for construction or repair work and who has not received the amount he claims is due under the contract may submit a verified written claim to the Director of the Office of State Construction of the Department of Administration for the amount the contractor claims is due. The Director may deny, allow, or compromise the claim, in whole or in part. A claim under this subsection is not a contested case under Chapter 150B of the General Statutes.

(c) A contractor who has completed a contract with a board for construction or repair work and who has not received the amount he claims is due under the contract may submit a verified written claim to the Director of the Office of State Construction of the Department of Administration for the amount the contractor claims is due. The claim shall be submitted within 60 days after the contractor receives a final statement of the board's disposition of his claim and shall state the factual basis for the claim.

The Director shall investigate a submitted claim within 90 days of receiving the claim, or within any longer time period upon which the Director and the contractor agree. The contractor may appear before the Director, either in person or through counsel, to present facts and arguments in support of his claim. The Director may allow, deny, or compromise the claim, in whole or in part. The Director shall give the contractor a written statement of the Director's decision on the contractor's claim.

A contractor who is dissatisfied with the Director's decision on a claim submitted under this subsection may commence a contested case on the claim under Chapter 150B of the General Statutes. The contested case shall be commenced within 60 days of receiving the Director's written statement of the decision.

(c1) A contractor who is dissatisfied with the Director's decision on a claim submitted under subsection (c) of this section may commence a contested case on the claim under Chapter 150B of the General Statutes. The contested case shall be commenced within 60 days of receiving the Director's written statement of the decision.

(d) As to any portion of a claim that is denied by the Director, the contractor may, in lieu of the procedures set forth in the preceding subsection of this section, within six months of receipt of the Director's final decision, institute a civil action for the sum he claims to be entitled to under the contract by filing a verified complaint and the issuance of a summons in the Superior Court of Wake County or in the superior court of any county where the work under the contract was performed. The procedure shall be the same as in all civil actions except that all issues shall be tried by the judge, without a jury.

(e) The provisions of this section are part of every contract for construction or repair work made by a board and a contractor. A provision in a contract that conflicts with this section is invalid. (1965, c. 1022; 1967, c. 860; 1969, c. 950, s. 1; 1973, c. 1423; 1975, c. 879, s. 46; 1981, c. 577; 1983, c. 761, s. 190; 1985, c. 746, s. 18; 1987, c. 847, s. 4; 1989, c. 40, s. 1; 1991, c. 103, s. 1; 1997-412, s. 7; 2001-496, s. 8(c); 2005-300, s. 1.)

§ 143-135.4. Authority of Department of Administration not repealed.

Nothing contained in this Article shall be construed as contravening or repealing any authorities given by statute to the Department of Administration. (1967, c. 860; 1975, c. 879, s. 46.)

§ 143-135.5. State policy; cooperation in promoting the use of small, minority, physically handicapped and women contractors; purpose.

(a)   It is the policy of this State to encourage and promote the use of small, minority, physically handicapped and women contractors in State construction projects. All State agencies, institutions and political subdivisions shall cooperate with the Department of Administration and all other State agencies, institutions and political subdivisions in efforts to encourage and promote the use of small, minority, physically handicapped and women contractors in achieving the purpose of this Article, which is the effective and economical construction of public buildings.

(b)   It is the policy of this State not to accept bids or proposals from, nor to engage in business with, any business that, within the last two years, has been finally found by a court or an administrative agency of competent jurisdiction to have unlawfully discriminated on the basis of race, gender, religion, national origin, age, physical disability, or any other unlawful basis in its solicitation, selection, hiring, or treatment of another business. (1983, c. 692, s. 1; 2001-496, s. 5.2.)

§ 143-135.6. Adjustment and resolution of community college board construction contract claim.

(a)   A contractor who has not completed a contract with a board of a community college for construction or repair work and who has not received the amount he claims is due under the contract may follow the claims procedure in G.S. 143-135.3(b) that is available to a contractor who has contracted with a State board.

(b)   A contractor who has completed a contract with a board of a community college for construction or repair work and who has not received the amount he claims is due under the contract may follow the same claims procedure in G.S. 143-135.3(c) that is available to a contractor who has contracted with a State board.

(c)   A contractor who is dissatisfied with the Director's decision on any portion of a claim submitted pursuant to subsection (b) of this section may, within six months of receipt of the Director's final decision, institute a civil action for the sum he claims to be entitled to under the contract in the Superior Court of Wake County or in the superior court of any county where the work under the contract was performed. The procedure shall be the same as in all civil actions except that all issues shall be tried by the judge, without a jury. A contractor may not commence an action under Chapter 150B of the General Statutes.

(d)   The provisions of this section are part of every contract for construction or repair work made by a board of a community college and a contractor. A provision in a contract that conflicts with this section is invalid.

(e)   For the purposes of this section, the following definitions shall apply, unless the context indicates otherwise:

(1)   "Community college" has the same meaning as in G.S. 115D-2(2).

(2)   "Contract for construction or repair work" has the same meaning as in G.S. 143-135.3(a).

(3)   "Contractor" means any person, firm, association, or corporation which has contracted for architectural, engineering, or other professional services in connection with construction or repair work, as well as those persons who have contracted to perform the construction or repair work.

(f)   The provisions of this section are applicable only to community college buildings subject to G.S. 143-341(3). (1989, c. 40, s. 2.)

§ 143-135.7. Safety officers.

Each contract for a State capital improvement project, as defined in Article 8B of this Chapter, shall require the contractor to designate a responsible person as safety officer to inspect the project site for unsafe health and safety hazards, to report these hazards to the contractor for correction, and to provide other safety and health measures on the project site as required by the terms and conditions of the contract. (1991 (Reg. Sess., 1992), c. 893, s. 3.)

§ 143-135.8. Prequalification.

Bidders may be prequalified for any public construction project. (1995, c. 367, s. 8.)

§ 143-135.9. Best Value procurements.

(a) Definitions. - The following definitions apply in this section:

(1) Best Value procurement. - The selection of a contractor based on a determination of which proposal offers the best trade-off between price and performance, where quality is considered an integral performance factor. The award decision is made based on multiple factors, including: total cost of ownership, meaning the cost of acquiring, operating, maintaining, and supporting a product or service over its projected lifetime; the evaluated technical merit of the vendor's proposal; the vendor's past performance; and the evaluated probability of performing the requirements stated in the solicitation on time, with high quality, and in a manner that accomplishes the stated business objectives and maintains industry standards compliance.

(2) Government-Vendor partnership. - A mutually beneficial contractual relationship between State government and a contractor, wherein the two share risk and reward, and value is added to the procurement of needed goods or services.

(3) Repealed by Session Laws 2013-188, s. 1, effective June 26, 2013.

(4) Solution-Based solicitation. - A solicitation in which the requirements are stated in terms of how the product or service being purchased should accomplish the business objectives, rather than in terms of the technical design of the product or service.

(b) Intent. - The intent of Best Value procurement is to enable contractors to offer and the agency to select the most appropriate solution to meet the business objectives defined in the solicitation and to keep all parties focused on the desired outcome of a procurement.

(c) Information Technology. - The acquisition of information technology by the State of North Carolina shall be conducted using the Best Value procurement method. For purposes of this section, business process reengineering, system design, and technology implementation may be combined into a single solicitation. For acquisitions which the procuring agency and the Division of Purchase and Contracts or the Office of Information Technology Services, as applicable, deem to be highly complex or determine that the optimal solution to the business problem at hand is not known, the use of Solution-Based Solicitation and Government-Vendor Partnership is authorized and encouraged. Any county, city, town, or subdivision of the State may acquire information technology pursuant to this section.

(d)   Repealed by Session Laws 2009-320, s. 1, effective July 24, 2009.

(e)   North Carolina Zoological Park. - The acquisition of goods and services under a contract entered pursuant to the exemption of G.S. 143-129.8A(a) by the Department of Environment and Natural Resources on behalf of the North Carolina Zoological Park may be conducted using the Best Value procurement method. For acquisitions which the procuring agency deems to be highly complex, the use of Government-Vendor partnership is authorized. (1998-189, s. 1; 1999-434, s. 15; 1999-456, s. 39; 2009-329, s. 1.2; 2013-188, s. 1.)

Article 8A.

Board of State Contract Appeals.

§§ 143-135.10 through 143-135.24: Repealed by Session Laws 1987, c. 847, s. 5.

Article 8B.

State Building Commission.

§ 143-135.25. State Building Commission - Creation; staff; membership; appointments; terms; vacancies; chairman; compensation.

(a)   A State Building Commission is created within the Department of Administration to develop procedures to direct and guide the State's capital facilities development and management program and to perform the duties created under this Article.

(b)   The State Construction Office of the Department of Administration shall provide staff to the State Building Commission. The chairman of the

Commission shall provide direction to the State Construction Office on its work for the Commission.

The director of the State Construction Office shall be a registered engineer or licensed architect and shall be technically qualified by educational background and professional experience in building design, construction, or facilities management. The administrative head shall be appointed by the Secretary of the Department of Administration.

(c)   The Commission shall consist of nine members qualified and appointed as follows:

(1)   A licensed architect whose primary practice is or was in the design of buildings, chosen from among not more than three persons nominated by the North Carolina Chapter of the American Institute of Architects, appointed by the Governor.

(2)   A registered engineer whose primary practice is or was in the design of engineering systems for buildings, chosen from among not more than three persons nominated by the Consulting Engineers Council and the Professional Engineers of North Carolina, appointed by the General Assembly upon the recommendation of the President Pro Tempore of the Senate in accordance with G.S. 120-121.

(3)   A licensed building contractor whose primary business is or was in the construction of buildings, or an employee of a company holding a general contractor's license, chosen from among not more than three persons nominated by the Carolinas AGC (Associated General Contractors), appointed by the General Assembly upon the recommendation of the Speaker of the House of Representatives in accordance with G.S. 120-121.

(4)   A licensed electrical contractor whose primary business is or was in the installation of electrical systems for buildings, chosen from among not more than three persons nominated by the North Carolina Association of Electrical Contractors, and the Carolinas Electrical Contractors' Association, appointed by the Governor.

(5)   A public member appointed by the General Assembly upon the recommendation of the President Pro Tempore of the Senate in accordance with G.S. 120-121.

(6) A licensed mechanical contractor whose primary business is or was in the installation of mechanical systems for buildings, chosen from among not more than three persons nominated by the North Carolina Association of Plumbing, Heating, Cooling Contractors, appointed by the General Assembly upon the recommendation of the Speaker of the House of Representatives in accordance with G.S. 120-121.

(7) An employee of the university system currently involved in the capital facilities development process, chosen from among not more than three persons nominated by the Board of Governors of The University of North Carolina, appointed by the Governor.

(8) A public member who is knowledgeable in the building construction or building maintenance area, appointed by the General Assembly upon the recommendation of the President Pro Tempore of the Senate in accordance with G.S. 120-121.

(9) A representative of local government, chosen from among not more than two persons nominated by the North Carolina Association of County Commissioners and two persons nominated by the North Carolina League of Municipalities, appointed by the General Assembly upon recommendation of the Speaker of the House of Representatives in accordance with G.S. 120-121.

The members shall be appointed for staggered three-year terms: The initial appointments to the Commission shall be made within 15 days of the effective date of this act [April 14, 1987]. The initial terms of members appointed pursuant to subdivisions (1), (2), and (3) shall expire June 30, 1990; the initial terms of members appointed pursuant to (4), (5), and (6) shall expire June 30, 1989; and the initial terms of members appointed pursuant to (7), (8), and (9) shall expire June 30, 1988. Members may serve no more than six consecutive years. In making new appointments or filling vacancies, the Governor shall ensure that minorities and women are represented on the Commission.

Vacancies in appointments made by the Governor shall be filled by the Governor for the remainder of the unexpired terms. Vacancies in appointments made by the General Assembly shall be filled in accordance with G.S. 120-122. Persons appointed to fill vacancies shall qualify in the same manner as persons appointed for full terms.

The chairman of the Commission shall be elected by the Commission. The Secretary of State shall serve as chairman until a chairman is elected.

(d) The Commission shall meet at least four times a year on or about January 15, April 15, July 15, and October 15. The Commission shall also meet upon the call of the chairman, or upon call of at least five members. The Secretary of State shall call the first meeting within 30 days of the effective date of this act; the first order of business at the first meeting shall be the election of a chairman by the Commission.

(e) Members of the Commission who are not State officers or employees shall receive per diem of one hundred dollars ($100.00) a day when the Commission meets and shall be reimbursed for travel and subsistence as provided in G.S. 138-5. Members who are State officers or employees shall be reimbursed for travel and subsistence as provided in G.S. 138-6. (1987, c. 71, s. 1; 1989, c. 42; 1991, c. 314, s. 1; 1991 (Reg. Sess., 1992), c. 893, s. 2; 1995, c. 367, s. 9; c. 490, s. 52; 1997-495, s. 85.1.)

§ 143-135.26. Powers and duties of the Commission.

The State Building Commission shall have the following powers and duties with regard to the State's capital facilities development and management program:

(1) To adopt rules establishing standard procedures and criteria to assure that the designer selected for each State capital improvement project, the consultant selected for planning and studies of an architectural and engineering nature associated with a capital improvement project or a future capital improvement project and a construction manager at risk selected for each capital improvement project has the qualifications and experience necessary for that capital improvement project or the proposed planning or study project. The rules shall provide that the State Building Commission, after consulting with the funded agency, is responsible and accountable for the final selection of the designer, consultant or construction manager at risk except when the General Assembly or The University of North Carolina is the funded agency. When the General Assembly is the funded agency, the Legislative Services Commission is responsible and accountable for the final selection of the designer, consultant, or the construction manager at risk and when the University is the funded agency, it shall be subject to the rules adopted hereunder, except it is responsible and accountable for the final selection of the designer, consultant, or construction manager at risk. All designers and consultants shall be selected within 60 days of the date funds are appropriated for a project by the General Assembly or the date of project authorization by the Director of the Budget;

provided, however, the State Building Commission may grant an exception to this requirement upon written request of the funded agency if (i) no site was selected for the project before the funds were appropriated or (ii) funds were appropriated for advance planning only; provided, further, the Director of the Budget, after consultation with the State Construction Office, may waive the 60-day requirement for the purpose of minimizing project costs through increased competition and improvements in the market availability of qualified contractors to bid on State capital improvement projects. The Director of the Budget also may, after consultation with the State Construction Office, schedule the availability of design and construction funds for capital improvement projects for the purpose of minimizing project costs through increased competition and improvements in the market availability of qualified contractors to bid on State capital improvement projects.

The State Building Commission shall submit a written report to the Joint Legislative Commission on Governmental Operations on the Commission's selection of a designer for a project within 30 days of selecting the designer.

(2)   To adopt rules for coordinating the plan review, approval, and permit process for State capital improvement and community college buildings, as defined in subdivision (4) of this section. The rules shall provide for a specific time frame for plan review and approval and permit issuance by each agency, consistent with applicable laws. The time frames shall be established to provide for expeditious review, approval, and permitting of State capital improvement projects and community college buildings. To further expedite the plan review, approval, and permit process, the State Building Commission shall develop a standard memorandum of understanding to be executed by the funded agency and all reviewing agencies for each State capital improvement project. The memorandum of understanding, at minimum, shall include provisions for establishing:

a.   The type and frequency of plan reviews.

b.   The submittal dates for each plan review.

c.   The estimated plan review time for each review and reviewing agency.

d.   A schedule of meeting dates.

(2a) To adopt rules exempting specified types of State capital improvement projects, including community college buildings as defined in subdivision (4) of this section, from plan review.

(3) To adopt rules for establishing a post-occupancy evaluation, annual inspection and preventive maintenance program for all State buildings.

(4) To develop procedures for evaluating the work performed by designers and contractors on State capital improvement projects and those community college buildings, as defined in G.S. 143-336, requiring the estimated expenditure for construction or repair work for which public bidding is required under G.S. 143-129, and for use of the evaluations as a factor affecting designer selections and determining qualification of contractors to bid on State capital improvement projects and community college buildings.

(5) To continuously study and recommend ways to improve the effectiveness and efficiency of the State's capital facilities development and management program.

(6) To request designers selected prior to April 14, 1987, whose plans for the projects have not been approved to report to the Commission on their progress on the projects. The Department of Administration shall provide the Commission with a list of all such projects.

(7) To appoint an advisory board, if the Commission deems it necessary, to assist the Commission in its work. No one other than the Commission may appoint an advisory board to assist or advise it in its work.

(8) To review the State's provisions for ensuring the safety and health of employees involved with State capital improvement projects, and to recommend to the appropriate agencies and to the General Assembly, after consultation with the Commissioner of Labor, changes in the terms and conditions of construction contracts, State regulations, or State laws that will enhance employee safety and health on these projects.

(9) To authorize a State agency, a local governmental unit, or any other entity subject to the provisions of G.S. 143-129 to use a method of contracting not authorized under G.S. 143-128. An authorization under this subdivision for an alternative contracting method shall be granted only under the following conditions:

a. An authorization shall apply only to a single project.

b. The entity seeking authorization must demonstrate to the Commission that the alternative contracting method is necessary because the project cannot be reasonably completed under the methods authorized under G.S. 143-128 or for such other reasons as the Commission, pursuant to its rules and criteria, deems appropriate and in the public's interest.

b1. The entity includes in its bid or proposal requirements that the contractor will file a plan for making a good faith effort to reach the minority participation goal set out in G.S. 143-128.2.

c. The authorization must be approved by a majority of the members of the Commission present and voting.

The Commission shall not waive the requirements of G.S. 143-129 or G.S. 143-132 for public contracts unless otherwise authorized by law.

(10) To adopt rules governing review and final approval of plans that are submitted to the State Construction Office pursuant to G.S. 58-31-40. The rules shall provide for the manner of submission of the plan by the owner, the type of structural work that may be completed by the owner pursuant to G.S. 58-31-40(c), and the expeditious review or completion of review of the plan in a manner that ensures that the building will meet the fire safety requirements of G.S. 58-31-40(b).

(11) To develop dispute resolution procedures, including mediation, for subcontractors under any of the construction methods authorized under G.S. 143-128(a1) on State capital improvement projects, including building projects of The University of North Carolina, and community college buildings as defined in subdivision (4) of this section, for use by any public entity that has not developed its own dispute resolution process.

(12) To adopt rules governing the use of open-end design agreements for State capital improvement projects and community college buildings as defined in subdivision (4) of this section, where the expenditure of public money does not exceed the amount specified in G.S. 143-64.34(b) or (c).

(13) To submit an annual report of its activities to the Governor and the Joint Legislative Commission on Governmental Operations. (1987, c. 71, s. 1; c. 721, s. 2; c. 830, s. 79(a); 1989, c. 50; 1989 (Reg. Sess., 1990), c. 889; 1991 (Reg.

Sess., 1992), c. 893, s. 1; 1993, c. 561, s. 29; 1995, c. 367, s. 10; 1996, 2nd Ex. Sess., c. 18, s. 10.1; 2001-496, s. 11; 2005-370, s. 2; 2007-446, s. 4.)

§ 143-135.27. Definition of capital improvement project.

As used in this Article, "State capital improvement project" means the construction of and any alteration, renovation, or addition to State buildings, as defined in G.S. 143-336, for which State funds, as defined in G.S. 143C-1-1, are used and which is required by G.S. 143-129 to be publicly advertised. (1987, c. 71, s. 1; 2001-442, s. 4; 2006-203, s. 87; 2008-195, s. 11.)

§ 143-135.28. Conflict of interest.

If any member of the Commission shall be interested either directly or indirectly, or shall be an officer or employee of or have an ownership interest in any firm or corporation interested directly or indirectly, in any contract authorized by the Commission, that interest shall be disclosed to the Commission and set forth in the minutes of the Commission, and the member having the interest may not participate on behalf of the Commission in the authorization of that contract. (1987, c. 71, s. 1.)

§ 143-135.29. Reserved for future codification purposes.

§ 143-135.30. Reserved for future codification purposes.

§ 143-135.31. Reserved for future codification purposes.

§ 143-135.32. Reserved for future codification purposes.

§ 143-135.33. Reserved for future codification purposes.

§ 143-135.34. Reserved for future codification purposes.

Article 8C.

Performance Standards for Sustainable, Energy-Efficient Public Buildings.

§ 143-135.35. Findings; legislative intent.

The General Assembly finds that public buildings can be built and renovated using sustainable, energy-efficient methods that save money, reduce negative environmental impacts, improve employee and student performance, and make employees and students more productive. The main objectives of sustainable, energy-efficient design are to avoid resource depletion of energy, water, and raw materials; prevent environmental degradation caused by facilities and infrastructure throughout their life cycle; and create buildings that are livable, comfortable, safe, and productive. It is the intent of the General Assembly that State-owned buildings and buildings of The University of North Carolina and the North Carolina Community College System be improved by establishing specific performance standards for sustainable, energy-efficient public buildings. These performance standards should be based upon recognized, consensus standards that are supported by science and have a demonstrated performance record. The General Assembly also intends, in order to ensure that the economic and environmental objectives of this Article are achieved, that State agencies, The University of North Carolina, and the North Carolina Community College System determine whether the performance standards are met for major facility construction and renovation projects, measure utility and maintenance costs, and verify whether these standards result in savings. Also, it is the intent of the General Assembly to establish a priority to use North Carolina-based resources, building materials, products, industries, manufacturers, and businesses to provide economic development to North Carolina and to meet the objectives of this Article. (2008-203, s. 1.)

§ 143-135.36. Definitions.

As used in this section, the following definitions apply unless the context requires otherwise:

(1)   "ASHRAE" means the American Society of Heating, Refrigerating and Air-Conditioning Engineers, Inc.

(2)   "Commission" means to document and to verify throughout the construction process whether the performance of a building, a component of a

building, a system of a building, or a component of a building system meets specified objectives, criteria, and agency project requirements.

(3) "Department" means the Department of Administration.

(4) "Institutions of higher education" means the constituent institutions of The University of North Carolina, the regional institutions as defined in G.S. 115D-2, and the community colleges as defined in G.S. 115D-2.

(5) "Major facility construction project" means a project to construct a building larger than 20,000 gross square feet of occupied or conditioned space, as defined in the North Carolina State Building Code adopted under Article 9 of Chapter 143 of the General Statutes. "Major facility construction project" does not include a project to construct a transmitter building or a pumping station.

(6) "Major facility renovation project" means a project to renovate a building when the cost of the project is greater than fifty percent (50%) of the insurance value of the building prior to the renovation and the renovated portion of the building is larger than 20,000 gross square feet of occupied or conditioned space, as defined in the North Carolina State Building Code. "Major facility renovation project" does not include a project to renovate a transmitter building or a pumping station. "Major facility renovation project" does not include a project to renovate a building having historic, architectural, or cultural significance under Part 4 of Article 2 of Chapter 143B of the General Statutes.

(7) "Public agency" means every State office, officer, board, department, and commission and institutions of higher education.

(8) "Weather-based irrigation controller" means an irrigation control device that utilizes local weather and landscape conditions to tailor irrigation system schedules to irrigation needs specific to site conditions. (2008-203, s. 1; 2011-394, s. 8(a).)

§ 143-135.37. Energy and water use standards for public major facility construction and renovation projects; verification and reporting of energy and water use.

(a) Program Established. - The Sustainable Energy-Efficient Buildings Program is established within the Department to be administered by the

Department. This program applies to any major facility construction or renovation project of a public agency that is funded in whole or in part from an appropriation in the State capital budget or through a financing contract as defined in G.S. 142-82.

(a1) Net Savings Required. - The requirements of this section apply to a major facility construction or renovation project only if the Department determines that the application of the requirements to the project will result in an anticipated net savings. There is an anticipated net savings if the cost of construction or renovation in accordance with the requirements of this section plus the estimated operating costs for the first 10 years post-construction would be less than the cost of construction or renovation if the project were not subject to the requirements of this section plus the estimated operating costs for the first 10 years post-construction. All third-party certification costs before and after construction or renovation shall be included in determining construction and operating costs. Renovation projects that will include guaranteed energy savings contracts, as defined by G.S. 143-64.17, and executed in accordance with the provisions of Part 2 of Article 3B of Chapter 143 of the General Statutes, are exempt from the requirements of this subsection.

(b) Energy-Efficiency Standard. - For every major facility construction project of a public agency, the building shall be designed and constructed so that the calculated energy consumption is at least thirty percent (30%) less than the energy consumption for the same building as calculated using the energy-efficiency standard in ASHRAE 90.1-2004. For every major facility renovation project of a public agency, the renovated building shall be designed and constructed so that the calculated energy consumption is at least twenty percent (20%) less than the energy consumption for the same renovated building as calculated using the energy-efficiency standard in ASHRAE 90.1-2004. For the purposes of this subsection, any exception or special standard for a specific type of building found in ASHRAE 90.1-2004 is included in the ASHRAE 90.1-2004 standard.

(c) Indoor Potable Water Use Standard. - For every major facility construction or renovation project of a public agency, the water system shall be designed and constructed so that the calculated indoor potable water use is at least twenty percent (20%) less than the indoor potable water use for the same building as calculated using the fixture performance requirements related to plumbing under the 2006 North Carolina State Building Code.

(c1) Outdoor Potable Water Use Standard. - For every major facility construction project of a public agency, the water system shall be designed and constructed so that the calculated sum of the outdoor potable water use and the harvested stormwater use is at least fifty percent (50%) less than the sum of the outdoor potable water use and the harvested stormwater use for the same building as calculated using the performance requirements related to plumbing under the 2006 North Carolina State Building Code. Weather-based irrigation controllers shall be used for irrigation systems for major facility construction projects. For every major facility renovation project of a public agency, the Department shall determine on a project-by-project basis what reduced level of outdoor potable use or harvested stormwater use, if any, is a feasible requirement for the project. The Department shall not require a greater reduction than is required under this subsection for a major facility construction project. To reduce the potable outdoor water as required under this subsection, weather-based irrigation controllers, landscape materials that are water use efficient, and irrigation strategies that include reuse and recycling of the water may be used.

(d) Performance Verification. - In order to be able to verify performance of a building component or an energy or water system component, the construction contract shall include provisions that require each building component and each energy and water system component to be commissioned, and these provisions shall be included at the earliest phase of the construction process as possible and in no case later than the schematic design phase of the project. Such commissioning shall continue through the initial operation of the building. The project design and construction teams and the public agency shall jointly determine what level of commissioning is appropriate for the size and complexity of the building or its energy and water system components.

(e) Separate Utility Meters. - In order to be able to monitor the initial cost and the continuing costs of the energy and water systems, a separate meter for each electricity, natural gas, fuel oil, and water utility shall be installed at each building undergoing a major facility construction or renovation project. Each meter shall be installed in accordance with the United States Department of Energy guidelines issued under section 103 of the Energy Policy Act of 2005 (Pub. L. 109-58, 119 Stat. 594 (2005)). Starting with the first month of facility operation, the public agency shall compare data obtained from each of these meters by month and by year with the applicable energy-efficiency standard under subsection (b) of this section and the applicable water use standard for the project under subsection (c) of this section and report annually no later than August 1 of each year to the Office of State Construction within the Department.

If the average energy use or the average water use over the initial 12-month period of facility operation exceeds the applicable energy-efficiency standard under subsection (b) of this section or exceeds the applicable water use standard under subsection (c) of this section by fifteen percent (15%) or more, the public agency shall investigate the actual energy or water use, determine the cause of the discrepancy, and recommend corrections or modifications to meet the applicable standard.

(f) Locally Sourced Materials. - To achieve sustainable building standards as required by this section, a major facility construction or renovation project may utilize a building rating system so long as the rating system (i) provides certification credits for, (ii) provides a preference to be given to, (iii) does not disadvantage, and (iv) promotes building materials or furnishings, including masonry, concrete, steel, textiles, or wood that are manufactured or produced within the State. (2008-203, s. 1; 2011-394, s. 8(b); 2013-242, s. 1.)

§ 143-135.38. Use of other standard when standard not practicable.

When the Department, public agency, and the design team determine that the energy-efficiency standard or the water use standard required under G.S. 143-135.37 is not practicable for a major facility construction or renovation project, then it must be determined by the State Building Commission if the standard is not practicable for the major facility construction or renovation project. If the State Building Commission determines the standard is not practicable for that project, the State Building Commission shall determine which standard is practicable for the design and construction for that major facility construction or renovation project. If a standard required under G.S. 143-135.37 is not followed for that project, the State Building Commission shall report this information and the reasons to the Department within 90 days of its determination. (2008-203, s. 1.)

§ 143-135.39. Guidelines for administering the Sustainable Energy-Efficient Buildings Program.

(a) Policies and Technical Guidelines. - The Department, in consultation with public agencies, shall develop and issue policies and technical guidelines to implement this Article for public agencies. The purpose of these policies and guidelines is to establish procedures and methods for complying with the energy-efficiency standard or the water use standard for major facility construction and renovation projects under G.S. 143-135.37.

(b) Preproposal Conference. - As provided in the request for proposals for construction services, the public agency may hold a preproposal conference for prospective bidders to discuss compliance with, and achievement of, the energy-efficiency standard or the water use standard required under G.S. 143-135.37 for prospective respondents.

(c) Advisory Committee. - The Department shall create a sustainable, energy-efficient buildings advisory committee comprised of representatives from the design and construction industry involved in public works contracting, personnel from the public agencies responsible for overseeing public works projects, and others at the Department's discretion to provide advice on implementing this Article. Among other duties, the advisory committee shall make recommendations regarding the education and training requirements under subsection (d) of this section, make recommendations regarding specific education and training criteria that are appropriate for the various roles with respect to, and levels of involvement in, a major facility construction or renovation project subject to this Article or the roles regarding the operation and maintenance of the facility, and make recommendations regarding developing a process whereby the Department receives ongoing evaluations and feedback to assist the Department in implementing this Article so as to effectuate the purpose of this Article. Further, the advisory committee may make recommendations to the Department regarding whether it is advisable to strengthen standards for energy efficiency or water use under this Article, whether it is advisable and feasible to add additional criteria to achieve greater sustainability in the construction and renovation of public buildings, or whether it is advisable and feasible to expand the scope of this Article to apply to additional types of publicly financed buildings or to smaller facility projects.

(d) Education and Training Requirements. - The Department shall review the advisory committee's recommendations under subsection (c) of this section regarding education and training. For each of the following, the Department shall develop education and training requirements that are consistent with the purpose of this Article and that are appropriate for the various roles with respect to, and level of involvement in, a major facility construction or renovation project or the roles regarding the operation and maintenance of the facility:

(1) The chief financial officers of public agencies.

(2) For each public agency that is responsible for the payment of the agency's utilities, the facility managers of these public agencies.

(3) The capital project coordinators of public agencies.

(4) Architects.

(5) Mechanical design engineers.

(e) Performance Review. - Annually the Department shall conduct a performance review of the Sustainable Energy-Efficient Buildings Program. The performance review shall include at least all of the following:

(1) Identification of the costs of implementing energy-efficiency and water use standards in the design and construction of major facility construction and renovation projects subject to this Article.

(2) Identification of operating savings attributable to the implementation of energy-efficiency and water use standards, including, but not limited to, savings in utility and maintenance costs.

(3) Identification of any impacts on employee productivity from using energy-efficiency and water use standards.

(4) Evaluation of the effectiveness of the energy-efficiency and water use standards established by this Article.

(5) Whether stricter standards or additional criteria for sustainable buildings should be used other than the standards under G.S. 143-135.37.

(6) Whether the Sustainable Energy-Efficient Buildings Program should be expanded to include additional public agencies, to include additional types of projects, or to include smaller major facility construction or renovation projects.

(7) Any recommendations for any other changes regarding sustainable, energy-efficient building standards that may be supported by the Department's findings.

(f) Report on Performance Review. - Each year, the Department shall include in its consolidated report under subsection (g) of this section a report of its findings under the performance review under subsection (e) of this section.

(g) Consolidated Report Required. - The Department shall consolidate the report required under subsection (f) of this section, the report under G.S. 143-135.37(e), the report, if any, from the State Building Commission under G.S. 143-135.38, and the report under G.S. 143-135.40 into one report. No later than October 1 of each year, this consolidated report shall be transmitted to the Chairs of the General Government Appropriations Subcommittees of both the Senate and the House of Representatives, the Environmental Review Commission, and the Joint Legislative Commission on Governmental Operations. The Department shall include any recommendations for administrative or legislative proposals that would better fulfill the legislative intent of this Article.

(h) Authority to Adopt Rules or Architectural or Engineering Standards. - The Department may adopt rules to implement this Article. The Department may adopt architectural or engineering standards as needed to implement this Article. (2008-203, s. 1.)

§ 143-135.40. Monitor construction standards and sustainable building standards.

(a) The Department shall monitor the development of construction standards and sustainable building standards to determine whether there is any standard that the Department determines would better fulfill the intent of the Sustainable Energy-Efficient Buildings Program to achieve sustainable, energy-efficient public buildings than the standards under G.S. 143-135.37, and, if so, whether this Article should be amended to provide for the use of any different standards or the use of any additional standards to address additional aspects of sustainable, energy-efficient buildings. Additional standards monitored shall address consideration of site development, material and resource selection, and indoor environmental quality to enhance the health or productivity of building occupants. Also, the Department shall monitor the development of improved energy-efficiency standards developed by the American Society of Heating, Refrigerating and Air-Conditioning Engineers, the ASHRAE standards, shall monitor whether the State Building Code Council adopts any other energy-efficiency standards for inclusion in the State Building Code that result in greater energy efficiency and increased energy savings in major facility construction and renovation projects under this Article, and shall monitor other standards for sustainable, energy-efficient buildings that are based upon recognized, consensus standards based on science and demonstrated performance.

(b) Each year, the Department shall report the results of its monitoring under this section, including any recommendations for administrative or legislative proposals. (2008-203, s. 1.)

Article 9.

Building Code Council and Building Code.

§ 143-136. Building Code Council created; membership.

(a) Creation; Membership; Terms. - There is hereby created a Building Code Council, which shall be composed of 17 members appointed by the Governor, consisting of two registered architects, one licensed general contractor, one licensed general contractor specializing in residential construction, one licensed general contractor specializing in coastal residential construction, one registered engineer practicing structural engineering, one registered engineer practicing mechanical engineering, one registered engineer practicing electrical engineering, one licensed plumbing and heating contractor, one municipal or county building inspector, one licensed liquid petroleum gas dealer/contractor involved in the design of natural and liquid petroleum gas systems who has expertise and experience in natural and liquid petroleum gas piping, venting and appliances, a representative of the public who is not a member of the building construction industry, a licensed electrical contractor, a registered engineer on the engineering staff of a State agency charged with approval of plans of State-owned buildings, a municipal elected official or city manager, a county commissioner or county manager, and an active member of the North Carolina fire service with expertise in fire safety. In selecting the municipal and county members, preference should be given to members who qualify as either a registered architect, registered engineer, or licensed general contractor. Of the members initially appointed by the Governor, three shall serve for terms of two years each, three shall serve for terms of four years each, and three shall serve for terms of six years each. Thereafter, all appointments shall be for terms of six years. The Governor may remove appointive members at any time. Neither the architect nor any of the above named engineers shall be engaged in the manufacture, promotion or sale of any building material, and any member who shall, during his term, cease to meet the qualifications for original appointment (through ceasing to be a practicing member of the profession indicated or otherwise) shall thereby forfeit his membership on the Council. In making new appointments or filling vacancies, the Governor shall ensure that minorities and women are represented on the Council.

The Governor may make appointments to fill the unexpired portions of any terms vacated by reason of death, resignation, or removal from office. In making such appointment, he shall preserve the composition of the Council required above.

(b) Compensation. - Members of the Building Code Council other than any who are employees of the State shall receive seven dollars ($7.00) per day, including necessary time spent in traveling to and from their place of residence within the State to any place of meeting or while traveling on official business of the Council. In addition, all members shall receive mileage and subsistence according to State practice while going to and from any place of meeting, or when on official business of the Council. (1957, c. 1138; 1965, c. 1145; 1969, c. 1229, s. 1; 1971, c. 323; 1979, c. 863; 1989, c. 25, s. 3; 1991 (Reg. Sess., 1992), c. 895, s. 2; 1998-57, s. 1.)

§ 143-137. Organization of Council; rules; meetings; staff; fiscal affairs.

(a) First Meeting; Organization; Rules. - Within 30 days after its appointment, the Building Code Council shall meet on call of the Commissioner of Insurance. The Council shall elect from its appointive members a chairman and such other officers as it may choose, for such terms as it may designate in its rules. The Council shall adopt such rules not inconsistent herewith as it may deem necessary for the proper discharge of its duties. The chairman may appoint members to such committees as the work of the Council may require. In addition, the chairman shall establish and appoint ad hoc code revision committees to consider and prepare revisions and amendments to the Code volumes. Each ad hoc committee shall consist of members of the Council, licensed contractors, and design professionals most affected by the Code volume for which the ad hoc committee is responsible, and members of the public. The subcommittees shall meet upon the call of their respective chairs and shall report their recommendations to the Council.

(b) Meetings. - The Council shall meet regularly, at least once every six months, at places and dates to be determined by the Council. Special meetings may be called by the chairman on his own initiative and must be called by him at the request of two or more members of the Council. All members shall be notified by the chairman in writing of the time and place of regular and special meetings at least seven days in advance of such meeting. Seven members shall constitute a quorum. All meetings shall be open to the public.

(c) Staff. - Personnel of the Division of Engineering of the Department of Insurance shall serve as a staff for the Council. Such staff shall have the duties of

(1) Keeping an accurate and complete record of all meetings, hearings, correspondence, laboratory studies, and technical work performed by or for the Council, and making these records available for public inspection at all reasonable times;

(2) Handling correspondence for the Council.

(d) Fiscal Affairs of the Council. - All funds for the operations of the Council and its staff shall be appropriated to the Department of Insurance for the use of the Council. All such funds shall be held in a separate or special account on the books of the Department of Insurance, with a separate financial designation or code number to be assigned by the Department of Administration or its agent. Expenditures for staff salaries and operating expenses shall be made in the same manner as the expenditure of any other Department of Insurance funds. The Department of Insurance may hire such additional personnel as may be necessary to handle the work of the Building Code Council, within the limits of funds appropriated for the Council and with the approval of the Council. (1957, c. 269, s. 1; c. 1138; 1987, c. 827, s. 219; 1987 (Reg. Sess., 1988), c. 975, s. 7; 1997-26, s. 4.)

§ 143-138. North Carolina State Building Code.

(a) Preparation and Adoption. - The Building Code Council may prepare and adopt, in accordance with the provisions of this Article, a North Carolina State Building Code. Before the adoption of the Code, or any part of the Code, the Council shall hold at least one public hearing. A notice of the public hearing shall be published in the North Carolina Register at least 15 days before the date of the hearing. Notwithstanding G.S. 150B-2(8a)h., the North Carolina State Building Code as adopted by the Building Code Council is a rule within the meaning of G.S. 150B-2(8a) and shall be adopted in accordance with the procedural requirements of Article 2A of Chapter 150B of the General Statutes.

The Council shall request the Office of State Budget and Management to prepare a fiscal note for a proposed Code change that has a substantial economic impact, as defined in G.S. 150B-21.4(b1), or that increases the cost of residential housing by eighty dollars ($80.00) or more per housing unit. The change can become effective only in accordance with G.S. 143-138(d). Neither the Department of Insurance nor the Council shall be required to expend any monies to pay for the preparation of any fiscal note under this section by any person outside of the Department or Council unless the Department or Council contracts with a third-party vendor to prepare the fiscal note.

(b) Contents of the Code. - The North Carolina State Building Code, as adopted by the Building Code Council, may include reasonable and suitable classifications of buildings and structures, both as to use and occupancy; general building restrictions as to location, height, and floor areas; rules for the lighting and ventilation of buildings and structures; requirements concerning means of egress from buildings and structures; requirements concerning means of ingress in buildings and structures; rules governing construction and precautions to be taken during construction; rules as to permissible materials, loads, and stresses; rules governing chimneys, heating appliances, elevators, and other facilities connected with the buildings and structures; rules governing plumbing, heating, air conditioning for the purpose of comfort cooling by the lowering of temperature, and electrical systems; and such other reasonable rules pertaining to the construction of buildings and structures and the installation of particular facilities therein as may be found reasonably necessary for the protection of the occupants of the building or structure, its neighbors, and members of the public at large.

(b1) Fire Protection; Smoke Detectors. - The Code may regulate activities and conditions in buildings, structures, and premises that pose dangers of fire, explosion, or related hazards. Such fire prevention code provisions shall be considered the minimum standards necessary to preserve and protect public health and safety, subject to approval by the Council of more stringent provisions proposed by a municipality or county as provided in G.S. 143-138(e). These provisions may include regulations requiring the installation of either battery-operated or electrical smoke detectors in every dwelling unit used as rental property, regardless of the date of construction of the rental property. For dwelling units used as rental property constructed prior to 1975, smoke detectors shall have an Underwriters' Laboratories, Inc., listing or other equivalent national testing laboratory approval, and shall be installed in accordance with either the standard of the National Fire Protection Association or the minimum protection designated in the manufacturer's instructions, which the property owner shall retain or provide as proof of compliance.

(b2) Carbon Monoxide Detectors. - The Code (i) may contain provisions requiring the installation of either battery-operated or electrical carbon monoxide detectors in every dwelling unit having a fossil-fuel burning heater, appliance, or fireplace, and in any dwelling unit having an attached garage and (ii) shall contain provisions requiring the installation of electrical carbon monoxide detectors at a lodging establishment. Violations of this subsection and rules adopted pursuant to this subsection shall be punishable in accordance with subsection (h) of this section and G.S. 143-139. In particular, the rules shall provide:

(1) For dwelling units, carbon monoxide detectors shall be those listed by a nationally recognized testing laboratory that is OSHA-approved to test and certify to American National Standards Institute/Underwriters Laboratories Standards ANSI/UL2034 or ANSI/UL2075 and shall be installed in accordance with either the standard of the National Fire Protection Association or the minimum protection designated in the manufacturer's instructions, which the property owner shall retain or provide as proof of compliance. A carbon monoxide detector may be combined with smoke detectors if the combined detector does both of the following: (i) complies with ANSI/UL2034 or ANSI/UL2075 for carbon monoxide alarms and ANSI/UL217 for smoke detectors; and (ii) emits an alarm in a manner that clearly differentiates between detecting the presence of carbon monoxide and the presence of smoke.

(2) For lodging establishments, carbon monoxide detectors shall be installed in every enclosed space having a fossil fuel burning heater, appliance, or fireplace and in any enclosed space, including a sleeping room, that shares a common wall, floor, or ceiling with an enclosed space having a fossil fuel burning heater, appliance, or fireplace. Carbon monoxide detectors shall be (i) listed by a nationally recognized testing laboratory that is OSHA-approved to test and certify to American National Standards Institute/Underwriters Laboratories Standards ANSI/UL2034 or ANSI/UL2075, (ii) installed in accordance with either the standard of the National Fire Protection Association or the minimum protection designated in the manufacturer's instructions, which the lodging establishment shall retain or provide as proof of compliance, (iii) receive primary power from the building's wiring, where such wiring is served from a commercial source, and (iv) receive power from a battery when primary power is interrupted. A carbon monoxide detector may be combined with smoke detectors if the combined detector complies with the requirements of this subdivision for carbon monoxide alarms and ANSI/UL217 for smoke detectors. For purposes of this subsection, "lodging establishment" means any hotel,

motel, tourist home, or other establishment permitted under authority of G.S. 130A-248 to provide lodging accommodations for pay to the public.

(b3)   Applicability of the Code. - Except as provided by subsections (b4) and (c1) of this section, the Code may contain provisions regulating every type of building or structure, wherever it might be situated in the State.

(b4)   Exclusion for Certain Farm Buildings. - Building rules do not apply to (i) farm buildings that are located outside the building-rules jurisdiction of any municipality, (ii) farm buildings that are located inside the building-rules jurisdiction of any municipality if the farm buildings are greenhouses, (iii) a primitive camp, or (iv) a primitive farm building. For the purposes of this subsection:

(1)   A "farm building" shall include any structure used or associated with equine activities, including, but not limited to, the care, management, boarding, or training of horses and the instruction and training of riders. Structures that are associated with equine activities include, but are not limited to, free standing or attached sheds, barns, or other structures that are utilized to store any equipment, tools, commodities, or other items that are maintained or used in conjunction with equine activities. The specific types of equine activities, structures, and uses set forth in this subdivision are for illustrative purposes, and should not be construed to limit, in any manner, the types of activities, structures, or uses that may be considered under this subsection as exempted from building rules. A farm building that might otherwise qualify for exemption from building rules shall remain subject only to an annual safety inspection by the applicable city or county building inspection department of any grandstand, bleachers, or other spectator-seating structures in the farm building. An annual safety inspection shall include an evaluation of the overall safety of spectator-seating structures as well as ensuring the spectator-seating structure's compliance with any building codes related to the construction of spectator-seating structures in effect at the time of the construction of the spectator-seating.

(2)   A "greenhouse" is a structure that has a glass or plastic roof, has one or more glass or plastic walls, has an area over ninety-five percent (95%) of which is used to grow or cultivate plants, is built in accordance with the National Greenhouse Manufacturers Association Structural Design manual, and is not used for retail sales. Additional provisions addressing distinct life safety hazards shall be approved by the local building-rules jurisdiction.

(3) A "farm building" shall include any structure used for the display and sale of produce, no more than 1,000 square feet in size, open to the public for no more than 180 days per year, and certified by the Department of Agriculture and Consumer Services as a Certified Roadside Farm Market.

(4) A "primitive camp" shall include any structure primarily used or associated with outdoor camping activities, including structures used for educational, instructional, or recreational purposes for campers and for management training, that are (i) not greater than 4,000 square feet in size and (ii) are not intended to be occupied for more than 24 hours consecutively. "Structures primarily used or associated with outdoor camping activities" include, but are not limited to, shelters, tree stands, outhouses, sheds, rustic cabins, campfire shelters, picnic shelters, tents, tepees or other indigenous huts, support buildings used only for administrative functions and not for activities involving campers or program participants, and any other structures that are utilized to store any equipment, tools, commodities, or other items that are maintained or used in conjunction with outdoor camping activities such as hiking, fishing, hunting, or nature appreciation, regardless of material used for construction. The specific types of primitive camping activities, structures, and uses set forth in this subdivision are for illustrative purposes and should not be construed to limit, in any manner, the types of activities, structures, or uses that are exempted from building rules.

(5) A "primitive farm building" shall include any structure used for activities, instruction, training, or reenactment of traditional or heritage farming practices. "Primitive farm buildings" include, but are not limited to, sheds, barns, outhouses, doghouses, or other structures that are utilized to store any equipment, tools, commodities, livestock, or other items supporting farm management. These specific types of farming activities, structures, and uses set forth by this subdivision are for illustrative purposes and should not be construed to limit in any manner the types of activities, structures, or uses that are exempted from building rules.

(6) A "farm building" shall not lose its status as a farm building because it is used for public or private events, including, but not limited to, weddings, receptions, meetings, demonstrations of farm activities, meals, and other events that are taking place on the farm because of its farm or rural setting.

(b5) Exclusion for Certain Minor Activities in Residential and Farm Structures. - No building permit shall be required under the Code or any local variance thereof approved under subsection (e) for any construction, installation, repair, replacement, or alteration costing five thousand dollars ($5,000) or less in any single family residence or farm building unless the work involves: the addition, repair, or replacement of load bearing structures; the addition (excluding replacement of same capacity) or change in the design of plumbing; the addition, replacement or change in the design of heating, air conditioning, or electrical wiring, devices, fixtures (excluding repair or replacement of electrical lighting devices and fixtures of the same type), appliances (excluding replacement of water heaters, provided that the energy use rate or thermal input is not greater than that of the water heater which is being replaced, and there is no change in fuel, energy source, location, capacity, or routing or sizing of venting and piping), or equipment, the use of materials not permitted by the North Carolina Uniform Residential Building Code; or the addition (excluding replacement of like grade of fire resistance) of roofing. The exclusions from building permit requirements set forth in this paragraph for electrical lighting devices and fixtures and water heaters shall apply only to work performed on a one- or two-family dwelling. In addition, exclusions for electrical lighting devices and fixtures and electric water heaters shall apply only to work performed by a person licensed under G.S. 87-43 and exclusions for water heaters, generally, to work performed by a person licensed under G.S. 87-21.

(b6)   No State Agency Permit. - No building permit shall be required under such Code from any State agency for the construction of any building or structure, the total cost of which is less than twenty thousand dollars ($20,000), except public or institutional buildings.

(b7)   Appendices. - For the information of users thereof, the Code shall include as appendices the following:

(1)   Any rules governing boilers adopted by the Board of Boiler and Pressure Vessels Rules,

(2)   Any rules relating to the safe operation of elevators adopted by the Commissioner of Labor, and

(3)   Any rules relating to sanitation adopted by the Commission for Public Health which the Building Code Council believes pertinent.

The Code may include references to such other rules of special types, such as those of the Medical Care Commission and the Department of Public Instruction as may be useful to persons using the Code. No rule issued by any agency other than the Building Code Council shall be construed as a part of the Code, nor supersede that Code, it being intended that they be presented with the Code for information only.

(b8) Exclusion for Certain Utilities. - Nothing in this Article shall extend to or be construed as being applicable to the regulation of the design, construction, location, installation, or operation of (1) equipment for storing, handling, transporting, and utilizing liquefied petroleum gases for fuel purposes or anhydrous ammonia or other liquid fertilizers, except for liquefied petroleum gas from the outlet of the first stage pressure regulator to and including each liquefied petroleum gas utilization device within a building or structure covered by the Code, or (2) equipment or facilities, other than buildings, of a public utility, as defined in G.S. 62-3, a cable television company, or an electric or telephone membership corporation, including without limitation poles, towers, and other structures supporting electric, cable television, or communication lines.

(b9) Exclusion for Industrial Machinery. - Nothing in this Article shall extend to or be construed as being applicable to the regulation of the design, construction, location, installation, or operation of industrial machinery. However, if during the building code inspection process, an electrical inspector has any concerns about the electrical safety of a piece of industrial machinery, the electrical inspector may refer that concern to the Occupational Safety and Health Division in the North Carolina Department of Labor but shall not withhold the certificate of occupancy nor mandate third-party testing of the industrial machinery based solely on this concern. For the purposes of this paragraph, "industrial machinery" means equipment and machinery used in a system of operations for the explicit purpose of producing a product or acquired by a State-supported center providing testing, research, and development services to manufacturing clients. The term does not include equipment that is permanently attached to or a component part of a building and related to general building services such as ventilation, heating and cooling, plumbing, fire suppression or prevention, and general electrical transmission.

(b10) Replacement Water Heaters. - The Code may contain rules concerning minimum efficiency requirements for replacement water heaters, which shall consider reasonable availability from manufacturers to meet installation space requirements and may contain rules concerning energy efficiency that require all hot water plumbing pipes that are larger than one-fourth of an inch to be insulated.

(b11)   School Seclusion Rooms. - No State, county, or local building code or regulation shall prohibit the use of special locking mechanisms for seclusion rooms in the public schools approved under G.S. 115C-391.1(e)(1)e., provided that the special locking mechanism shall be constructed so that it will engage only when a key, knob, handle, button, or other similar device is being held in position by a person, and provided further that, if the mechanism is electrically or electronically controlled, it automatically disengages when the building's fire alarm is activated. Upon release of the locking mechanism by a supervising adult, the door must be able to be opened readily.

(b12)   Cisterns. - The Code may include rules pertaining to the construction or renovation of residential or commercial buildings and structures that permit the use of cisterns to provide water for flushing toilets and for outdoor irrigation. No State, county, or local building code or regulation shall prohibit the use of cisterns to provide water for flushing toilets and for outdoor irrigation. As used in this subsection, "cistern" means a storage tank that is watertight; has smooth interior surfaces and enclosed lids; is fabricated from nonreactive materials such as reinforced concrete, galvanized steel, or plastic; is designed to collect rainfall from a catchment area; may be installed indoors or outdoors; and is located underground, at ground level, or on elevated stands.

(b13)   Migrant Housing. - The Council shall provide for an exemption from any requirements in the fire prevention code for installation of an automatic sprinkler system applicable to buildings meeting all of the following:

(1)   Has one floor.

(2)   Meets all requirements of 29 C.F.R. § 1910.142, as amended.

(3)   Meets all requirements of Article 19 of Chapter 95 of the General Statutes and rules implementing that Article.

For purposes of this subsection, "migrant housing" and "migrant" shall be defined as in G.S. 95-223.

(b14)   [Exclusion for Routine Maintenance. -] No building permit shall be required under the Code for routine maintenance on fuel dispensing pumps and other dispensing devices. For purposes of this subsection, "routine maintenance" includes repair or replacement of hoses, O-rings, nozzles, or emergency breakaways.

(c) Standards to Be Followed in Adopting the Code. - All regulations contained in the North Carolina State Building Code shall have a reasonable and substantial connection with the public health, safety, morals, or general welfare, and their provisions shall be construed reasonably to those ends. Requirements of the Code shall conform to good engineering practice. The Council may use as guidance, but is not required to adopt, the requirements of the International Building Code of the International Code Council, the Standard Building Code of the Southern Building Code Congress International, Inc., the Uniform Building Code of the International Conference of Building Officials, the National Building Code of the Building Officials and Code Administrators, Inc., the National Electric Code, the Life Safety Code, the National Fuel Gas Code, the Fire Prevention Code of the National Fire Protection Association, the Safety Code for Elevators and Escalators, and the Boiler and Pressure Vessel Code of the American Society of Mechanical Engineers, and standards promulgated by the American National Standards Institute, Standards Underwriters' Laboratories, Inc., and similar national or international agencies engaged in research concerning strength of materials, safe design, and other factors bearing upon health and safety.

(c1) Exemptions for Private Clubs and Religious Organizations. - The North Carolina State Building Code and the standards for the installation and maintenance of limited-use or limited-access hydraulic elevators under this Article shall not apply to private clubs or establishments exempted from coverage under Title II of the Civil Rights Act of 1964, 42 U.S.C. § 2000a, et seq., or to religious organizations or entities controlled by religious organizations, including places of worship. A nonreligious organization or entity that leases space from a religious organization or entity is not exempt under this subsection.

(d) Amendments of the Code. - The Building Code Council may periodically revise and amend the North Carolina State Building Code, either on its own motion or upon application from any citizen, State agency, or political subdivision of the State. In addition to the periodic revisions or amendments made by the Council, the Council shall revise the North Carolina State Building Code: Residential Code for One- and Two-Family Dwellings, including provisions applicable to One- and Two-Family Dwellings from the NC Energy Code, NC Electrical Code, NC Fuel Gas Code, NC Plumbing Code, and NC Mechanical Code only every six years, to become effective the first day of January of the following year, with at least six months between adoption and effective date. The first six-year revision under this subsection shall be adopted to become effective January 1, 2019, and every six years thereafter. In adopting any amendment, the Council shall comply with the same procedural requirements and the same standards set forth above for adoption of the Code. The Council, through the Department of Insurance, shall publish in the North Carolina Register and shall post on the Council's Web site all appeal decisions made by the Council and all formal opinions at least semiannually. The Council, through the Department of Insurance, shall also publish at least semiannually in the North Carolina Register a statement providing the accurate Web site address and information on how to find additional commentary and interpretation of the Code.

(e) Effect upon Local Codes. - Except as otherwise provided in this section, the North Carolina State Building Code shall apply throughout the State, from the time of its adoption. Approved rules shall become effective in accordance with G.S. 150B-21.3. However, any political subdivision of the State may adopt a fire prevention code and floodplain management regulations within its jurisdiction. The territorial jurisdiction of any municipality or county for this purpose, unless otherwise specified by the General Assembly, shall be as follows: Municipal jurisdiction shall include all areas within the corporate limits of the municipality and extraterritorial jurisdiction areas established as provided in G.S. 160A-360 or a local act; county jurisdiction shall include all other areas of the county. No such code or regulations, other than floodplain management regulations and those permitted by G.S. 160A-436, shall be effective until they have been officially approved by the Building Code Council as providing adequate minimum standards to preserve and protect health and safety, in accordance with the provisions of subsection (c) above. Local floodplain regulations may regulate all types and uses of buildings or structures located in flood hazard areas identified by local, State, and federal agencies, and include provisions governing substantial improvements, substantial damage, cumulative substantial improvements, lowest floor elevation, protection of mechanical and electrical systems, foundation construction, anchorage, acceptable flood resistant materials, and other measures the political subdivision deems necessary considering the characteristics of its flood hazards and vulnerability. In the absence of approval by the Building Code Council, or in the event that approval is withdrawn, local fire prevention codes and regulations shall have no force and effect. Provided any local regulations approved by the local governing body which are found by the Council to be more stringent than the adopted statewide fire prevention code and which are found to regulate only activities and conditions in buildings, structures, and premises that pose dangers of fire, explosion or related hazards, and are not matters in conflict with the State Building Code, shall be approved. Local governments may enforce the fire prevention code of the State Building Code using civil remedies authorized under G.S. 143-139, 153A-123, and 160A-175. If the Commissioner of Insurance or other State official with responsibility for enforcement of the Code institutes a civil action pursuant to G.S. 143-139, a local government may not institute a civil action under G.S. 143-139, 153A-123, or 160A-175 based upon the same violation. Appeals from the assessment or imposition of such civil remedies shall be as provided in G.S. 160A-434.

A local government may not adopt any ordinance in conflict with the exemption provided by subsection (c1) of this section. No local ordinance or regulation shall be construed to limit the exemption provided by subsection (c1) of this section.

(f)   Repealed by Session Laws 1989, c. 681, s. 3.

(g)   Publication and Distribution of Code. - The Building Code Council shall cause to be printed, after adoption by the Council, the North Carolina State Building Code and each amendment thereto. It shall, at the State's expense, distribute copies of the Code and each amendment to State and local governmental officials, departments, agencies, and educational institutions, as is set out in the table below. (Those marked by an asterisk will receive copies only on written request to the Council.)

OFFICIAL OR AGENCY	NUMBER OF COPIES
State Departments and Officials	
Governor	1
Lieutenant Governor	1
Auditor	1
Treasurer	1
Secretary of State	1
Superintendent of Public Instruction	1

Attorney General (Library)... 1

Commissioner of Agriculture... 1

Commissioner of Labor... 1

Commissioner of Insurance... 1

Department of Environment and Natural Resources... 1

Department of Health and Human Services.. 1

Division of Juvenile Justice of the Department of Public Safety........................ 1

Board of Transportation.. 1

Utilities Commission... 1

Department of Administration... 1

Clerk of the Supreme Court... 1

Clerk of the Court of Appeals.. 1

Department of Cultural Resources [State Library].. 1

Supreme Court Library... 1

Legislative Library... 1

Office of Administrative Hearings.. 1

Rules Review Commission... 1

Schools

All state-supported colleges and universities

in the State of North Carolina.. * 1 each

Local Officials

Clerks of the Superior Courts.. 1 each

Chief Building Inspector of each incorporated

municipality or county... 1

In addition, the Building Code Council shall make additional copies available at such price as it shall deem reasonable to members of the general public. The proceeds from sales of the Building Code shall be credited to the Insurance Regulatory Fund under G.S. 58-6-25.

(h) Violations. - Any person who shall be adjudged to have violated this Article or the North Carolina State Building Code, except for violations of occupancy limits established by either, shall be guilty of a Class 3 misdemeanor and shall upon conviction only be liable to a fine, not to exceed fifty dollars ($50.00), for each offense. Each 30 days that such violation continues shall constitute a separate and distinct offense. Violation of occupancy limits established pursuant to the North Carolina State Building Code shall be a Class 3 misdemeanor. Any violation incurred more than one year after another conviction for violation of the occupancy limits shall be treated as a first offense for purposes of establishing and imposing penalties.

(i) Section 1008 of Chapter X of Volume 1 of the North Carolina State Building Code, Title "Special Safety to Life Requirements Applicable to Existing High-Rise Buildings" as adopted by the North Carolina State Building Code Council on March 9, 1976, as ratified and adopted as follows:

SECTION 1008-SPECIAL SAFETY TO LIFE REQUIREMENTS APPLICABLE TO EXISTING HIGH-RISE BUILDINGS

1008 - GENERAL.

(a) Applicability. - Within a reasonable time, as fixed by "written order" of the building official, and except as otherwise provided in subsection (j) of this section every building the [then] existing, that qualifies for classification under Table 1008.1 shall be considered to be a high-rise building and shall be provided with safety to life facilities as hereinafter specified. All other buildings shall be considered as low-rise. NOTE: The requirements of Section 1008 shall be considered as minimum requirements to provide for reasonable safety to life requirements for existing buildings and where possible, the owner and designer should consider the provisions of Section 506 applicable to new high-rise buildings.

(b)   Notification of Building Owner. - The Department of Insurance will send copies of amendments adopted to all local building officials with the suggestion that all local building officials transmit to applicable building owners in their jurisdiction copies of adopted amendments, within six months from the date the amendments are adopted, with the request that each building owner respond to the local building official how he plans to comply with these requirements within a reasonable time.

NOTE: Suggested reasonable time and procedures for owners to respond to the building official's request is as follows:

(1)   The building owner shall, upon receipt of written request from the building official on compliance procedures within a reasonable time, submit an overall plan required by 1008(c) below within one year and within the time period specified in the approved overall plan, but not to exceed five years after the overall plan is approved, accomplish compliance with this section, as evidenced by completion of the work in accordance with approved working drawings and specifications and by issuance of a new Certificate of Compliance by the building official covering the work. Upon approval of building owner's overall plan, the building official shall issue a "written order", as per 1008(a) above, to comply with Section 1008 in accordance with the approved overall plan.

(2)   The building official may permit time extensions beyond five years to accomplish compliance in accordance with the overall plan when the owner can show just cause for such extension of time at the time the overall plan is approved.

(3)   The local building official shall send second request notices as per 1008(b) to building owners who have made no response to the request at the end of six months and a third request notice to no response building owners at the end of nine months.

(4)   If the building owner makes no response to any of the three requests for information on how the owner plans to comply with Section 1008 within 12 months from the first request, the building official shall issue a "written order" to

the building owner to provide his building with the safety to life facilities as required by this section and to submit an overall plan specified by (1) above within six months with the five-year time period starting on the date of the "written order".

(5) For purposes of this section, the Construction Section of the Division of Health Service Regulation, Department of Health and Human Services, will notify all non-State owned I-Institutional buildings requiring licensure by the Division of Health Service Regulation and coordinate compliance requirements with the Department of Insurance and the local building official.

(c) Submission of Plans and Time Schedule for Completing Work. - Plans and specifications, but not necessarily working drawings covering the work necessary to bring the building into compliance with this section shall be submitted to the building official within a reasonable time. (See suggested time in NOTE of Section 1008(b) above). A time schedule for accomplishing the work, including the preparation of working drawings and specifications shall be included. Some of the work may require longer periods of time to accomplish than others, and this shall be reflected in the plan and schedule.

NOTE: Suggested Time Period For Compliance:

SUGGESTED TIME PERIOD FOR COMPLIANCE

TIME FOR ITEM COMPLETION	CLASS I (SECTION)	CLASS II (SECTION)	CLASS III (SECTION)
Signs in Elevator Lobbies and Elevator Cabs 180 days	1008.2(h)	1008.3(h)	1008.4(h)
Emergency Evacuation Plan 180 days	1008(b)	NOTE:	
Corridor Smoke Detectors			

(Includes alternative door closers) 1 year	1008.2(c)	1008.3(c)	1008.4(c)
Manual Fire Alarm 1 year	1008.2(a)	1008.3(a)	1008.4(a)
Voice Communication System Required 2 years	1008.2(b)	1008.3(b)	1008.4(b)
Smoke Detectors Required 1 year	1008.2(c)	1008.3(c)	1008.4(c)
Protection and Fire Stopping for Vertical Shafts 3 years	1008.2(f)	1008.3(f)	1008.4(f)
Special Exit Requirements- Number, Location and Illumination to be in accordance with Section 1007 3 years	1008.2(e)	1008.3(e)	1008.4(e)
Emergency Electrical Power Supply 4 years	1008.2(d)	1008.3(d)	1008.4(d)
Special Exit Facilities Required 5 years	1008.2(e)	1008.3(e)	1008.4(e)

Compartmentation for			
Institutional Buildings 5 years	1008.2(f)	1008.3(f)	1008.4(f)
Emergency Elevator			
Requirements 5 years	1008.2(h)	1008.3(h)	1008.4(h)
Central Alarm Facility			
Required 5 years		1008.3(i)	1008.4(i)
Areas of Refuge Required			
on Every Eighth Floor 5 years			1008.4(j)
Smoke Venting 5 years			1008.4(k)
Fire Protection of			
Electrical Conductors 5 years			1008.4(l)
Sprinkler System Required 5 years			1008.4(m)

(d) Building Official Notification of Department of Insurance. - The building official shall send copies of written notices he sends to building owners to the Engineering and Building Codes Division for their files and also shall file an annual report by August 15th of each year covering the past fiscal year setting forth the work accomplished under the provisions of this section.

(e) Construction Changes and Design of Life Safety Equipment. - Plans and specifications which contain construction changes and design of life safety equipment requirements to comply with provisions of this section shall be prepared by a registered architect in accordance with provisions of Chapter 83A of the General Statutes or by a registered engineer in accordance with provisions of Chapter 89C of the General Statutes or by both an architect and engineer particularly qualified by training and experience for the type of work involved. Such plans and specifications shall be submitted to the Engineering and Building Codes Division of the Department of Insurance for approval. Plans and specifications for I-Institutional buildings licensed by the Division of Health Service Regulation as noted in (b) above shall be submitted to the Construction Section of that Division for review and approval.

(f) Filing of Test Reports and Maintenance on Life Safety Equipment. - The engineer performing the design for the electrical and mechanical equipment, including sprinkler systems, must file the test results with the Engineering and Building Codes Division of the Department of Insurance, or to the agency designated by the Department of Insurance, that such systems have been tested to indicate that they function in accordance with the standards specified in this section and according to design criteria. These test results shall be a prerequisite for the Certificate of Compliance required by (b) above. Test results for I-Institutional shall be filed with the Construction Section, Division of Health Service Regulation. It shall be the duty and responsibility of the owners of Class I, II and III buildings to maintain smoke detection, fire detection, fire control, smoke removal and venting as required by this section and similar emergency systems in proper operating condition at all times. Certification of full tests and inspections of all emergency systems shall be provided by the owner annually to the fire department.

(g) Applicability of Chapter X and Conflicts with Other Sections. - The requirements of this section shall be in addition to those of Sections 1001 through 1007; and in case of conflict, the requirements affording the higher degree of safety to life shall apply, as determined by the building official.

(h) Classes of Buildings and Occupancy Classifications. - Buildings shall be classified as Class I, II or III according to Table 1008.1. In the case of mixed occupancies, for this purpose, the classification shall be the most restrictive one resulting from the application of the most prevalent occupancies to Table 1008.1.

FOOTNOTE: Emergency Plan. - Owners, operators, tenants, administrators or managers of high-rise buildings should consult with the fire authority having jurisdiction and establish procedures which shall include but not necessarily be limited to the following:

(1) Assignment of a responsible person to work with the fire authority in the establishment, implementation and maintenance of the emergency pre-fire plan.

(2) Emergency plan procedures shall be supplied to all tenants and shall be posted conspicuously in each hotel guest room, each office area, and each schoolroom.

(3) Submission to the local fire authority of an annual renewal or amended emergency plan.

(4) Plan should be completed as soon as possible.

1008.1 - ALL EXISTING BUILDINGS SHALL BE CLASSIFIED AS CLASS I, II AND III ACCORDING TO TABLE 1008.1.

TABLE 1008.1

Scope

CLASS	OCCUPANCY GROUP (3)(4)	FLOOR GRADE HEIGHT (2)	OCCUPIED ABOVE AVERAGE EXCEEDING
average less	Group R-Residential Group B-Business Group E-Educational		60' but less than 120' above grade or 6 but

213

CLASS I	Group A-Assembly	than 12 stories
	Group H-Hazardous	average grade.
	Group I-Institutional-Restrained	

	Group I-Institutional-Unrestrained	36' but less than 60' above
		average grade or 3 but less than
		6 stories above
average grade. Group R-Residential	120' but less than 250' above	
	Group B-Business	average grade or 12 but less
	Group E-Educational	than 25 stories above average
CLASS II	Group A-Assembly	grade.
	Group H-Hazardous	
	Group I-Institutional-Restrained	
	Group I-Institutional-Unrestrained	60' but less than 250' above
		average grade or 6 but less than
		25 stories above
average grade. Group R-Residential		250' or 25 stories above average

                Group B-Business   grade.

CLASS III   Group E-Educational

                Group I-Institutional

                Group A-Assembly

                Group H-Hazardous

NOTE 1: The entire building shall comply with this section when the building has an occupied floor above the height specified, except that portions of the buildings which do not exceed the height specified are exempt from this section, subject to the following provisions:

(a)   Low-rise portions of Class I buildings must be separated from high-rise portions by one-hour construction.

(b)   Low-rise portions of Class II and III buildings must be separated from high-rise portions by two-hour construction.

(c)   Any required exit from the high-rise portion which passes through the low-rise portions must be separated from the low-rise portion by the two-hour construction.

NOTE 2: The height described in Table 1008.1 shall be measured between the average grade outside the building and the finished floor of the top occupied story.

NOTE 3: Public parking decks meeting the requirements of Section 412.7 and less than 75 feet in height are exempt from the requirements of this section when there is no other occupancy above or below such deck.

NOTE 4: Special purpose equipment buildings, such as telephone equipment buildings housing the equipment only, with personnel occupant load limited to persons required to maintain the equipment may be exempt from any or all of these requirements at the discretion of the Engineering and Building Codes Division provided such special purpose equipment building is separated from other portions of the building by two-hour fire rated construction.

1008.2-REQUIREMENTS FOR EXISTING CLASS I BUILDINGS.

All Class I buildings shall be provided with the following:

(a)   An approved manual fire alarm system, meeting the requirements of Section 1125 and applicable portions of NFPA 71, 72A, 72B, 72C or 72D, shall be provided unless the building is fully sprinklered or equipped with an approved automatic fire detection system connected to the fire department.

(b)   All Class I buildings shall meet the requirements of Sections 1001-1007.

(c)   Smoke Detectors Required. - At least one approved listed smoke detector tested in accordance with UL-167, capable of detecting visible and invisible particles of combustion shall be installed as follows:

(1)   All buildings classified as institutional, residential and assembly occupancies shall be provided with listed smoke detectors in all required exit corridors spaced no further than 60' on center or more than 15' from any wall. Exterior corridors open to the outside are not required to comply with this requirement. If the corridor walls have one-hour fire resistance rating with all openings protected with 1-3/4 inch solid wood core or hollow metal door or equivalent and all corridor doors are equipped with approved self-closing devices, the smoke detectors in the corridor may be omitted. Detectors in corridors may be omitted when each dwelling unit is equipped with smoke detectors which activate the alarm system.

(2)   In every mechanical equipment, boiler, electrical equipment, elevator equipment or similar room unless the room is sprinklered or the room is separated from other areas by two-hour fire resistance construction with all openings therein protected with approved fire dampers and Class B fire doors. (Approved listed fire (heat) detectors may be submitted for these rooms.)

(3)   In the return air portion of every air conditioning and mechanical ventilation system that serves more than one floor.

(4)   The activation of any detector shall activate the alarm system, and shall cause such other operations as required by this Code.

(5)   The annunciator shall be located near the main entrance or in a central alarm and control facility.

NOTE 1: Limited area sprinklers may be supplied from the domestic water system provided the domestic water system is designed to support the design flow of the largest number of sprinklers in any one of the enclosed areas. When supplied by the domestic water system, the maximum number of sprinklers in any one enclosed room or area shall not exceed 20 sprinklers which must totally protect the room or area.

(d)   Emergency Electrical Power Supply. - An emergency electrical power supply shall be provided to supply the following for a period of not less than two hours. An emergency electrical power supply may consist of generators, batteries, a minimum of two remote connections to the public utility grid supplied by multiple generating stations, a combination of the above.

(1)   Emergency, exit and elevator cab lighting.

(2)   Emergency illumination for corridors, stairs, etc.

(3)   Emergency Alarms and Detection Systems. - Power supply for fire alarm and fire detection. Emergency power does not need to be connected to fire alarm or detection systems when they are equipped with their own emergency power supply from float or trickle charge battery in accordance with NFPA standards.

(e)   Special Exit Requirements. - Exits and exitways shall meet the following requirements:

(1)   Protection of Stairways Required. - All required exit stairways shall be enclosed with noncombustible one-hour fire rated construction with a minimum of 1¾ inch solid core wood door or hollow metal door or 20 minute UL listed doors as entrance thereto. (See Section 1007.5).

(2)   Number and Location of Exits. - All required exit stairways shall meet the requirements of Section 1007 to provide for proper number and location and proper fire rated enclosures and illumination of and designation for means of egress.

(3)   Exit Outlets. - Each required exit stair shall exit directly outside or through a separate one-hour fire rated corridor with no openings except the necessary openings to exit into the fire rated corridor and from the fire rated corridor and such openings shall be protected with 1¾ inch solid wood core or hollow metal door or equivalent unless the exit floor level and all floors below are equipped with an approved automatic sprinkler system meeting the requirements of NFPA No. 13.

(f) Smoke Compartments Required for I-Institutional Buildings. - Each occupied floor shall be divided into at least two compartments with each compartment containing not more than 30 institutional occupants. Such compartments shall be subdivided with one-half hour fire rated partitions which shall extend from outside wall to outside wall and from floor to and through any concealed space to the floor slab or roof above and meet the following requirements:

(1) Maximum area of any smoke compartment shall be not more than 22,500 square feet in area with both length and width limited to 150 feet.

(2) At least one smoke partition per floor regardless of building size forming two smoke zones of approximately equal size.

(3) All doors located in smoke partitions shall be properly gasketed to insure a substantial barrier to the passage of smoke and gases.

(4) All doors located in smoke partitions shall be no less than 1¾ inch thick solid core wood doors with UL, ¼ inch wire glass panel in metal frames. This glass panel shall be a minimum of 100 square inches and a maximum of 720 square inches.

(5) Every door located in a smoke partition shall be equipped with an automatic closer. Doors that are normally held in the open position shall be equipped with an electrical device that shall, upon actuation of the fire alarm or smoke detection system in an adjacent zone, close the doors in that smoke partition.

(6) Glass in all corridor walls shall be ¼", UL approved, wire glass in metal frames in pieces not to exceed 1296 square inches.

(7) Doors to all patient rooms and treatment areas shall be a minimum of 1¾ inch solid core wood doors except in fully sprinklered buildings.

(g) Protection and Fire Stopping for Vertical Shafts. - All vertical shafts extending more than one floor including elevator shafts, plumbing shafts, electrical shafts and other vertical openings shall be protected with noncombustible one-hour fire rated construction with shaft wall openings protected with 1¾ inch solid core wood door or hollow metal door. Vertical shafts (such as electrical wiring shafts) which have openings such as ventilated doors on each floor must be fire stopped at the floor slab level with noncombustible materials having a fire resistance rating not less than one hour to provide an effective barrier to the passage of smoke, heat and gases from floor to floor through such shafts.

EXCEPTION: Shaft wall openings protected in accordance with NFPA No. 90A and openings connected to metal ducts equipped with approved fire dampers within the shaft wall openings do not need any additional protection.

(h)   Signs in Elevator Lobbies and Elevator Cabs. - Each elevator lobby call station on each floor shall have an emergency sign located adjacent to the call button and each elevator cab shall have an emergency sign located adjacent to the floor status indicator. The required emergency sign shall be readable at all times and shall be a minimum of 1/2" high block letters with the words: "IN CASE OF FIRE DO NOT USE ELEVATOR - USE THE EXIT STAIRS" or other words to this effect.

1008.3 - REQUIREMENTS FOR EXISTING CLASS II BUILDINGS.

All Class II buildings must meet the following requirements:

(a)   Manual Fire Alarm. - Provide manual fire alarm system in accordance with Section 1008.2(a). In addition, buildings so equipped with sprinkler alarm system or automatic fire detection system must have at least one manual fire alarm station near an exit on each floor as a part of such sprinkler or automatic fire detection and alarm system. Such manual fire alarm systems shall report a fire by floor.

(b)   Voice Communication System Required. - An approved voice communication system or systems operated from the central alarm and control facilities shall be provided and shall consist of the following:

(1)   One-Way Voice Communication Public Address System Required. - A one-way voice communication system shall be established on a selective basis which can be heard clearly by all occupants in all exit stairways, elevators, elevator lobbies, corridors, assembly rooms and tenant spaces.

NOTE 1: This system shall function so that in the event of one circuit or speaker being damaged or out of service, the remainder of the system shall continue to be operable.

NOTE 2: This system shall include provisions for silencing the fire alarm devices when the loud speakers are in use, but only after the fire alarm devices have operated initially for not less than 15 seconds.

(c)   Smoke Detectors Required. - Smoke detectors are required as per Section 1008.2(c). The following are additional requirements:

(1)   Storage rooms larger than 24 square feet or having a maximum dimension of over eight feet shall be provided with approved fire detectors or smoke detectors installed in an approved manner unless the room is sprinklered.

(2)   The actuation of any detectors shall activate the fire alarm system.

(d)   Emergency Electrical Power Supply. - An emergency electrical power supply shall be provided to supply the following for a period of not less than two hours. An emergency electrical power supply may consist of generators, batteries, a minimum of two remote connections to the public utility grid supplied by multiple generating stations, a combination of the above. Power supply shall furnish power for items listed in Section 1008.2(d) and the following:

(1)   Pressurization Fans. - Fans to provide required pressurization, smoke venting or smoke control for stairways.

(2)   Elevators. - The designated emergency elevator.

(e)   Special Exit Facilities Required. - The following exit facilities are required:

(1)   The special exit facilities required in 1008.2(e) are required. All required exit stairways shall be enclosed with noncombustible two-hour fire rated construction with a minimum of 1 1/2 hour Class B-labeled doors as entrance thereto: (See Section 1007.5).

(2)   Smoke-Free Stairways Required. - At least one stairway shall be a smoke free stairway in accordance with Section 1104.2 or at least one stairway shall be pressurized to between 0.15 inch and 0.35 inch water column pressure with all doors closed. Smoke-free stairs and pressurized stairs shall be identified with signs containing letters a minimum of 1/2 inch high containing the words "PRIMARY EXIT STAIRS" unless all stairs are smoke free or pressurized. Approved exterior stairways meeting the requirements of Chapter XI or

approved existing fire escapes meeting the requirements of Chapter X with all openings within 10 feet protected with wire glass or other properly designed stairs protected to assure similar smoke-free vertical egress may be permitted. All required exit stairways shall also meet the requirements of Section 1008.2(e).

(3) If stairway doors are locked from the stairway side, keys shall be provided to unlock all stairway doors on every eighth floor leading into the remainder of the building and the key shall be located in a glass enclosure adjacent to the door at each floor level (which may sound an alarm when the glass is broken). When the key unlocks the door, the hardware shall be of the type that remains unlocked after the key is removed. Other means, approved by the building official may be approved to enable occupants and fire fighters to readily unlock stairway doors on every eighth floor that may be locked from the stairwell side. The requirements of this section may be eliminated in smoke-free stairs and pressurized stairs provided fire department access keys are provided in locations acceptable to the local fire authority.

(f) Compartmentation for I-Institutional Buildings Required. - See Section 1008.2(f).

(g) Protection and Fire Stopping for Vertical Shafts. - All vertical shafts extending more than one floor including elevator shafts, plumbing shafts, electrical shafts and other vertical openings shall be protected with noncombustible two-hour fire rated construction with Class B-labeled door except for elevator doors which shall be hollow metal or equivalent. All vertical shafts which are not so enclosed must be fire stopped at each floor slab with noncombustible materials having a fire resistance rating of not less than two hours to provide an effective barrier to the passage of smoke, heat and gases from floor to floor through such shaft.

EXCEPTION: Shaft wall openings protected in accordance with NFPA No. 90A and openings connected to metal ducts equipped with approved fire dampers within the shaft wall opening do not need any additional protection.

(h) Emergency Elevator Requirements.

(1) Elevator Recall. - Each elevator shall be provided with an approved manual return. When actuated, all cars taking a minimum of one car at a time, in each group of elevators having common lobby, shall return directly at normal car speed to the main floor lobby, or to a smoke-free lobby leading most directly to

the outside. Cars that are out of service are exempt from this requirement. The manual return shall be located at the main floor lobby.

NOTE: Manually operated cars are considered to be in compliance with this provision if each car is equipped with an audible or visual alarm to signal the operator to return to the designated level.

(2) Identification of Emergency Elevator. - At least one elevator shall be identified as the emergency elevator and shall serve all floor levels. NOTE: This elevator will have a manual control in the cab which will override all other controls including floor call buttons and door controls.

(3) Signs in Elevator Lobbies and Elevator Cabs. - Each elevator lobby call station on each floor shall have an emergency sign located adjacent to the call button and each elevator cab shall have an emergency sign located adjacent to the floor status indicator. These required emergency signs shall be readable at all times and shall be a minimum of 1/2 inch high block letters with the words: "IN CASE OF FIRE DO NOT USE ELEVATOR - USE THE EXIT STAIRS" or other words to this effect.

(i) Central Alarm Facility Required. - A central alarm facility accessible at all times to fire department personnel or attended 24 hours a day, shall be provided and shall contain the following:

(1) Facilities to automatically transmit manual and automatic alarm signals to the fire department either directly or through a signal monitoring service.

(2) Public service telephone.

(3) Fire detection and alarm systems annunciator panels to indicate the type of signal and the floor or zone from which the fire alarm is received. These signals shall be both audible and visual with a silence switch for the audible.

NOTE: Detectors in HVAC systems used for fan shut down need not be annunciated.

(4) Master keys for access from all stairways to all floors.

(5) One-way voice emergency communications system controls.

1008.4 - REQUIREMENTS FOR EXISTING CLASS III BUILDINGS.

All Class III Buildings shall be provided with the following:

(a)   Manual Fire Alarm System. - A manual fire alarm system meeting the requirements of Section 1008.3(a).

(b)   Voice Communication System Required. - An approved voice communication system or systems operated from the central alarm and control facilities shall be provided and shall consist of the following:

(1)   One-Way Voice Communication Public Address System Required. - A one-way voice communication system shall be established on a selective or general basis which can be heard clearly by all occupants in all elevators, elevator lobbies, corridors, and rooms or tenant spaces exceeding 1,000 sq. ft. in area.

NOTE 1: This system shall be designed so that in the event of one circuit or speaker being damaged or out of service the remainder of the system shall continue to be operable.

NOTE 2: This system shall include provisions for silencing the fire alarm devices when the loud speakers are in use, but only after the fire alarm devices have operated initially for not less than 15 seconds.

(2)   Two-way system for use by both fire fighters and occupants at every fifth level in stairways and in all elevators.

(3)   Within the stairs at levels not equipped with two-way voice communications, signs indicating the location of the nearest two-way device shall be provided.

NOTE: The one-way and two-way voice communication systems may be combined.

(c)   Smoke Detectors Required. - Approved listed smoke detectors shall be installed in accordance with Section 1008.3(c) and in addition, such detectors shall terminate at the central alarm and control facility and be so designed that it will indicate the fire floor or the zone on the fire floor.

(d)   Emergency Electrical Power Supply. - Emergency electrical power supply meeting the requirements of Section 1008.3(d) to supply all emergency equipment required by Section 1008.3(d) shall be provided and in addition, provisions shall be made for automatic transfer to emergency power in not more than ten seconds for emergency illumination, emergency lighting and emergency communication systems. Provisions shall be provided to transfer power to a second designated elevator located in a separate shaft from the primary emergency elevator. Any standpipe or sprinkler system serving occupied floor areas 400 feet or more above grade shall be provided with on-site generated power or diesel driven pump.

(e)   Special Exit Requirements. - All exits and exitways shall meet the requirements of Section 1008.3(e).

(f)   Compartmentation of Institutional Buildings Required. - See Section 1008.2(f).

(g)   Protection and Fire Stopping for Vertical Shafts. - Same as Class II buildings. See Section 1008.3(g).

(h)   Emergency Elevator Requirements.

(1)   Primary Emergency Elevator. - At least one elevator serving all floors shall be identified as the emergency elevator with identification signs both outside and inside the elevator and shall be provided with emergency power to meet the requirements of Section 1008.3(c).

NOTE: This elevator will have a manual control in the cab which will override all other controls including floor call buttons and door controls.

(2)   Elevator Recall. - Each elevator shall be provided with an approved manual return. When actuated, all cars taking a minimum of one car at a time, in each group of elevators having common lobby, shall return directly at normal car speed to the main floor lobby or to a smoke-free lobby leading most directly to the outside. Cars that are out of service are exempt from this requirement. The manual return shall be located at the main floor lobby.

NOTE: Manually operated cars are considered to be in compliance with this provision if each car is equipped with an audible or visual alarm to signal the operator to return to the designated level.

(3)   Signs in Elevator Lobbies and Elevator Cabs. - Each elevator lobby call station on each floor shall have an emergency sign located adjacent to the call button and each elevator cab shall have an emergency sign located adjacent to

the floor status indicator. These required emergency signs shall be readable at all times and have a minimum of ½" high block letters with the words: "IN CASE OF FIRE, UNLESS OTHERWISE INSTRUCTED, DO NOT USE THE ELEVATOR - USE THE EXIT STAIRS" or other words to this effect.

(4) Machine Room Protection. - When elevator equipment located above the hoistway is subject to damage from smoke particulate matter, cable slots entering the machine room shall be sleeved beneath the machine room floor to inhibit the passage of smoke into the machine room.

(5) Secondary Emergency Elevator. - At least one elevator located in separate shaft from the Primary Emergency Elevator shall be identified as the "Secondary Emergency Elevator" with identification signs both outside and inside the elevator. It will serve all occupied floors above 250 feet and shall have all the same facilities as the primary elevator and will be capable of being transferred to the emergency power system.

NOTE: Emergency power supply can be sized for nonsimultaneous use of the primary and secondary emergency elevators.

(i) Central Alarm and Control Facilities Required.

(1) A central alarm facility accessible at all times to Fire Department personnel or attended 24 hours a day, shall be provided. The facility shall be located on a completely sprinklered floor or shall be enclosed in two-hour fire resistive construction. Openings are permitted if protected by listed 1½ hour Class B-labeled closures or water curtain devices capable of a minimum discharge of three gpm per lineal foot of opening. The facility shall contain the following:

(i) Facilities to automatically transmit manual and automatic alarm signals to the fire department either directly or through a signal monitoring service.

(ii) Public service telephone.

(iii) Direct communication to the control facility.

(iv) Controls for the voice communication systems.

(v)   Fire detection and alarm system annunciator panels to indicate the type of signal and the floor or zone from which the fire alarm is received, those signals, shall be both audible and visual with a silence switch for the audible.

NOTE: Detectors in HVAC systems used for fan shut down need not be annunciated.

(2)   A control facility (fire department command station) shall be provided at or near the fire department response point and shall contain the following:

(i)   Elevator status indicator.

NOTE: Not required in buildings where there is a status indicator at the main elevator lobby.

(ii)   Master keys for access from all stairways to all floors.

(iii)   Controls for the two-way communication system.

(iv)   Fire detection and alarm system annunciator panels to indicate the type of signal and the floor or zone from which the fire alarm is received.

(v)   Direct communication to the central alarm facility.

(3)   The central alarm and control facilities may be combined in a single approved location. If combined, the duplication of facilities and the direct communication system between the two may be deleted.

(j)   Areas of Refuge Required. - Class III buildings shall be provided with a designated "area of refuge" at the 250 ft. level and on at least every eighth floor or fraction thereof above that level to be designed so that occupants above the 250 ft. level can enter at all times and be safely accommodated in floor areas meeting the following requirements unless the building is completely sprinklered:

(1)   Identification and Size. - These areas of refuge shall be identified on the plans and in the building as necessary. The area of refuge shall provide not less than 3 sq. ft. per occupant for the total number of occupants served by the area based on the occupancy content calculated by Section 1105. A minimum of two percent (2%) of the number of occupants on each floor shall be assumed to be handicapped and no less than 16 sq. ft. per handicapped occupant shall be

provided. Smoke proof stairways meeting the requirements of Section 1104.2 and pressurized stairways meeting the requirements of Section 1108.3(e)(2) may be used for ambulatory occupants at the rate of 3 sq. ft. of area of treads and landings per person, but in no case shall the stairs count for more than one-third of the total occupants. Doors leading to designated areas of refuge from stairways or other areas of the building shall not have locking hardware or shall be automatically unlocked upon receipt of any manual or automatic fire alarm signal.

(2)　Pressurized. - The area of refuge shall be pressurized with 100% fresh air utilizing the maximum capacity of existing mechanical building air conditioning system without recirculation from other areas or other acceptable means of providing fresh air into the area.

(3)　Fire Resistive Separation. - Walls, partitions, floor assemblies and roof assemblies separating the area of refuge from the remainder of the building shall be noncombustible and have a fire resistance rating of not less than one hour. Duct penetrations shall be protected as required for penetrations of shafts. Metallic piping and metallic conduit may penetrate or pass through the separation only if the openings around the piping or conduit are sealed on each side of the penetrations with impervious noncombustible materials to prevent the transfer of smoke or combustion gases from one side of the separation to the other. The fire door serving as a horizontal exit between compartments shall be so installed, fitted and gasketed to provide a barrier to the passage of smoke.

(4)　Access Corridors. - Any corridor leading to each designated area of refuge shall be protected as required by Sections 1104 and 702. The capacity of an access corridor leading to an area of refuge shall be based on 150 persons per unit width as defined in Section 1105.2. An access corridor may not be less than 44 inches in width. The width shall be determined by the occupant content of the most densely populated floor served. Corridors with one-hour fire resistive separation may be utilized for area of refuge at the rate of three sq. ft. per ambulatory occupant provided a minimum of one cubic ft. per minute of outside air per square foot of floor area is introduced by the air conditioning system.

(5)　Penetrations. - The continuity of the fire resistance at the juncture of exterior walls and floors must be maintained.

(k)　Smoke Venting. - Smoke venting shall be accomplished by one of the following methods in nonsprinklered buildings:

(1) In a nonsprinklered building, the heating, ventilating and air conditioning system shall be arranged to exhaust the floor of alarm origin at its maximum exhausting capacity without recirculating air from the floor of alarm origin to any other floor. The system may be arranged to accomplish this either automatically or manually. If the air conditioning system is also used to pressurize the areas of refuge, this function shall not be compromised by using the system for smoke removal.

(2) Venting facilities shall be provided at the rate of 20 square feet per 100 lineal feet or 10 square feet per 50 lineal feet of exterior wall in each story and distributed around the perimeter at not more than 50 or 100 foot intervals openable from within the fire floor. Such panels and their controls shall be clearly identified.

(3) Any combination of the above two methods or other approved designs which will produce equivalent results and which is acceptable to the building official.

(l) Fire Protection of Electrical Conductors. - New electrical conductors furnishing power for pressurization fans for stairways, power for emergency elevators and fire pumps required by Section 1008.4(d) shall be protected by a two-hour fire rated horizontal or vertical enclosure or structural element which does not contain any combustible materials. Such protection shall begin at the source of the electrical power and extend to the floor level on which the emergency equipment is located. It shall also extend to the emergency equipment to the extent that the construction of the building components on that floor permits. New electrical conductors in metal raceways located within a two-hour fire rated assembly without any combustible therein are exempt from this requirement.

(m) Automatic Sprinkler Systems Required.

(1) All areas which are classified as Group M-mercantile and Group H-hazardous shall be completely protected with an automatic sprinkler system.

(2) All areas used for commercial or institutional food preparation and storage facilities adjacent thereto shall be provided with an automatic sprinkler system.

(3) An area used for storage or handling of hazardous substances shall be provided with an automatic sprinkler system.

(4) All laboratories and vocational shops in Group E, Educational shall be provided with an automatic sprinkler system.

(5) Sprinkler systems shall be in strict accordance with NFPA No. 13 and the following requirements:

The sprinkler system must be equipped with a water flow and supervisory signal system that will transmit automatically a water flow signal directly to the fire department or to an independent signal monitoring service satisfactory to the fire department.

(j) Subsection (i) of this section does not apply to business occupancy buildings as defined in the North Carolina State Building Code except that evacuation plans as required on page 8, lines 2 through 16 [Section 1008, footnote following subsection (h)], and smoke detectors as required for Class I Buildings as required by Section 1008.2, page 11, lines 5 through 21 [Section 1008.2, subdivision (c)(1)]; Class II Buildings as required by Section 1008.3, page 17, lines 17 through 28 and page 18, lines 1 through 10 [Section 1008.3, subsections (c) and (d)]; and Class III Buildings, as required by Section 1008.4, lines 21 through 25 [Section 1008.4, subsection (c)] shall not be exempted from operation of this act as applied to business occupancy buildings, except that the Council shall adopt rules that allow a business occupancy building built prior to 1953 to have a single exit to remain if the building complies with the Building Code on or before December 31, 2006.

(j1) A nonbusiness occupancy building built prior to the adoption of the 1953 Building Code that is not in compliance with Section 402.1.3.5 of Volume IX of the Building Code or Section 3407.2.2 of Volume I of the Building Code must comply with the applicable sections by December 31, 2006.

(j2) Pursuant to Article 9G of Chapter 143 of the General Statutes, the Building Code Council is authorized to review and endorse proposals for the construction of tall buildings or structures in areas surrounding major military installations, as those terms are defined in G.S. 143-151.71.

(k) For purposes of use in the Code, the term "Family Care Home" shall mean an adult care home having two to six residents.

(l) When any question arises as to any provision of the Code, judicial notice shall be taken of that provision of the Code. (1957, c. 1138; 1969, c. 567; c. 1229, ss. 2-6; 1971, c. 1100, ss. 1, 2; 1973, c. 476, ss. 84, 128, 138, 152; c.

507, s. 5; 1981, c. 677, s. 3; c. 713, ss. 1, 2; 1981 (Reg. Sess., 1982), c. 1282, s. 20.2D; c. 1348, s. 1; 1983, c. 614, s. 3; 1985, c. 576, s. 1; c. 622, s. 2; c. 666, s. 39; 1989, c. 25, s. 2; c. 681, ss. 2, 3, 9, 10, 18, 19; c. 727, ss. 157, 158; 1991 (Reg. Sess., 1992), c. 895, s. 1; 1993, c. 329, ss. 1, 3; c. 539, s. 1009; 1994, Ex. Sess., c. 24, s. 14(c); 1995, c. 111, s. 1; c. 242, s. 1; c. 507, s. 27.8(r); c. 535, s. 30; 1997-26, ss. 1-3, 5; 1997-443, ss. 11A.93, 11A.94, 11A.118(a), 11A.119(a); 1998-57, s. 2; 1998-172, s. 1; 1998-202, s. 4(u); 1999-456, s. 40; 2000-137, s. 4(x); 2000-140, s. 93.1(a); 2001-141, ss. 1, 2, 3, 4; 2001-421, ss. 1.1, 1.2, 1.5; 2001-424, s. 12.2(b); 2002-144, s. 5; 2003-221, s. 6; 2003-284, s. 22.2; 2004-124, ss. 21.1, 21.2; 2005-205, s. 6; 2007-182, ss. 1, 2; 2007-529, s. 1; 2007-542, s. 1; 2008-176, s. 2; 2008-219, s. 1; 2009-79, s. 1(a)-(c); 2009-243, s. 1; 2009-532, s. 1; 2009-570, s. 18; 2010-97, s. 6(b); 2011-145, s. 19.1(mm); 2011-364, s. 1; 2012-34, s. 1; 2012-187, s. 16.1; 2013-75, s. 1; 2013-118, ss. 2, 3; 2013-206, s. 2; 2013-265, s. 18; 2013-413, ss. 19(a), 41.)

§ 143-138.1. Introduction and instruction of the North Carolina Building Code; posting of written commentaries and interpretations on Department of Insurance Web site.

(a) Prior to the effective date of Code changes pursuant to G.S. 143-138, the State Building Code Council and Department of Insurance shall provide for instructional classes for the various trades affected by the Code. The Department of Insurance shall develop the curriculum for each class but shall consult the affected licensing boards and trade organizations. The curriculum shall include explanations of the rationale and need for each Code amendment or revision. Classes may also be conducted by, on behalf of, or in cooperation with licensing boards, trade associations, and professional societies. The Department of Insurance may charge fees sufficient to recover the costs it incurs under this section. The Council shall ensure that courses are accessible to persons throughout the State.

(b) The Department of Insurance shall post and maintain on its Web site written commentaries and written interpretations made and given by staff to the North Carolina Building Code Council and the Department for each section of the North Carolina Building Code. (1997-26, s. 6; 2013-118, s. 3.5.)

§ 143-139. Enforcement of Building Code.

(a) Procedural Requirements. - Subject to the provisions set forth herein, the Building Code Council shall adopt such procedural requirements in the North Carolina State Building Code as shall appear reasonably necessary for adequate enforcement of the Code while safeguarding the rights of persons subject to the Code.

(b) General Building Regulations. - The Insurance Commissioner shall have general supervision, through the Division of Engineering of the Department of Insurance, of the administration and enforcement of all sections of the North Carolina State Building Code pertaining to plumbing, electrical systems, general building restrictions and regulations, heating and air conditioning, fire protection, and the construction of buildings generally, except those sections of the Code, the enforcement of which is specifically allocated to other agencies by subsections (c) through (e) below. The Insurance Commissioner, by means of the Division of Engineering, shall exercise his duties in the enforcement of the North Carolina State Building Code (including local building codes which have superseded the State Building Code in a particular political subdivision pursuant to G.S. 143-138(e)) in cooperation with local officials and local inspectors duly appointed by the governing body of any municipality or board of county commissioners pursuant to Part 5 of Article 19 of Chapter 160A of the General Statutes or Part 4 of Article 18 of Chapter 153A of the General Statutes, or any other applicable statutory authority.

(b1) Remedies. - In case any building or structure is maintained, erected, constructed, or reconstructed or its purpose altered, so that it becomes in violation of this Article or of the North Carolina State Building Code, either the local enforcement officer or the State Commissioner of Insurance or other State official with responsibility under this section may, in addition to other remedies, institute any appropriate action or proceeding to: (i) prevent the unlawful maintenance, erection, construction, or reconstruction or alteration of purpose, or overcrowding, (ii) restrain, correct, or abate the violation, or (iii) prevent the occupancy or use of the building, structure, or land until the violation is corrected. In addition to the civil remedies set out in G.S. 160A-175 and G.S. 153A-123, a county, city, or other political subdivision authorized to enforce the North Carolina State Building Code within its jurisdiction may, for the purposes stated in (i) through (iii) of this subsection, levy a civil penalty for violation of the fire prevention code of the North Carolina State Building Code, which penalty may be recovered in a civil action in the nature of debt if the offender does not pay the penalty within a prescribed period of time after the offender has been cited for the violation. If the Commissioner or other State official institutes an action or proceeding under this section, a county, city, or other political subdivision may not institute a civil action under this section based upon the same violation. Appeals from the imposition of any remedy set forth herein, including the imposition of a civil penalty by a county, city, or other political subdivision, shall be as provided in G.S. 160A-434.

(c) Boilers. - The Bureau of Boiler Inspection of the Department of Labor shall have general supervision of the administration and enforcement of those sections of the North Carolina State Building Code which pertain to boilers of the types enumerated in Article 7 of Chapter 95 of the General Statutes.

(d) Elevators. - The Department of Labor shall have general supervision of the administration and enforcement of those sections of the North Carolina State Building Code which pertain to elevators, moving stairways, and amusement devices such as merry-go-rounds, roller coasters, Ferris wheels, etc.

(e) State Buildings. - With respect to State buildings, the Department of Administration shall have general supervision, through the Office of State Construction, of the administration and enforcement of all sections of the North Carolina State Building Code pertaining to plumbing, electrical systems, general building restrictions and regulations, heating and air conditioning, fire protection, and the construction of buildings generally, except those sections of the Code the enforcement of which is specifically allocated to other agencies by subsections (c) and (d) of this section, and shall also exercise all remedies as provided in subsection (b1) of this section. The Department of Administration shall be the only agency with the authority to seek remedies pursuant to this section with respect to State buildings. Except as provided herein, nothing in this subsection shall be construed to abrogate the authority of the Commissioner of Insurance under G.S. 58-31-40 or any other provision of law. (1957, c. 1138; 1963, c. 811; 1989, c. 681, s. 11; 1993, c. 329, s. 2; 2009-474, ss. 3, 4.)

§ 143-139.1. Certification of manufactured buildings, structures or components by recognized independent testing laboratory; minimum standards for modular homes.

(a) Certification. - The State Building Code may provide, in circumstances deemed appropriate by the Building Code Council, for testing, evaluation, inspection, and certification of buildings, structures or components manufactured off the site on which they are to be erected, by a recognized independent testing laboratory having follow-up inspection services approved by the Building Code Council. Approval of such buildings, structures or components shall be evidenced by labels or seals acceptable to the Council. All building units, structures or components bearing such labels or seals shall be deemed to meet the requirements of the State Building Code and this Article without further inspection or payment of fees, except as may be required for the enforcement of the Code relative to the connection of units and components and enforcement of local ordinances governing zoning, utility connections, and foundations permits. The Building Code Council shall adopt and may amend from time to time such reasonable and appropriate rules and regulations as it deems necessary for approval of agencies offering such testing, evaluation, inspection, and certification services and for overseeing their operations. Such rules and regulations shall include provisions to insure that such agencies are independent and free of any potential conflicts of interest which might influence their judgment in exercising their functions under the Code. Such rules and regulations may include a schedule of reasonable fees to cover administrative expenses in approving and overseeing operations of such agencies and may require the posting of a bond or other security satisfactory to the Council guaranteeing faithful performance of duties under the Code.

The Building Code Council may also adopt rules to insure that any person that is not licensed, in accordance with G.S. 87-1, and that undertakes to erect a North Carolina labeled manufactured modular building, meets the manufacturer's installation instructions and applicable provisions of the State Building Code. Any such person, before securing a permit to erect a modular building, shall provide the code enforcement official proof that he has in force for each modular building to be erected a $5,000 surety bond insuring compliance with the regulations of the State Building Code governing installation of modular buildings.

(b) Minimum Standards for Modular Homes. - To qualify for a label or seal under subsection (a) of this section, a single-family modular home must meet or exceed the following construction and design standards:

(1) Roof pitch. - For homes with a single predominant roofline, the pitch of the roof shall be no less than five feet rise for every 12 feet of run.

(2) Eave projection. - The eave projections of the roof shall be no less than 10 inches, which may not include a gutter around the perimeter of the home, unless the roof pitch is 8/12 or greater.

(3) Exterior wall. - The minimum height of the exterior wall shall be at least seven feet six inches for the first story.

(4) Siding and roofing materials. - The materials and texture for the exterior materials shall be compatible in composition, appearance, and durability to the exterior materials commonly used in standard residential construction.

(5) Foundations. - The home shall be designed to require foundation supports around the perimeter. The supports may be in the form of piers, pier and curtain wall, piling foundations, a perimeter wall, or other approved perimeter supports. (1971, c. 1099; 1989, c. 653, s. 2; 2003-400, s. 17.)

§ 143-139.2. Enforcement of insulation requirements; certificate for occupancy; no electric service without compliance.

(a) In addition to other enforcement provisions set forth in this Chapter, no single family or multi-unit residential building on which construction is begun in North Carolina on or after January 1, 1978, shall be occupied until it has been certified as being in compliance with the minimum insulation standards for residential construction, as prescribed in the North Carolina State Building Code or as approved by the Building Code Council as provided in G.S. 143-138(e).

(b) No public supplier of electric service, including regulated public utilities, municipal electric service and electric membership corporations, shall connect for electric service to an occupant any residential building on which construction is begun on or after January 1, 1978, unless said building complies with the insulation requirements of the North Carolina State Building Code or of local building codes approved by the Building Codes Council as provided in G.S. 143-138(e), and has been certified for occupancy in compliance with the minimum insulation standards of the North Carolina State Building Code or of any local modification approved as provided in G.S. 143-138(e), by a person designated as an inspector pursuant to subsection (a) of this section.

(c) This section shall apply only in any county or city that elects to enforce the insulation and energy utilization standards of the State Building Code pursuant to G.S. 143-151.27. (1977, c. 792, s. 7; 1983, c. 377, s. 1.)

§ 143-139.3. Inspection of liquified petroleum gas piping systems for residential structures.

If the test required under the North Carolina State Building Code for a liquified petroleum gas piping system serving a one or two-family residential dwelling is not performed by a qualified code enforcement official, as defined in G.S. 143-151.8(a)(5), the contractor who installed the system shall verify that the system complies with the test requirements and shall certify the results, in writing, to the code official. (1993, c. 356, s. 3.)

§ 143-140. Hearings before enforcement agencies as to questions under Building Code.

Any person desiring to raise any question under this Article or under the North Carolina State Building Code shall be entitled to a technical interpretation from the appropriate enforcement agency, as designated in the preceding section. Upon request in writing by any such person, the enforcement agency through an appropriate official shall within a reasonable time provide a written interpretation, setting forth the facts found, the decision reached, and the reasons therefor. In the event of dissatisfaction with such decision, the person affected shall have the options of:

(1)   Appealing to the Building Code Council or

(2)   Appealing directly to the Superior Court, as provided in G.S. 143-141. (1957, c. 1138; 1989, c. 681, s. 4.)

§ 143-140.1. Appeals of alternative design construction and methods.

Alternative designs and construction shall follow the State Building Code. In the event of a dispute between a local authority having jurisdiction and the designer or owner-representative regarding alternative designs and construction, and notwithstanding any other section within this Article, appeals by the designer or owner-representative on matters pertaining to alternative design construction or methods shall be heard by the Department of Insurance Engineering Division. The Department of Insurance Engineering Division shall issue its decision regarding an appeal filed under this section within 10 business days. The

Commissioner of Insurance shall adopt rules in furtherance of this section. (2007-507, s. 18.)

§ 143-141. Appeals to Building Code Council.

(a) Method of Appeal. - Whenever any person desires to take an appeal to the Building Code Council from the decision of a State enforcement agency relating to any matter under this Article or under the North Carolina State Building Code, he shall within 30 days after such decision give written notice to the Building Code Council through the Division of Engineering of the Department of Insurance that he desires to take an appeal. A copy of such notice shall be filed at the same time with the enforcement agency from which the appeal is taken. The chairman of the Building Code Council shall fix a reasonable time and place for a hearing, giving reasonable notice to the appellant and to the enforcement agency. Such hearing shall be not later than the next regular meeting of the Council. The Building Code Council shall thereupon conduct a full and complete hearing as to the matters in controversy, after which it shall within a reasonable time give a written decision setting forth its findings of fact and its conclusions.

(b) Interpretations of the Code. - The Building Code Council shall have the duty, in hearing appeals, to give interpretations of such provisions of the Building Code as shall be pertinent to the matter at issue. Where the Council finds that an enforcement agency was in error in its interpretation of the Code, it shall remand the case to the agency with instructions to take such action as it directs. Interpretations by the Council and local enforcement officials shall be based on a reasonable construction of the Code provisions.

(c) Variations of the Code. - Where the Building Code Council finds on appeal that materials or methods of construction proposed to be used are as good as those required by the Code, it shall remand the case to the enforcement agency with instructions to permit the use of such materials or methods of construction. The Council shall thereupon immediately initiate procedures for amending the Code as necessary to permit the use of such materials or methods of construction.

(d) Further Appeals to the Courts. - Whenever any person desires to take an appeal from a decision of the Building Code Council or from the decision of an enforcement agency (with or without an appeal to the Building Code Council), he may take an appeal either to the Wake County Superior Court or to the superior court of the county in which the proposed building is to be situated, in accordance with the provisions of Chapter 150B of the General Statutes. (1957, c. 1138; 1973, c. 1331, s. 3; 1987, c. 827, s. 1; 1997-26, s. 7.)

§ 143-142. Further duties of the Building Code Council.

(a)   Recommended Statutory Changes. - It shall be the duty of the Building Code Council to make a thorough study of the building laws of the State, including both the statutes enacted by the General Assembly and the rules and regulations adopted by State and local agencies. On the basis of such study, the Council shall recommend to the 1959 and subsequent General Assemblies desirable statutory changes to simplify and improve such laws.

(b)   Recommend Changes in Enforcement Procedures. - It shall be the duty of the Building Code Council to make a thorough and continuing study of the manner in which the building laws of the State are enforced by State, local, and private agencies. On the basis of such studies, the Council may recommend to the General Assembly any statutory changes necessary to improve and simplify the enforcement machinery. The Council may also advise State agencies as to any changes in administrative practices which could be made to improve the enforcement of building laws without statutory changes. (1957, c. 1138.)

§ 143-143. Effect on certain existing laws.

Nothing in this Article shall be construed as abrogating or otherwise affecting the power of any State department or agency to promulgate regulations, make inspections, or approve plans in accordance with any other applicable provisions of law not in conflict with the provisions herein. (1957, c. 1138.)

§ 143-143.1. Repealed by Session Laws 1971, c. 882, s. 1.

§ 143-143.2. Electric wiring of houses, buildings, and structures.

The electric wiring of houses or buildings for lighting or for other purposes shall conform to the requirements of the State Building Code, which includes the

National Electric Code and any amendments and supplements thereto as adopted and approved by the State Building Code Council, and any other applicable State and local laws. In order to protect the property of citizens from the dangers incident to defective electric wiring of buildings, it shall be unlawful for any firm or corporation to allow any electric current for use in any newly erected building to be turned on without first having had an inspection made of the wiring by the appropriate official electrical inspector or inspection department and having received from that inspector or department a certificate approving the wiring of such building. It shall be unlawful for any person, firm, or corporation engaged in the business of selling electricity to furnish initially any electric current for use in any building, unless said building shall have first been inspected by the appropriate official electrical inspector or inspection department and a certificate given as above provided. In the event that there is no legally appointed inspector or inspection department with jurisdiction over the property involved, the two preceding sentences shall have no force or effect. As used in this section, "building" includes any structure. (1905, c. 506, s. 23; Rev., s. 3001; C.S., s. 2763; 1969, c. 1229, s. 7; 1989, c. 681, s. 20.)

§ 143-143.3. Temporary toilet facilities at construction sites.

(a) Suitable toilet facilities shall be provided and maintained in a sanitary condition during construction. An adequate number of facilities must be provided for the number of employees at the construction site. There shall be at least one facility for every two contiguous construction sites. Such facilities may be portable, enclosed, chemically treated, tank-tight units. Portable toilets shall be enclosed, screened, and weatherproofed with internal latches. Temporary toilet facilities need not be provided on-site for crews on a job site for no more than one working day and having transportation readily available to nearby toilet facilities.

(b) It shall be the duty of the Building Code Council to establish standards to carry out the provisions of subsection (a) of this section not inconsistent with the requirements for toilet facilities at construction sites established pursuant to federal occupational safety and health rules. (1993, c. 528.)

§ 143-143.4. Door lock exemption for certain businesses.

(a) Notwithstanding this Article or any other law to the contrary, any business entity licensed to sell automatic weapons as a federal firearms dealer that is in the business of selling firearms or ammunition and that operates a firing range which rents firearms and sells ammunition shall be exempt from the door lock requirements of Chapter 10 of Volume 1 of the North Carolina State Building Code when issued a permit to that effect by the Department of Insurance in accordance with this section.

(b) The Department of Insurance shall issue a permit to a business entity specified in subsection (a) of this section for an exemption from the door lock requirements of Chapter 10 of Volume 1 of the North Carolina State Building Code if all of the following conditions are met:

(1) The building or facility in which business is conducted has a sales floor and customer occupancy space that is contained on one floor and is no larger than 15,000 square feet of retail sales space. Retail sales space is that area where firearms or ammunition are displayed and merchandised for sale to the public.

(2) The building or facility in which business is conducted is equipped with an approved smoke, fire, and break-in alarm system installed and operated in accordance with rules adopted by the Department of Insurance. An approved smoke, fire, or break-in alarm system does not have to include an automatic door unlocking mechanism triggered when the smoke, fire, or break-in alarm system is triggered.

(3) The owner or operator of the business will provide to all applicable employees within 10 days of the issuance of the permit under this section or at the time the employee is hired, whichever time is later, a written facility locking plan applicable for the close of business each day.

(4) Each entrance to the building or facility in which business is conducted is posted with a sign conspicuously located that warns that the building is exempt from the door lock requirements of the State Building Code, and that after business hours the building or facility's doors will remain locked from the inside even in the case of fire.

(5) Payment of a permit fee of five hundred dollars ($500.00) to the Department of Insurance.

(c) The Department of Insurance shall file a copy of the permit issued in accordance with subsection (b) of this section with all local law enforcement and fire protection agencies that provide protection for the business entity.

(d) The Department of Insurance shall be responsible for any inspections necessary for the issuance of permits under this section and, in conjunction with local inspection departments, shall be responsible for periodic inspections to ensure compliance with the requirements of this section. The Department of Insurance may contract with local inspection departments to conduct inspections under this subsection.

(e) The Department of Insurance shall revoke a permit issued under this section upon a finding that the requirements for the original issuance of the permit are not being complied with.

(f) Appeals of decisions of the Department of Insurance regarding the issuance or revocation of permits under this section shall be in accordance with Chapter 150B of the General Statutes.

(g) For the purposes of this section, "business entity" has the same meaning as in G.S. 59-102.

(h) In addition to the provisions of G.S. 143-138(h), the owner or operator of any business entity who is issued a permit as a door lock exempt business in accordance with subsection (b) of this section who fails to comply with the permit requirements of subsection (b) of this section shall be subject to a civil penalty of five hundred dollars ($500.00) for the first offense, one thousand dollars ($1,000) for the second offense, and five thousand dollars ($5,000) for the third and subsequent offenses, except when the building or facility in which business is conducted is in compliance with the door lock requirements of Chapter 10 of Volume 1 of the North Carolina State Building Code. Penalties authorized in this subsection shall be imposed by the city or county in which the violation occurs. Each day the building or facility in which business is conducted is not in compliance with the provisions of this subsection constitutes a separate offense.

(i) The Department of Insurance shall adopt rules to implement this section. (2001-324, s. 1.)

§ 143-143.5. Access to toilets in shopping malls.

Notwithstanding any other law or rule, a horizontal travel distance of 300 feet for access to public use toilets in covered mall buildings shall be allowed. (2004-199, s. 37(a); 2005-289, s. 2.)

§ 143-143.6. Expired pursuant to Session Laws 2007-82, s. 2, effective July 1, 2009.

§ 143-143.7: Reserved for future codification purposes.

Article 9A.

North Carolina Manufactured Housing Board - Manufactured Home Warranties.

Part 1. Duties, Warranties, Purchase Transaction.

§ 143-143.8. Purpose.

The General Assembly finds that manufactured homes have become a primary housing resource for many of the citizens of North Carolina. The General Assembly finds further that it is the responsibility of the manufactured home industry to provide homes which are of reasonable quality and safety and to offer warranties to buyers that provide a means of remedying quality and safety defects in manufactured homes. The General Assembly also finds that it is in the public interest to provide a means for enforcing such warranties.

Consistent with these findings and with the legislative intent to promote the general welfare and safety of manufactured home residents in North Carolina, the General Assembly finds that the most efficient and economical way to assure safety, quality and responsibility is to require the licensing and bonding of all segments of the manufactured home industry. The General Assembly also finds that it is reasonable and proper for the manufactured home industry to cooperate with the Commissioner of Insurance, through the establishment of the North Carolina Manufactured Housing Board, to provide for a comprehensive framework for industry regulations. (1981, c. 952, s. 2; 1999-393, s. 1; 2005-451, s. 1.)

§ 143-143.9. Definitions.

The following definitions apply in this Part:

(1)   Bank. - A federally insured financial institution including institutions defined under G.S. 53C-1-4(4), savings and loan associations, credit unions, savings banks and other financial institutions chartered under this or any other state law or chartered under federal law.

(1a)   Board. - The North Carolina Manufactured Housing Board.

(2)   Buyer. - A person for whom a dealer performs, or is engaged to perform, any services or provides any products including the purchase and setup of a manufactured home for use as a residence or other related use.

(3)   Code. - Engineering standards adopted by the Commissioner.

(4)   Commissioner. - The Commissioner of Insurance of the State of North Carolina.

(5)   Department. - The Department of Insurance of the State of North Carolina.

(5a)   Deposit. - Any and all funds received by a dealer from a buyer or someone on behalf of a buyer for the performance of services or the provision of goods.

(5b)   Escrow or trust account. - An account with a bank that is designated as an escrow account or as a trust account and that is maintained by a dealer for the deposit of buyers' funds.

(5c)   Escrow or trust account funds. - Funds belonging to a person other than the dealer that are received by or placed under the control of the dealer in connection with the performance of services or the provision of products by a dealer for a buyer.

(5d)   Funds. - Any form of money, including cash, payment instruments such as checks, money orders, or sales drafts, and receipts from electronic fund transfers. The term does not include letters of credit or promissory notes.

(5e)   License. - A license issued under this Part.

(5f) Licensee. - A person who has been issued a license under this Part by the North Carolina Manufactured Housing Board.

(6) Manufactured home. - A structure, transportable in one or more sections, which, in the traveling mode, is eight feet or more in width or is 40 feet or more in length, or when erected on site, is 320 or more square feet, and which is built on a permanent chassis and designed to be used as a dwelling with or without a permanent foundation when connected to the required utilities, and includes the plumbing, heating, air conditioning and electrical systems contained therein.

(7) Manufactured home dealer or dealer. - Any person engaged in the business of buying or selling manufactured homes or offering or displaying manufactured homes for sale in North Carolina. Any person who buys or sells three or more manufactured homes in any 12-month period, or who offers or displays for sale three or more manufactured homes in any 12-month period shall be presumed to be a manufactured home dealer. The terms "selling" and "sale" include lease-purchase transactions. The term "manufactured home dealer" does not include banks and finance companies that acquire manufactured homes as an incident to their regular business.

(8) Manufactured home manufacturer or manufacturer. - Any person, resident or nonresident, who manufactures or assembles manufactured homes for sale to dealers in North Carolina.

(9) Manufactured home salesperson or salesperson. - Any person employed by a manufactured home dealer to sell manufactured homes to buyers. Manufactured home salesperson or salesperson also includes sales managers, lot managers, general managers, or others who manage or supervise salespersons.

(10) Person. - Any individual, natural persons, firm, partnership, association, corporation, legal representative or other recognized legal entity.

(11) Responsible party. - A manufacturer, dealer, supplier, or set-up contractor.

(12) Setup. - The operations performed at the occupancy site which render a manufactured home fit for habitation.

(13)   Set-up contractor. - A person who engages in the business of performing setups for compensation in North Carolina.

(14)   Substantial defect. - Any substantial deficiency in or damage to materials or workmanship occurring in a manufactured home which has been reasonably maintained and cared for in normal use. The term also means any structural element, utility system or component part of the manufactured home which fails to comply with the Code.

(15)   Supplier. - The original producer of completed components, including refrigerators, stoves, hot water heaters, dishwashers, cabinets, air conditioners, heating units, and similar components, and materials such as floor coverings, paneling, siding, trusses, and similar materials, which are furnished to a manufacturer or dealer for installation in the manufactured home prior to sale to a buyer. (1981, c. 952, s. 2; 1987, c. 429, ss. 4, 5, 19; 1999-393, s. 1; 2001-421, s. 2.1.; 2005-451, ss. 1, 2; 2012-56, s. 48.)

§ 143-143.10. Manufactured Housing Board created; membership; terms; meetings.

(a)   There is created the North Carolina Manufactured Housing Board within the Department. The Board shall be composed of 11 members as follows:

(1)   The Commissioner of Insurance or the Commissioner's designee.

(2)   A manufactured home manufacturer.

(3)   A manufactured home dealer.

(4)   A representative of the banking and finance industry.

(5)   A representative of the insurance industry.

(6)   A manufactured home supplier.

(7)   A set-up contractor.

(8)   Two representatives of the general public.

(9) A person who is employed with a HUD-approved housing counseling agency in the State.

(10) An accountant.

The Commissioner or the Commissioner's designee shall chair the Board. The Governor shall appoint to the Board the manufactured home manufacturer and the manufactured home dealer. The General Assembly upon the recommendation of the Speaker of the House of Representatives in accordance with G.S. 120-121 shall appoint to the Board the representative of the banking and finance industry, the employee of a HUD-approved housing counseling agency, and the representative of the insurance industry. The General Assembly upon the recommendation of the President Pro Tempore of the Senate in accordance with G.S. 120-121 shall appoint to the Board the manufactured home supplier, the accountant, and the set-up contractor. The Commissioner shall appoint two representatives of the general public. Except for the representatives from the general public and the persons appointed by the General Assembly, each member of the Board shall be appointed by the appropriate appointing authority from a list of nominees submitted to the appropriate appointing authority by the Board of Directors of the North Carolina Manufactured Housing Institute. At least three nominations shall be submitted for each position on the Board. The members of the Board shall be residents of the State.

The members of the Board shall serve for terms of three years. In the event of any vacancy of a position appointed by the Governor or Commissioner, the appropriate appointing authority shall appoint a replacement in the same manner as provided for the original appointment to serve the remainder of the unexpired term. Vacancies in appointments made by the General Assembly shall be filled in accordance with G.S. 120-122. In the event of any vacancy, the appropriate appointing authority shall appoint a replacement to serve the remainder of the unexpired term. Such appointment shall be made in the same manner as provided for the original appointment. No member of the Board shall serve more than two consecutive, three-year terms.

The members of the Board designated in subdivisions (8), (9), and (10) of this subsection shall have no current or previous financial interest connected with the manufactured housing industry. No member of the Board shall participate in any proceeding before the Board involving that member's own business.

Each member of the Board, except the Commissioner and any other State employee, shall receive per diem and allowances as provided with respect to occupational licensing boards by G.S. 93B-5. Fees collected by the Board under this Article shall be credited to the Insurance Regulatory Fund created under G.S. 58-6-25.

(b)   In accordance with the provisions of this Part, the Board shall have the following powers and duties:

(1)   To issue licenses to manufacturers, dealers, salespersons, and set-up contractors.

(2)   To require that an adequate bond or other security be posted by all licensees, except manufactured housing salespersons.

(3)   To receive and resolve complaints from buyers of manufactured homes and from persons in the manufactured housing industry, in connection with the warranty, warranty service, licensing requirements or any other provision under this Part.

(4)   To adopt rules in accordance with Chapter 150B of the General Statutes as are necessary to carry out the provisions of this Part.

(5)   To file against the bond posted by a licensee for warranty repairs and service on behalf of a buyer.

(6)   To request that the Department of Justice conduct criminal history checks of applicants for licensure pursuant to G.S. 114-19.13.

(7)   To conduct random audits of dealer escrow or trust accounts. (1981, c. 952, s. 2; 1983, c. 717, ss. 107-109, 114; 1987, c. 429, ss. 6, 7, 19, c. 827, s. 1; 1999-393, s. 1; 2002-144, s. 4; 2003-221, s. 1; 2003-400, s. 9; 2005-451, ss. 1, 3; 2011-330, s. 47(b).)

§ 143-143.10A. Criminal history checks of applicants for licensure.

(a)   Definitions. - The following definitions shall apply in this section:

(1) Applicant. - A person applying for licensure as a manufactured home manufacturer, dealer, salesperson, or set-up contractor.

(2) Criminal history. - A history of conviction of a state or federal crime, whether a misdemeanor or felony, that bears on an applicant's fitness for licensure under this Part. The crimes include the criminal offenses set forth in any of the following Articles of Chapter 14 of the General Statutes: Article 5, Counterfeiting and Issuing Monetary Substitutes; Article 5A, Endangering Executive and Legislative Officers; Article 6, Homicide; Article 7A, Rape and Other Sex Offenses; Article 8, Assaults; Article 10, Kidnapping and Abduction; Article 13, Malicious Injury or Damage by Use of Explosive or Incendiary Device or Material; Article 14, Burglary and Other Housebreakings; Article 15, Arson and Other Burnings; Article 16, Larceny; Article 17, Robbery; Article 18, Embezzlement; Article 19, False Pretenses and Cheats; Article 19A, Obtaining Property or Services by False or Fraudulent Use of Credit Device or Other Means; Article 19B, Financial Transaction Card Crime Act; Article 20, Frauds; Article 21, Forgery; Article 26, Offenses Against Public Morality and Decency; Article 26A, Adult Establishments; Article 27, Prostitution; Article 28, Perjury; Article 29, Bribery; Article 31, Misconduct in Public Office; Article 35, Offenses Against the Public Peace; Article 36A, Riots, Civil Disorders, and Emergencies; Article 39, Protection of Minors; Article 40, Protection of the Family; Article 59, Public Intoxication; and Article 60, Computer-Related Crime. The crimes also include possession or sale of drugs in violation of the North Carolina Controlled Substances Act in Article 5 of Chapter 90 of the General Statutes and alcohol-related offenses including sale to underage persons in violation of G.S. 18B-302 or driving while impaired in violation of G.S. 20-138.1 through G.S. 20-138.5. In addition to the North Carolina crimes listed in this subdivision, such crimes also include similar crimes under federal law or under the laws of other states.

(b) All applicants for licensure shall consent to a criminal history record check. Refusal to consent to a criminal history record check may constitute grounds for the Board to deny licensure to an applicant. The Board shall ensure that the State and national criminal history of an applicant is checked. Applicants shall obtain criminal record reports from one or more reporting services designated by the Board to provide criminal record reports. Each applicant is required to pay the designated service for the cost of the criminal record report. In the alternative, the Board may provide to the North Carolina Department of Justice the fingerprints of the applicant to be checked, a form signed by the applicant consenting to the criminal record check and the use of fingerprints and other identifying information required by the State or National Repositories of Criminal Histories, and any additional information required by the Department of Justice. The Board shall keep all information obtained pursuant to this section confidential.

(c)   If an applicant's criminal history record check reveals one or more convictions listed under subdivision (a)(2) of this section, the conviction shall not automatically bar licensure. The Board shall consider all of the following factors regarding the conviction:

(1)   The level of seriousness of the crime.

(2)   The date of the crime.

(3)   The age of the person at the time of the conviction.

(4)   The circumstances surrounding the commission of the crime, if known.

(5)   The nexus between the criminal conduct of the person and the job duties of the position to be filled.

(6)   The person's prison, jail, probation, parole, rehabilitation, and employment records since the date the crime was committed.

(7)   The subsequent commission by the person of a crime listed in subdivision (a)(2) of this section.

If, after reviewing these factors, the Board determines that the applicant's criminal history disqualifies the applicant for licensure, the Board may deny licensure of the applicant. The Board may disclose to the applicant information contained in the criminal history record check that is relevant to the denial. The Board shall not provide a copy of the criminal history record check to the applicant. The applicant shall have the right to appear before the Board to appeal the Board's decision. However, an appearance before the full Board shall constitute an exhaustion of administrative remedies in accordance with Chapter 150B of the General Statutes.

(d)   Limited Immunity. - The Board, its officers, and employees, acting in good faith and in compliance with this section, shall be immune from civil liability for denying licensure to an applicant based on information provided in the applicant's criminal history record check. (2003-400, s. 8; 2005-451, s. 1; 2007-416, s. 1; 2012-12, s. 2(vv).)

§ 143-143.11. License required; application for license.

(a) It shall be unlawful for any manufactured home manufacturer, dealer, salesperson, or set-up contractor to engage in business as such in this State without first obtaining a license from the Board for each place of business operated by the licensee, as provided in this Part. The fact that a person is licensed by the Board as a set-up contractor or a dealer does not preempt any other licensing boards' applicable requirements for that person.

(b) Application for the license shall be made to the Board at such time, in such form, and contain information the Board requires, and shall be accompanied by the fee established by the Board. The fee shall not exceed three hundred fifty dollars ($350.00) for each license issued. In addition to the license fee, the Board may also charge an applicant a fee to cover the cost of the criminal history record check required by G.S. 143-143.10A.

(c) In the application, the Board shall require information relating to the matters set forth in G.S. 143-143.13 as grounds for refusal of a license, and information relating to other pertinent matters consistent with safeguarding the public interest. All of this information shall be considered by the Board in determining the fitness of the applicant. Once the Board has determined that an applicant is fit, the Board must provide the applicant a license for each place of business operated by the applicant.

(d) All licenses shall expire, unless revoked or suspended, on June 30 of each year following the date of issue.

(e) Every licensee shall, on or before the first day of July of each year, obtain a renewal of a license for the next year by applying to the Board, completing the necessary hours of continuing education required under G.S. 143-143.11B, and paying the required renewal fee for each place of business operated by the licensee. The renewal fee shall not exceed three hundred fifty dollars ($350.00) for each license issued. Upon failure to renew by the first day of July, a license automatically expires. The license may be renewed at any time within one year after its lapse upon payment of the renewal fee and a late filing fee. The late filing fee shall not exceed three hundred fifty dollars ($350.00).

(f) Repealed by Session Laws 2005-297, s. 1, effective August 22, 2005.

(g) Notwithstanding the provisions of subsection (a), the Board may provide by rule that a manufactured home salesperson will be allowed to engage in business during the time period after making application for a license but before such license is granted.

(h)   As a prerequisite to obtaining a license under this Part, a person may be required to pass an examination prescribed by the Board that is based on the Code, this Part, and any other subject matter considered relevant by the Board. (1981, c. 952, s. 2; 1985, c. 487, s. 1; 1987, c. 429, s. 19; 1987 (Reg. Sess., 1988), c. 1039, ss. 2, 3; 1989, c. 485, s. 44; 1991, c. 644, s. 35; 1999-393, s. 1; 2003-400, s. 10; 2005-297, s. 1.; 2005-451, s. 1; 2009-451, s. 21.4.)

§ 143-143.11A. Notification of change of address, control of ownership, and bankruptcy.

(a)   Every applicant for a license shall inform the Board of the applicant's business address. Every licensee shall give written notification to the Board of any change in the licensee's business address, for whatever reason, within 10 business days after the licensee moves to a new address or a change in the address takes place. A violation of this subsection shall not constitute grounds for revocation, suspension, or non-renewal of a license or for the imposition of any other penalty by the Board.

(b)   Notwithstanding any other provision of law, whenever the Board is authorized or required to give notice to a licensee under this Part, the notice may be delivered personally to the licensee or sent by first-class mail to the licensee at the address provided to the Board under subsection (a) of this section. Notice shall be deemed given four days after mailing, and any Department employee may certify that notice has been given.

(c)   Every person licensed under this Part, except for a person licensed as a manufactured home salesperson, shall give written notification to the Board of any change in ownership or control of the licensee's business within 30 business days after the change. A "change in ownership or control" means the sale or conveyance of the capital stock of the business or of an owner's interest in the business, which operates to place a person or group of persons, not previously in control of the business, in effective control of the business. A violation of this subsection shall not constitute grounds for revocation, suspension, or nonrenewal of a license or for the imposition of any other penalty by the Board.

(d) Upon the filing for protection under the United States Bankruptcy Code by any licensee, or by any business in which the licensee holds a position of employment, management or ownership, the licensee shall notify the Board of the filing of protection within three business days after the filing. Upon the appointment of a receiver by a court of this State for any licensee, or for any business in which the licensee holds a position of employment, management, or ownership the licensee shall notify the Board of the appointment within three business days after the appointment. (1999-393, s. 1; 2000-122, s. 9; 2005-451, s. 1.)

§ 143-143.11B. Continuing education.

(a) The Board may establish programs and requirements of continuing education for licensees, but shall not require licensees to complete more than eight credit hours of continuing education. Before the renewal of a license, a licensee shall present evidence to the Board that the licensee has completed the required number of continuing education hours in courses approved by the Board during the two months immediately preceding the expiration of the licensee's license. No member of the Board shall provide or sponsor a continuing education course under this section while that person is serving on the Board.

(b) The Board may establish nonrefundable fees for the purpose of providing staff and resources to administer continuing education programs, and may establish nonrefundable course application fees, not to exceed one hundred fifty dollars ($150.00), for the Board's review and approval of proposed continuing education courses. The Board may charge the sponsor of an approved course a nonrefundable fee not to exceed seventy-five dollars ($75.00) for the annual renewal of course approval. The Board may also require a course sponsor to pay a fee, not to exceed five dollars ($5.00) per credit hour per licensee, for each licensee completing an approved continuing education course conducted by the sponsor. The Board may award continuing education credit for a course that has not been approved by the Board or for related educational activity and may prescribe the procedures for a licensee to submit information on the course or related educational activity for continuing education credit. The Board may charge the licensee a fee not to exceed fifty dollars ($50.00) for each course or activity submitted.

(c) The Board may adopt any reasonable rules not inconsistent with this Part to give purpose and effect to the continuing education requirement, including rules that govern:

(1) The content and subject matter of continuing education courses.

(2) The criteria, standards, and procedures for the approval of courses, course sponsors, and course instructors.

(3) The methods of instruction.

(4) The computation of course credit.

(5) The ability to carry forward course credit from one year to another.

(6) The waiver of or variance from the continuing education requirement for hardship or other reasons.

(7) The procedures for compliance and sanctions for noncompliance.

(d) The license of any person who fails to comply with the continuing education requirements under this section shall lapse. The Board may, for good cause shown, grant extensions of time to licensees to comply with these requirements. Any licensee who, after obtaining an extension, offers evidence satisfactory to the Board that he or she has satisfactorily completed the required continuing education courses shall be deemed in compliance with this section.

(e) A manufactured home manufacturer or manufacturer is exempt from the requirements of this section. (1999-393, s. 1; 2001-421, s. 2.2; 2005-451, s. 1.)

§ 143-143.12. Bond required.

(a) A person licensed as a manufactured home salesperson shall not be required to furnish a bond, but each applicant approved by the Board for license as a manufacturer, dealer, or set-up contractor shall furnish a corporate surety bond, cash bond or fixed value equivalent in the following amounts:

(1) For a manufacturer, two thousand dollars ($2,000) per manufactured home manufactured in the prior license year, up to a maximum of one hundred

thousand dollars ($100,000). When no manufactured homes were produced in the prior year, the amount required shall be based on the estimated number of manufactured homes to be produced during the current year.

(2) For a dealer who has one place of business, the amount shall be thirty-five thousand dollars ($35,000).

(3) For a dealer who has more than one place of business, the amount shall be twenty-five thousand dollars ($25,000) for each additional place of business.

(4) For a set-up contractor, the amount shall be ten thousand dollars ($10,000).

(b) A corporate surety bond shall be approved by the Board as to form and shall be conditioned upon the obligor faithfully conforming to and abiding by the provisions of this Part. A cash bond or fixed value equivalent shall be approved by the Board as to form and terms of deposits in order to secure the ultimate beneficiaries of the bond. A corporate surety bond shall be for a one-year period, and a new bond or a proper continuation certificate shall be delivered to the Board at the beginning of each subsequent one-year period.

(c) Any buyer of a manufactured home who suffers any loss or damage by any act of a licensee that constitutes a violation of this Part may institute an action to recover against the licensee and the surety.

(d) The Board may adopt rules to assure satisfaction of claims. (1981, c. 952, s. 2; 1985, c. 487, s. 2; 1987, c. 429, s. 19; c. 827, s. 223; 1999-393, s. 1; 2000-122, s. 8; 2005-451, s. 1.)

§ 143-143.13. Grounds for denying, suspending, or revoking licenses; civil penalties.

(a) A license may be denied, suspended or revoked by the Board on any one or more of the following grounds:

(1) Making a material misstatement in application for license.

(2) Failing to post an adequate corporate surety bond, cash bond or fixed value equivalent.

(3) Engaging in the business of manufactured home manufacturer, dealer, salesperson, or set-up contractor without first obtaining a license from the Board.

(4) Failing to comply with the warranty service obligations and claims procedure established by this Part.

(5) Failing to comply with the set-up requirements established by this Part.

(6) Failing or refusing to account for or to pay over moneys or other valuables belonging to others that have come into licensee's possession arising out of the sale of manufactured homes.

(6a) Failing to comply with the escrow or trust account provisions of Part 2 of this Article.

(7) Using unfair methods of competition or committing unfair or deceptive acts or practices.

(8) Failing to comply with any provision of this Part.

(9) Failing to appear for a hearing before the Board or for a prehearing conference with a person or persons designated by the Board after proper notice or failing to comply with orders of the Board issued pursuant to this Part.

(10) Employing unlicensed salespersons.

(11) Offering for sale manufactured homes manufactured or assembled by unlicensed manufacturers or selling manufactured homes to unlicensed dealers for sale to buyers in this State.

(12) Conviction of any crime listed in G.S. 143-143.10A.

(13) Having had a license revoked, suspended or denied by the Board; or having had a license revoked, suspended or denied by a similar entity in another state; or engaging in conduct in another state which conduct, if committed in this State, would have been a violation under this Part.

(14) Employing or contracting with any person to perform setups who is not licensed by the Board as a set-up contractor.

(15)   Failure to comply with the provisions of Chapters 47G and 47H of the General Statutes.

(b)   Repealed by Session Laws 1985, c. 666, s. 38.

(c)   In addition to the authority to deny, suspend, or revoke a license under this Part the Board may impose a civil penalty upon any person violating the provisions of this Part. Upon a finding by the Board of a violation of this Part, the Board shall order the payment of a penalty of not less than one hundred dollars ($100.00) nor more than five hundred dollars ($500.00). In determining the amount of the penalty, the Board shall consider the degree and extent of harm caused by the violation, the amount of money that inured to the benefit of the violator as a result of the violation, whether the violation was committed willfully, and the prior record of the violator in complying or failing to comply with laws, rules, or orders applicable to the violator. Each day during which a violation occurs shall constitute a separate offense. The penalty shall be payable to the Board. The Board shall remit the clear proceeds of penalties provided for in this subsection to the Civil Penalty and Forfeiture Fund in accordance with G.S. 115C-457.2.

Payment of the civil penalty under this section shall be in addition to payment of any other penalty for a violation of the criminal laws of this State. Nothing in this subsection shall prevent the Board from negotiating a mutually acceptable agreement with any person as to the status of the person's license or certificate or as to any civil penalty. (1981, c. 952, s. 2; 1985, c. 487, ss. 3 to 5; c. 666, s. 38; 1985 (Reg. Sess., 1986), c. 1027, s. 51; 1987, c. 429, s. 19; 1989, c. 485, s. 45; 1991, c. 644, s. 34; 1998-215, s. 92; 1999-393, s. 1; 2003-400, s. 11; 2005-451, ss. 1, 4; 2010-164, s. 5.)

§ 143-143.14. Hearings; rules.

(a)   License suspensions, revocations, and renewal refusals are subject to the provisions of Chapter 150B of the General Statutes.

(b)   If the Board finds that an applicant has not met the requirements for licensure, the Board shall refuse to issue the applicant a license and shall notify the applicant in writing of the denial and the grounds for the denial. The application may also be denied for any reason for which a license may be suspended or revoked or not renewed under G.S. 143-143.13. Within 30 days after receipt of a notification that an application for a license has been denied, the applicant may make a written request for a review by a member of the Department staff designated by the chair of the Board to determine the reasonableness of the Board's action. The review shall be completed without undue delay, and the applicant shall be notified promptly in writing as to the outcome of the review. Within 30 days after service of the notification as to the outcome, the applicant may make a written request for a hearing under Article 3A of Chapter 150B of the General Statutes if the applicant disagrees with the outcome.

(c)   The Board may adopt rules for hearings and prehearing conferences under this Part, and the rules may include provisions for prefiled evidence, the use of evidence, testimony of parties, prehearing statements, prehearing conference procedures, settlement conference procedures, discovery, subpoenas, sanctions, motions, intervention, consolidation of cases, continuances, and the rights and responsibilities of parties and witnesses. (1981, c. 952, s. 2; 1987, c. 429, s. 19; 1993, c. 504, s. 34; 1993 (Reg. Sess., 1994), c. 678, s. 34; 1999-393, s. 1; 2005-451, s. 1.)

§ 143-143.15. Set-up requirements.

(a)   Manufactured homes shall be set up in accordance with the standards adopted by the Commissioner.

(b)   If a manufactured home is insured against damage caused by windstorm and subsequently sustains windstorm damage that indicates the manufactured home was not set up in the manner required by this section, the insurer issuing the insurance policy on the manufactured home shall not be relieved from meeting the obligations specified in the insurance policy with respect to such damage on the basis that the manufactured home was not properly set up. (1981, c. 952, s. 2; 1987, c. 429, s. 8; 1999-393, s. 1; 2005-451, s. 1.)

§ 143-143.16. Warranties.

Each manufacturer, dealer and supplier of manufactured homes shall warrant each new manufactured home sold in this State in accordance with the warranty requirements prescribed by this section for a period of at least 12 months, measured from the date of delivery of the manufactured home to the buyer. The warranty requirements for each manufacturer, dealer, supplier and set-up contractor of manufactured homes are as follows:

(1) The manufacturer warrants that all structural elements, plumbing systems, heating, cooling and fuel burning systems, electrical systems, and any other components included by the manufacturer are manufactured and installed free from substantial defects.

(2) The dealer warrants:

a. That any modifications or alterations made to the manufactured home by the dealer or authorized by the dealer are free from substantial defects. Alterations or modifications made by a dealer shall relieve the manufacturer of warranty responsibility as to the item altered or modified and any resulting damage.

b. That a setup performed by the dealer on the manufactured home is performed in compliance with the Code.

c. That the setup and transportation of the manufactured home by the dealer did not result in substantial defects.

(3) The supplier warrants that any warranties generally offered in the ordinary sale of his product to consumers shall be extended to buyers of manufactured homes. The manufacturer's warranty shall remain in effect notwithstanding the existence of a supplier's warranty.

(4) The set-up contractor warrants that the manufactured home is set up in compliance with the Code and that the setup did not result in any substantial defects. (1981, c. 952, s. 2; 1987, c. 429, s. 9; 1999-393, s. 1; 2005-451, s. 1.)

§ 143-143.17. Presenting claims for warranties and substantial defects.

(a) Whenever a claim for warranty service or about a substantial defect is made to a licensee, it shall be handled as provided in this Part. The licensee shall make a record of the name and address of each claimant and the date, substance, and disposition of each claim about a substantial defect. The licensee may request that a claim be in writing, but must nevertheless record it as provided above, and may not delay service pending receipt of the written claim.

(b)   When the licensee notified is not the responsible party, he shall in writing immediately notify the claimant and the responsible party of the claim. When a responsible party is asked to remedy defects, it may not fail to remedy those defects because another party may also be responsible. Nothing in this section prevents a party from obtaining compensation by way of contribution or subrogation from another responsible party in accordance with any other provision of law or contract.

(c)   Within the time limits provided in this Part, the licensee shall either resolve the claim or determine that it is not justified. At any time a licensee determines that a claim for warranty service is not justified in whole or in part he shall immediately notify the claimant in writing that the claim or part of the claim is rejected and why, and shall inform the claimant that he is entitled to complain to the Board, for which a complete mailing address shall be provided. (1981, c. 952, s. 2; 1987, c. 429, s. 19; 1999-393, s. 1; 2005-451, s. 1.)

§ 143-143.18. Warranty service.

(a)   When a service agreement exists between or among a manufacturer, dealer and supplier to provide warranty service, the agreement shall specify which party is to remedy warranty defects. Every service agreement shall be in writing. Nothing contained in such an agreement shall relieve the responsible party, as provided by this Part, of responsibility to perform warranty service. However, any licensee undertaking by such agreement to perform the warranty service obligations of another shall thereby himself become responsible both to that other licensee and to the buyer for his failure adequately to perform as agreed.

(b)   When no service agreement exists for warranty service, the responsible party as designated by this Part is responsible for remedying the warranty defect.

(c)   A substantial defect shall be remedied within 45 days after the receipt of written notification from the claimant. If no written notification is given, the defect shall be remedied within 45 days after the mailing of notification by the Board, unless the claim is unreasonable or bona fide reasons exist for not remedying the defect within the 45-day period. The responsible party shall respond to the claimant in writing with a copy to the Board stating its reasons for not promptly remedying the defect and stating what further action is contemplated by the responsible party. Notwithstanding the foregoing provisions of this subsection, defects, which constitute an imminent safety hazard to life and health shall be remedied within five working days of receipt of the written notification of the warranty claim. An imminent safety hazard to life and health shall include but not be limited to (i) inadequate heating in freezing weather; (ii) failure of sanitary facilities; (iii) electrical shock, leaking gas; or (iv) major structural failure. The Board may suspend this five-day time period in the event of widespread defects or damage resulting from adverse weather conditions or other natural catastrophes.

(d)   When the person remedying the defect is not the responsible party as designated by the provisions of this Part, he shall be entitled to reasonable compensation paid to him by the responsible party. Conduct that coerces or requires a nonresponsible party to perform warranty service is a violation of this Part.

(e)   Warranty service shall be performed at the site at which the manufactured home is initially delivered to the buyer, except for components which can be removed for service without substantial expense or inconvenience to the buyer.

(f)   Any dealer, manufacturer or supplier may complain to the Board when warranty service obligations under this Part are not being enforced. (1981, c. 952, s. 2; 1987, c. 429, ss. 17, 19; 1999-393, s. 1; 2005-451, s. 1.)

§ 143-143.19. Dealer alterations.

(a)   No alteration or modification shall be made to a manufactured home by a dealer after shipment from the manufacturer's plant, unless such alteration or modification is authorized by this Part or the manufacturer. The dealer shall ensure that all authorized alterations and modifications are performed, if so required, by qualified persons as defined in subsection (d). An unauthorized alteration or modification performed by a dealer or his agent or employee shall place primary warranty responsibility for the altered or modified item upon the dealer. If the manufacturer fulfills or is required to fulfill the warranty on the altered or modified item, he shall be entitled to recover damages in the amount of his cost and attorney's fee from the dealer.

(b)   An unauthorized alteration or modification of a manufactured home by the owner or his agent shall relieve the manufacturer of responsibility to remedy defects caused by such alteration or modification. A statement to this effect, together with a warning specifying those alterations or modifications which should be performed only by qualified personnel in order to preserve warranty protection, shall be displayed clearly and conspicuously on the face of the warranty. Failure to display such statement shall result in warranty responsibility on the manufacturer.

(c)   The Board is authorized to adopt rules in accordance with Chapter 150B of the General Statutes that define the alterations or modifications which must be made by qualified personnel. The Board may require qualified personnel only for those alterations and modifications which could substantially impair the structural integrity or safety of the manufactured home.

(d)   In order to be designated as a person qualified to alter or modify a manufactured home, a person must comply with State licensing or competency requirements in skills relevant to performing alterations or modifications on manufactured homes. (1981, c. 952, s. 2; 1987, c. 429, s. 19; c. 827, s. 1; 1999-393, s. 1; 2005-451, s. 1.)

§ 143-143.20. Disclosure of manner used in determining length of manufactured homes.

In any advertisement or other communication regarding the length of a manufactured home, a manufacturer or dealer shall not include the coupling mechanism in describing the length of the home. (1981, c. 952, s. 2; 2005-451, s. 1.)

§ 143-143.20A. Display of pricing on manufactured homes.

(a)   If the manufacturer of a manufactured home publishes a manufacturer's suggested retail price, that price shall be displayed near the front entrance of the manufactured home.

(b)   Each manufactured home dealer shall prominently display a sign and provide to each buyer a notice, developed by the North Carolina Manufactured Housing Board, containing information about the Board, including how to file a consumer complaint with the Board and the warranties and protections provided for each new manufactured home under federal and State law. (2003-400, s. 6; 2005-451, s. 1.)

§ 143-143.21: Repealed by Session Laws 1993, c. 409, s. 6.

§ 143-143.21A. Purchase agreements; buyer cancellations.

(a)   A purchase agreement for a manufactured home shall include all of the following:

(1)   A description of the manufactured home and all accessories included in the purchase.

(2)   The purchase price for the home and all accessories.

(3)   The amount of deposit or other payment toward or payment of the purchase price of the manufactured home and accessories that is made by the buyer.

(4)   The date the retail purchase agreement is signed.

(5)   The estimated terms of financing the purchase, if any, including the estimated interest rate, number of years financed, and monthly payment.

(6)   The buyer's signature.

(7)   The dealer's signature.

(b)   The purchase agreement shall contain, in immediate proximity to the space reserved for the signature of the buyer and in at least ten point, all upper-case Gothic type, the following statement:

"I UNDERSTAND THAT I HAVE THE RIGHT TO CANCEL THIS PURCHASE BEFORE MIDNIGHT OF THE THIRD BUSINESS DAY AFTER THE DATE THAT I HAVE SIGNED THIS AGREEMENT. I UNDERSTAND THAT THIS

CANCELLATION MUST BE IN WRITING. IF I CANCEL THE PURCHASE AFTER THE THREE-DAY PERIOD, I UNDERSTAND THAT THE DEALER MAY NOT HAVE ANY OBLIGATION TO GIVE ME BACK ALL OF THE MONEY THAT I PAID THE DEALER. I UNDERSTAND ANY CHANGE TO THE TERMS OF THE PURCHASE AGREEMENT BY THE DEALER WILL CANCEL THIS AGREEMENT."

(c) At the time the deposit or other payment toward or payment for the purchase price is received by the dealer, the dealer shall give the buyer a copy of the purchase agreement and a completed form in duplicate, captioned "Notice of Cancellation," which shall be attached to the purchase agreement, be easily detachable, and explain the buyer's right to cancel the purchase and how that right can be exercised.

(d) The dealer shall return the deposit or other payment toward or payment for the purchase price to the buyer if the buyer cancels the purchase before midnight of the third business day after the date the buyer signed the purchase agreement or if any of the material terms of the purchase agreement are changed by the dealer. To make the cancellation effective, the buyer shall give the dealer written notice of the buyer's cancellation of the purchase. The dealer shall return the deposit or other payment toward or payment for the purchase price to the buyer within seven business days, or 15 business days when payment is by personal check, after receipt of the notice of cancellation or within three business days of any change by the dealer of the purchase agreement. For purposes of this section, "business day" means any day except Sunday and legal holidays. Each time the dealer gives the buyer a new set of financing terms, unless the financing terms are more favorable to the buyer, the buyer shall be given another three-day cancellation period. The dealer shall not commence setup procedures until after the final three-day cancellation period has expired.

(e) If the buyer cancels the purchase after the three-day cancellation period, but before the sale is completed, and if:

(1) The manufactured home is in the dealer's inventory, the dealer may retain from the deposit or other payment received from the buyer actual damages up to a maximum of ten percent (10%) of the purchase price; or

(2) The manufactured home is specially ordered from the manufacturer for the buyer, the dealer may retain actual damages up to the full amount of the buyer's deposit or other payment received from the buyer.

(f) Repealed by Session Laws 2005-451, s. 5, effective April 1, 2006. (1993, c. 409, s. 7; 1999-393, s. 1; 2003-400, s. 7; 2005-451, ss. 1, 5; 2006-259, s. 24.5.)

§ 143-143.21B. Dealer cancellation; deposit refund.

A dealer shall refund to a buyer the full amount of a deposit on the purchase of a manufactured home if the buyer has fulfilled his obligations under the purchase agreement and the dealer cancels the purchase at any time. (1998-211, s. 37; 2005-451, s. 1.)

§ 143-143.22. Inspection of service records.

The Board may inspect the service records of a manufacturer, dealer, supplier or set-up contractor relating to a written warranty claim or complaint made to the Board against the manufacturer, dealer, supplier, or set-up contractor. Every licensee shall send to the Board upon request within 10 days a copy of every document or record pertinent to any complaint or claim for service. (1981, c. 952, s. 2; 1999-393, s. 1; 2005-451, s. 1.)

§ 143-143.23. Other remedies not excluded.

Nothing in this Part, rules adopted by the Board, or any action of the Board shall limit any right or remedy available to the buyer or any power or duty of the Attorney General. (1981, c. 952, s. 2; 1987, c. 429, s. 19; 1999-393, s. 1; 2005-451, s. 1.)

§ 143-143.24. Engaging in business without license a Class 1 misdemeanor.

If any person shall unlawfully act as a manufactured home manufacturer, dealer, salesperson, or set-up contractor without first obtaining a license from the Board, as provided in this Part, he shall be guilty of a Class 1 misdemeanor.

(1985, c. 487, s. 6; 1987, c. 429, s. 19; 1993, c. 539, s. 1010; 1994, Ex. Sess., c. 24, s. 14(c); 1999-393, s. 1; 2005-451, s. 1.)

§ 143-143.25. Staff support for Board.

The Manufactured Building Division of the Department shall provide clerical and other staff services required by the Board; and shall administer and enforce all provisions of this Part and all rules adopted under this Part, subject to the direction of the Board; except for powers and duties delegated by this Part to local units of government, other State agencies, or to any persons. (1991, c. 644, s. 36; 1999-393, s. 1; 2005-451, s. 1.)

§§ 143-143.26 through 143-143.49: Reserved for future codification purposes.

Part 2. Buyer Deposit, Escrow or Trust Accounts.

§ 143-143.50. Escrow or trust account required.

(a) Dealers shall maintain buyers' deposits in an escrow or trust account with a bank. A dealer shall not commingle any other funds with buyers' deposits in the escrow or trust account.

(b) Dealers shall notify the Board in writing when the escrow or trust account is established. The notification shall include the name and number of the account and the name and location of the bank holding the account.

(c) All buyer funds shall be placed in the escrow or trust account no later than the close of the third banking business day after receipt.

(d) Dealers shall provide buyers with a receipt for all buyer deposits received by the dealer. The receipt shall include the amount of the buyer deposit, the date the deposit was provided to the dealer, and the name and address of the bank where the buyer's funds will be deposited. (2005-451, s. 6.)

§ 143-143.51. Use of escrow or trust funds; penalty for violations.

(a) Buyer funds in the dealer's escrow or trust account shall be held for the benefit of the buyer and may only be used for purposes authorized under the contractual obligations of the dealer to the buyer. No buyer funds in the dealer's escrow or trust account may be used by the dealer until after all the terms set forth in G.S. 143-143.21A are finalized and after the three-day right of cancellation period as set forth in G.S. 143-143.21A has expired. The dealer may use buyer funds to complete the steps necessary for site preparation of property, when approved in writing in advance by the buyer. Buyer funds in the dealer's escrow or trust account shall be promptly returned to the buyers when the buyer is entitled to return of the funds in accordance with G.S. 143-143.21A.

(b) Notwithstanding any other provision of law and in addition to any other sanction the Board may impose under this Article, if the Board finds that a dealer has used a buyer's funds for a purpose that is not authorized under subsection (a) of this section or if the Board finds that a dealer has failed to place deposits in the dealer's escrow or trust account, the Board may fine the dealer or order restitution to the buyer in an amount up to the amount that the dealer misappropriated or failed to place in the account. (2005-451, s. 6.)

§ 143-143.52. Minimum requirements for dealer records for escrow or trust accounts at banks.

The records required for escrow or trust accounts maintained at a bank shall consist of the following and be maintained for a period of five years from the date of purchase:

(1) All bank receipts or deposit slips listing the source and date of receipt of all funds deposited in the account and the name of the buyer to whom the funds belong.

(2) All cancelled checks or other instruments drawn on the account, or printed digital images thereof furnished by the bank, showing the amount, date, and recipient of the disbursement.

(3) All instructions or authorizations to transfer, disburse, or withdraw funds from the escrow or trust account.

(4) All bank statements and other documents received from the bank with respect to the escrow or trust account, including notices of return or dishonor of any instrument drawn on the account against insufficient funds.

(5) A ledger containing a record of receipts and disbursements for each buyer from whom and for whom funds are received and showing the current balance of funds held in the escrow or trust account for each buyer. (2005-451, s. 6.)

§ 143-143.53. Accountings for escrow or trust funds.

Upon the request of the buyer, the dealer shall provide to the buyer a written accounting of the receipts and disbursements of all escrow or trust funds upon the complete disbursement of the escrow or trust accounts. (2005-451, s. 6.)

§ 143-143.54. Audits and record inspection.

All financial records required by this Part shall be subject to audit for cause and to random audit at the discretion of and by the Board, the Commissioner, or the Attorney General. The Board may inspect these records periodically, without prior notice and may also inspect these records whenever the Board determines that the records are pertinent to an investigation of any complaint against a licensee. The dealer shall provide written authorization to the bank that holds the escrow or trust account to release any and all requested information relative to the account to the parties authorized under this section to inspect those records. (2005-451, s. 6.)

Article 9B.

Uniform Standards Code For Manufactured Homes.

§ 143-144. Short title.

This Article shall be known and may be cited as "The Uniform Standards for Manufactured Homes Act." (1969, c. 961, s. 1; 1985, c. 487, s. 7; 1987, c. 429, s. 19; 1999-393, s. 2.)

§ 143-145. Definitions.

The following definitions apply in this Article:

(1) Act. - The National Manufactured Housing Construction and Safety Standards Act of 1974, 42 U.S.C. § 5401, et seq., federal regulations adopted under the Act, and any laws enacted by the United States Congress that supersede or supplement the Act.

(2) Commissioner. - The Commissioner of Insurance of the State of North Carolina or an authorized designee of the Commissioner.

(3) Repealed by Session Laws 1999-393, s. 2.

(4) HUD. - The United States Department of Housing and Urban Development or any successor agency.

(5) Inspection department. - A North Carolina city or county building inspection department authorized by Chapter 160A or Chapter 153A of the General Statutes.

(6) Label. - The form of certification required by HUD to be permanently affixed to each transportable section of each manufactured home manufactured for sale to a purchaser in the United States to indicate that the manufactured home conforms to all applicable federal construction and safety standards.

(7) Manufactured home. - A structure, transportable in one or more sections, which in the traveling mode is eight body feet or more in width, or 40 body feet or more in length, or, when erected on site, is 320 or more square feet; and which is built on a permanent chassis and designed to be used as a dwelling, with or without permanent foundation when connected to the required utilities, including the plumbing, heating, air conditioning and electrical systems contained therein. "Manufactured home" includes any structure that meets all of

the requirements of this subsection except the size requirements and with respect to which the manufacturer voluntarily files a certification required by the Secretary of HUD and complies with the standards established under the Act.

For manufactured homes built before June 15, 1976, "manufactured home" means a portable manufactured housing unit designed for transportation on its own chassis and placement on a temporary or semipermanent foundation having a measurement of over 32 feet in length and over eight feet in width. "Manufactured home" also means a double-wide manufactured home, which is two or more portable manufactured housing units designed for transportation on their own chassis that connect on site for placement on a temporary or semipermanent foundation having a measurement of over 32 feet in length and over eight feet in width.

(8) Repealed by Session Laws 1999-393, s. 2. (1969, c. 961, s. 2; 1971, c. 1172, s. 1; 1985, c. 487, s. 7; 1987, c. 429, ss. 10, 19; 1999-393, s. 2.)

§ 143-146. Statement of policy; rule-making power.

(a) Manufactured homes, because of the manner of their construction, assembly and use and that of their systems, components and appliances (including heating, plumbing and electrical systems) like other finished products having concealed vital parts may present hazards to the health, life and safety of persons and to the safety of property unless properly manufactured. In the sale of manufactured homes, there is also the possibility of defects not readily ascertainable when inspected by purchasers. It is the policy and purpose of this State to provide protection to the public against those possible hazards, and for that purpose to forbid the manufacture and sale of new manufactured homes, which are not so constructed as to provide reasonable safety and protection to their owners and users. This Article provides to the Commissioner all necessary authority to enable the State to obtain approval as a State Administrative Agency under the provisions of the Act.

(b) through (d) Repealed by Session Laws 1999-393, s. 2.

(e) The Commissioner may adopt rules to carry out the provisions of the Act and this Article, including rules for consumer complaint procedures and rules for the enforcement of the standards and regulations established and adopted by

HUD under the Act. (1969, c. 961, s. 3; 1971, c. 1172, s. 2; 1979, c. 558, ss. 5, 6; 1985, c. 487, s. 7; 1987, c. 429, ss. 11, 12, 18, 19; 1999-393, s. 2.)

§ 143-147. Structures built under previous standards.

The legal status of any structure built before the effective date of the Act shall not be affected by any changes made in this Article by the General Assembly. (1969, c. 961, s. 4; 1971, c. 1172, s. 3; 1985, c. 487, s. 7; 1987, c. 429, s. 19; 1999-393, s. 2.)

§ 143-148. Certain structures excluded from coverage.

The Commissioner may by rule provide for the exclusion of certain structures by certification in accordance with the Act. (1969, c. 961, s. 5; 1971, c. 1172, s. 4; 1979, c. 558, s. 3; 1987, c. 429, s. 13; 1999-393, s. 2.)

§ 143-149. Necessity for obtaining label for purposes of sale.

No person shall sell or offer for sale any manufactured home in this State that does not have a label. It is a defense to any prosecution for a violation of this section if a person shows that a certificate of title for the manufactured home as required by G.S. 20-52 was obtained before June 15, 1976, or produces other satisfactory evidence on file with the North Carolina Division of Motor Vehicles that the manufactured home was manufactured before June 15, 1976. (1971, c. 1172, s. 5; 1985, c. 487, s. 7; 1999-393, s. 2.)

§ 143-150. No electricity to be furnished units not in compliance.

It is unlawful for any person to furnish electricity for use in any manufactured home without first ascertaining that the manufactured home and its electrical supply has been inspected pursuant to G.S. 143-139 by the inspection authority having jurisdiction and found to comply with the requirements of the State Electrical Code. The certificate of compliance issued by the inspection jurisdiction shall be accepted as evidence of compliance. (1971, c. 1172, s. 6; 1985, c. 487, s. 7; 1993, c. 504, s. 35; 1999-393, s. 2.)

§ 143-151. Penalties.

(a) Any person who is found by the Commissioner to have violated the provisions of the Act, this Article, or any rules adopted under this Article, shall be liable for a civil penalty not to exceed one thousand dollars ($1,000) for each violation. Each violation shall constitute a separate violation for each manufactured home or for each failure or refusal to allow or perform an act required by the Act, this Article, or any rules adopted under this Article. The maximum civil penalty may not exceed one million dollars ($1,000,000) for any related series of violations occurring within one year after the date of the first violation. In determining the amount of the penalty, the Commissioner shall consider the degree and extent of harm caused by the violation, the amount of money that inured to the benefit of the violator as a result of the violation, whether the violation was willful, and the prior record of the violator in complying or failing to comply with laws, rules, or orders applicable to the violator. The clear proceeds of civil penalties provided for in this section shall be remitted to the Civil Penalty and Forfeiture Fund in accordance with G.S. 115C-457.2.

(b) Any individual, or a director, officer or agent of a corporation who knowingly and willfully violates the Act, this Article, or any rules adopted under this Article in a manner that threatens the health or safety of any purchaser is guilty of a Class I felony. (1971, c. 1172, s. 7; 1979, c. 558, s. 1; 1985, c. 487, s. 7; 1987, c. 429, s. 19; 1993, c. 539, s. 1011; 1994, Ex. Sess., c. 24, s. 14(c); 1998-215, s. 93; 1999-393, s. 2.)

§ 143-151.1. Enforcement.

The Commissioner may initiate any appropriate action or proceeding to prevent, restrain, or correct any violation of the Act, this Article, or any rules adopted under this Article. The Commissioner, or any of his deputies or employees, upon showing proper credentials and in the discharge of their duties under this Article, or the Act, is authorized at reasonable hours and without advance notice to enter and inspect all factories, warehouses, or establishments in this State in which manufactured homes are manufactured, stored or held for sale. (1971, c.

1172, s. 8; 1979, c. 558, s. 2; 1985, c. 487, s. 7; 1987, c. 429, ss. 15, 18, 19; 1999-393, s. 2.)

§ 143-151.2. Fees.

(a) The Commissioner shall establish a monitoring inspection fee in an amount required by the Secretary of HUD. This monitoring inspection fee shall be an amount paid by each manufactured home manufacturer in this State for each manufactured home produced by the manufacturer in this State.

(b) The monitoring inspection fee shall be paid by the manufacturer to the Secretary of HUD or the Secretary's agent. (1979, c. 558, s. 4; 1985, c. 487, s. 7; 1987, c. 429, s. 18; 1999-393, s. 2.)

§ 143-151.3. Reports.

Each manufacturer, distributor, and dealer of manufactured homes shall establish and maintain such records, make such reports, and provide such information as the Commissioner or the Secretary of HUD may reasonably require to be able to determine whether the manufacturer, distributor, or dealer has acted or is acting in compliance with this Article, or the Act and shall, upon request of a person designated by the Commissioner or the Secretary of HUD, permit the person to inspect appropriate books, papers, records and documents relevant to determining whether the manufacturer, distributor, or dealer has acted or is acting in compliance with this Article or the Act, and any rules adopted by the Commissioner under this Article. (1979, c. 558, s. 4; 1985, c. 487, s. 7; 1987, c. 429, ss. 18, 19; 1999-393, s. 2.)

§ 143-151.4. Notification of defects and correction procedures.

Every manufacturer of manufactured homes shall provide for notification and correction procedures in any manufactured home produced by the manufacturer in accordance with the Act, this Article, and any rules adopted by the Commissioner. (1979, c. 558, s. 4; 1985, c. 487, s. 7; 1987, c. 429, s. 14; 1999-393, s. 2.)

§ 143-151.5. Prohibited acts.

(a) No person shall:

(1) Manufacture for sale, lease, sell, offer for sale or lease, or introduce or deliver, or import into the United States, any manufactured home that is manufactured on or after the effective date of any applicable manufactured home construction and safety standard under the Act or this Article and that does not comply with the standard, except as provided in subsections (b), (c), and (d) of this section.

(2) Fail or refuse to permit access to or copying of records, or fail to make reports or provide information, or fail or refuse to permit entry or inspection, as required under the Act or this Article.

(3) Fail to furnish notification of any defect as required by the Act or this Article.

(4) Fail to issue a label or issue a label if the person in the exercise of due care has reason to know that the label is false or misleading in a material respect.

(5) Fail to comply with a rule adopted or an order issued by the Commissioner under this Article.

(6) Issue a certification pursuant to G.S. 143-148 if the person in the exercise of due care has reason to know that the certification is false or misleading in a material respect.

(b) (1) Subdivision (a)(1) of this section does not apply to the sale, the offer for sale, or the introduction or delivery of any manufactured home after the first purchase of it in good faith for purposes other than resale.

(2) Subdivision (a)(1) of this section does not apply to any person who establishes that he did not have reason to know in the exercise of due care that the manufactured home was not in conformity with applicable manufactured home construction and safety standards.

(c) Subdivision (a)(1) of this section shall not apply to any person who, before the first purchase, holds a certificate of compliance issued by the manufacturer or importer of the manufactured home to the effect that the manufactured home conforms to all applicable manufactured home construction and safety standards, unless the person knows that the manufactured home does not so conform. (1979, c. 558, s. 4; 1985, c. 487, s. 7; 1987, c. 429, ss. 16, 19; 1999-393, s. 2.)

§ 143-151.6. Reserved for future codification purposes.

§ 143-151.7. Reserved for future codification purposes.

Article 9C.

North Carolina Code Officials Qualification Board.

§ 143-151.8. Definitions.

(a)   As used in this Article, unless the context otherwise requires:

(1)   "Board" means the North Carolina Code Officials Qualification Board.

(2)   "Code" means the North Carolina State Building Code and related local building rules approved by the Building Code Council enacted, adopted or approved under G.S. 143-138, any resolution adopted by a federally recognized Indian Tribe under G.S. 153A-350.1 in which the Tribe adopts the North Carolina State Building Code and related local building rules, and the standards adopted by the Commissioner of Insurance under G.S. 143-143.15(a).

(3)   "Code enforcement" means the examination and approval of plans and specifications, or the inspection of the manner of construction, workmanship, and materials for construction of buildings and structures and components thereof, or the enforcement of fire code regulations as an employee of the State or local government or as an employee of a federally recognized Indian Tribe employed to perform inspections on tribal lands under G.S. 153A-350.1, as an individual contracting with the State or a local government or a federally recognized Indian Tribe who performs inspections on tribal lands under G.S. 153A-350.1 to conduct inspections, or as an individual who is employed by a company contracting with a county or a city to conduct inspections, except an employee of the State Department of Labor engaged in the administration and enforcement of those sections of the Code which pertain to boilers and

elevators, to assure compliance with the State Building Code and related local building rules.

(4) "Local inspection department" means the agency or agencies of local government, or any government agency of a federally recognized Indian Tribe under G.S. 153A-350.1, with authority to make inspections of buildings and to enforce the Code and other laws, ordinances, and rules enacted by the State and the local government or a federally recognized Indian Tribe under G.S. 153A-350.1, which establish standards and requirements applicable to the construction, alteration, repair, or demolition of buildings, and conditions that may create hazards of fire, explosion, or related hazards.

(5) "Qualified Code-enforcement official" means a person qualified under this Article to engage in the practice of Code enforcement.

(b) For purposes of this Article, the population of a city or county shall be determined according to the most current federal census, unless otherwise specified. (1977, c. 531, s. 1; 1987, c. 827, ss. 224, 225; 1989, c. 681, s. 15; 1993, c. 232, s. 4.1; 1999-78, s. 2; 1999-372, s. 5; 2001-421, s. 2.4.)

§ 143-151.9. North Carolina Code Officials Qualification Board established; members; terms; vacancies.

(a) There is hereby established the North Carolina Code Officials Qualification Board in the Department of Insurance. The Board shall be composed of 20 members appointed as follows:

(1) One member who is a city or county manager;

(2) Two members, one of whom is an elected official representing a city over 5,000 population and one of whom is an elected official representing a city under 5,000 population;

(3) Two members, one of whom is an elected official representing a county over 40,000 population and one of whom is an elected official representing a county under 40,000 population;

(4) Two members serving as building officials with the responsibility for administering building, plumbing, electrical and heating codes, one of whom serves a county and one of whom serves a city;

(5) One member who is a registered architect;

(6) One member who is a registered engineer;

(7) Two members who are licensed general contractors, at least one of whom specializes in residential construction;

(8) One member who is a licensed electrical contractor;

(9) One member who is a licensed plumbing or heating contractor;

(10) One member selected from the faculty of the North Carolina State University School of Engineering and one member selected from the faculty of the School of Engineering of the North Carolina Agricultural and Technical State University;

(11) One member selected from the faculty of the School of Government at the University of North Carolina at Chapel Hill;

(12) One member selected from the Community Colleges System Office;

(13) One member selected from the Division of Engineering and Building Codes in the Department of Insurance; and,

(14) One member who is a local government fire prevention inspector and one member who is a citizen of the State.

The various categories shall be appointed as follows: (1), (2), (3), and (14) by the Governor; (4), (5), and (6) by the General Assembly upon the recommendation of the President Pro Tempore in accordance with G.S. 120-121; (7), (8), and (9) by the General Assembly upon the recommendation of the Speaker of the House of Representatives in accordance with G.S. 120-121; (10) by the deans of the respective schools of engineering of the named universities; (11) by the Dean of the School of Government at the University of North Carolina at Chapel Hill; (12) by the President of the Community Colleges System; and (13) by the Commissioner of Insurance.

(b) The members shall be appointed for staggered terms and the initial appointments shall be made prior to September 1, 1977, and the appointees shall hold office until July 1 of the year in which their respective terms expire and until their successors are appointed and qualified as provided hereafter:

For the terms of one year: the members from subdivisions (1), (6) and (10) of subsection (a), and one member from subdivision (3).

For the terms of two years: the member from subdivision (11) of subsection (a), one member from subdivision (2), one member from subdivision (4), one member from subdivision (7), and one member from subdivision (14).

For the terms of three years: the members from subdivisions (8) and (12) of subsection (a), one member from subdivision (2), one member from subdivision (4), and one member from subdivision (14).

For the terms of four years: the members from subdivisions (5), (9) and (13) of subsection (a), one member from subdivision (3), and one member from subdivision (7).

Thereafter, as the term of each member expires, his successor shall be appointed for a term of four years. Notwithstanding the appointments for a term of years, each member shall serve at the will of the Governor.

Members of the Board who are public officers shall serve ex officio and shall perform their duties on the Board in addition to the duties of their office.

(c) Vacancies in the Board occurring for any reason shall be filled for the unexpired term by the person making the appointment. (1977, c. 531, s. 1; 1987, c. 564, s. 28; 1989, c. 681, s. 16; 1995, c. 490, s. 12(a); 1999-84, s. 22; 2006-264, s. 29(m).)

§ 143-151.10. Compensation.

Members of the Board who are State officers or employees shall receive no salary for serving on the Board, but shall be reimbursed for their expenses in accordance with G.S. 138-6. Members of the Board who are full-time salaried public officers or employees other than State officers or employees shall receive no salary for serving on the Board, but shall be reimbursed for subsistence and travel expenses in accordance with G.S. 138-5(a)(2) and (3). All other members of the Board shall receive compensation and reimbursement for expenses in accordance with G.S. 138-5(a). (1977, c. 531, s. 1.)

§ 143-151.11. Chairman; vice-chairman; other officers; meetings; reports.

(a)   The members of the Board shall select one of their members as chairman upon its creation, and shall select the chairman each July 1 thereafter.

(b)   The Board shall select a vice-chairman and such other officers and committee chairmen from among its members, as it deems desirable, at the first regular meeting of the Board after its creation and at the first regular meeting after July 1 of each year thereafter. Provided, nothing in this subsection shall prevent the creation or abolition of committees or offices of the Board, other than the office of vice-chairman, as the need may arise at any time during the year.

(c)   The Board shall hold at least four regular meetings per year upon the call of the chairman. Special meetings shall be held upon the call of the chairman or the vice-chairman, or upon the written request of four members of the Board.

(d)   The activities and recommendations of the Board with respect to standards for Code officials training and certification shall be set forth in regular and special reports made by the Board. Additionally, the Board shall present special reports and recommendations to the Governor or the General Assembly, or both, as the need may arise or as the Governor or the General Assembly may request. (1977, c. 531, s. 1.)

§ 143-151.12. Powers.

In addition to powers conferred upon the Board elsewhere in this Article, the Board shall have the power to:

(1)   Adopt rules necessary to administer this Article;

(1a) Require State agencies, local inspection departments, and local governing bodies to submit reports and information about the employment, education, and training of Code-enforcement officials;

(2) Establish minimum standards for employment as a Code-enforcement official: (i) in probationary or temporary status, and (ii) in permanent positions;

(3) Certify persons as being qualified under the provisions of this Article to be Code-enforcement officials, including persons employed by a federally recognized Indian Tribe to perform inspections on tribal lands under G.S. 153A-350.1;

(4) Consult and cooperate with counties, municipalities, agencies of this State, other governmental agencies, and with universities, colleges, junior colleges, community colleges and other institutions concerning the development of Code-enforcement training schools and programs or courses of instruction;

(5) Establish minimum standards and levels of education or equivalent experience for all Code-enforcement instructors, teachers or professors;

(6) Conduct and encourage research by public and private agencies which shall be designed to improve education and training in the administration of Code enforcement;

(7) Adopt and amend bylaws, consistent with law, for its internal management and control; appoint such advisory committees as it may deem necessary; and enter into contracts and do such other things as may be necessary and incidental to the exercise of its authority pursuant to this Article; and,

(8) Make recommendations concerning any matters within its purview pursuant to this Article. (1977, c. 531, s. 1; 1987, c. 564, s. 15; c. 827, s. 226; 1999-78, s. 3.)

§ 143-151.13. Required standards and certificates for Code-enforcement officials.

(a) No person shall engage in Code enforcement under this Article unless that person possesses one of the following types of certificates, currently valid, issued by the Board attesting to that person's qualifications to engage in Code enforcement: (i) a standard certificate; (ii) a limited certificate provided for in subsection (c) of this section; or (iii) a probationary certificate provided for in subsection (d) of this section. To obtain a standard certificate, a person must pass an examination, as prescribed by the Board or by a contracting party under G.S. 143-151.16(d), that is based on the North Carolina State Building Code and administrative procedures required for Code enforcement. The Board may issue a standard certificate of qualification to each person who successfully completes the examination. The certificate authorizes that person to engage in Code enforcement and to practice as a qualified Code-enforcement official in North Carolina. The certificate of qualification shall bear the signatures of the chairman and secretary of the Board.

(b) The Board shall issue one or more standard certificates to each Code-enforcement official demonstrating the qualifications set forth in subsection (b1) of this section. Standard certificates are available for each of the following types of qualified Code-enforcement officials:

(1) Building inspector.

(2) Electrical inspector.

(3) Mechanical inspector.

(4) Plumbing inspector.

(5) Fire inspector.

(b1) The holder of a standard certificate may practice Code enforcement only within the inspection area and level described upon the certificate issued by the Board. A Code-enforcement official may qualify and hold one or more certificates. These certificates may be for different levels in different types of positions as defined in this section and in rules adopted by the Board.

(b2) A Code-enforcement official holding a certificate indicating a specified level of proficiency in a particular type of position may hold a position calling for that type of qualification anywhere in the State. With respect to all types of Code-enforcement officials, those with Level I, Level II, or Level III certificates shall be qualified to inspect and approve only those types and sizes of buildings as specified in rules adopted by the Board.

(c) A Code-enforcement official holding office as of the date specified in this subsection for the county or municipality by which he is employed, shall not be required to possess a standard certificate as a condition of tenure or continued employment but shall be required to complete such in-service training as may be prescribed by the Board. At the earliest practicable date, such official shall receive from the Board a limited certificate qualifying him to engage in Code enforcement at the level, in the particular type of position, and within the governmental jurisdiction in which he is employed. The limited certificate shall be valid only as an authorization for the official to continue in the position he held on the applicable date and shall become invalid if he does not complete in-service training within two years following the applicable date in the schedule below, according to the governmental jurisdiction's population as published in the 1970 U.S. Census:

Counties and Municipalities over 75,000 population - July 1, 1979

Counties and Municipalities between 50,001 and 75,000 - July 1, 1981

Counties and Municipalities between 25,001 and 50,000 - July 1, 1983

Counties and Municipalities 25,000 and under - July 1, 1985

All fire prevention inspectors holding office - July 1, 1989. Fire prevention inspectors have until July 1, 1993, to complete in-service training.

An official holding a limited certificate can be promoted to a position requiring a higher level certificate only upon issuance by the Board of a standard certificate or probationary certificate appropriate for such new position.

(d) The Board may provide for the issuance of probationary or temporary certificates valid for such period (not less than one year nor more than three years) as specified by the Board's rules, or until June 30, 1983, whichever is later, to any Code-enforcement official newly employed or newly promoted who lacks the qualifications prescribed by the Board as prerequisite to applying for a standard certificate under subsection (a). No official may have a probationary or temporary certificate extended beyond the specified period by renewal or otherwise. The Board may provide for appropriate levels of probationary or temporary certificates and may issue these certificates with such special conditions or requirements relating to the place of employment of the person holding the certificate, his supervision on a consulting or advisory basis, or other matters as the Board may deem necessary to protect the public safety and health.

(e) The Board shall, without requiring an examination, issue a standard certificate to any person who is currently certified as a county electrical inspector pursuant to G.S. 153A-351. The certificate issued by the Board shall authorize the person to serve at the electrical inspector level approved by the Commissioner of Insurance in G.S. 153A-351.

(f) The Board shall issue a standard certificate to any person who is currently licensed to practice as a(n):

(1) Architect, registered pursuant to Chapter 83A;

(2) General contractor, licensed pursuant to Article 1 of Chapter 87;

(3) Plumbing or heating contractor, licensed pursuant to Article 2 of Chapter 87;

(4) Electrical contractor, licensed pursuant to Article 4 of Chapter 87; or,

(5) Professional engineer, registered pursuant to Chapter 89C;

provided the person successfully completes a short course, as prescribed by the Board, relating to the State Building Code regulations and Code-enforcement administration. The standard certificate shall authorize the person to practice as a qualified Code-enforcement official in a particular type of position at the level determined by the Board, based on the type of license or registration held in any profession specified above. (1977, c. 531, s. 1; 1979, cc. 521, 829; 1983, c. 90; 1987, c. 827, ss. 225, 227; 1989, c. 681, s. 17; 1989 (Reg. Sess., 1990), c. 1021, s. 5; 1991, c. 133, s. 1; 2007-120, s. 1; 2008-124, s. 8.1.)

§ 143-151.13A. Professional development program for officials.

(a) As used in this section, "official" means a qualified Code-enforcement official as that term is defined in G.S. 143-151.8.

(b) The Board may establish professional development requirements for officials as a condition of the renewal or reactivation of their certificates. The purposes of these professional development requirements are to assist officials in maintaining professional competence in their enforcement of the Code and to assure the health, safety, and welfare of the citizens of North Carolina. An official subject to this section shall present evidence to the Board at each certificate renewal after initial certification, that during the 12 months before the certificate expiration date, the official has completed the required number of credit hours in courses approved by the Board. Annual continuing education hour requirements shall be determined by the Board but shall not be more than six credit hours.

(c) The Board may require an individual who earns a certificate under programs established in G.S. 143-151.13 to complete professional development courses, not to exceed six hours in each technical area of certification, within one year after that individual is first employed by a city or county inspection department.

(d) As a condition of reactivating a standard or limited certificate, the Board may require the completion of professional development courses within one year after reemployment as an official as follows:

(1) An individual who has been on inactive status for more than two years and who has not been continuously employed by a city or county inspection department during the period of inactive status shall complete professional development courses not to exceed 12 hours for each technical area in which the individual is certified.

(2) An individual who has been on inactive status for more than two years and who has been continuously employed by a city or county inspection department during the period of inactive status shall complete professional development courses not to exceed six hours for each technical area in which the individual is certified.

(3) An individual who has been on inactive status for two years or less shall complete professional development courses not to exceed four hours for each technical area in which the individual is certified.

(e) The Board may, for good cause shown, grant extensions of time to officials to comply with these requirements. An official who, after obtaining an extension under this subsection, offers evidence satisfactory to the Board that the official has satisfactorily completed the required professional development courses, is in compliance with this section.

(f)   The Board may adopt rules to implement this section, including rules that govern:

(1)   The content and subject matter of professional development courses.

(2)   The criteria, standards, and procedures for the approval of courses, course sponsors, and course instructors.

(3)   The methods of instruction.

(4)   The computation of course credit.

(5)   The ability to carry-forward course credit from one year to another.

(6)   The waiver of or variance from the professional development required for hardship or other reasons.

(7)   The procedures for compliance and sanctions for noncompliance. (2005-102, s. 1.)

§ 143-151.14. Comity.

The Board may, without requiring an examination, grant a standard certificate as a qualified Code-enforcement official for a particular type of position and level to any person who, at the time of application, is certified as a qualified Code-enforcement official by a similar board of another state, district or territory where standards are acceptable to the Board and not lower than those required by this Article. A fee of not more than twenty dollars ($20.00), as determined by the Board, must be paid by the applicant to the Board for the issuance of a certificate under the provisions of this section. The provisions of G.S. 143-151.16(b) relating to renewal fees and late renewals shall apply to every person granted a standard certificate in accordance with this section. (1977, c. 531, s. 1; 2007-120, s. 2.)

§ 143-151.15. Return of certificate to Board; reissuance by Board.

A certificate issued by the Board under this Article is valid as long as the person certified is employed by the State of North Carolina or any political subdivision thereof as a Code-enforcement official, or is employed by a federally recognized Indian Tribe to perform inspections on tribal lands under G.S. 153A-350.1 as a Code-enforcement official. When the person certified leaves that employment for any reason, he shall return the certificate to the Board. If the person subsequently obtains employment as a Code-enforcement official in any governmental jurisdiction described above, the Board may reissue the certificate to him. The provisions of G.S. 143-151.16(b) relating to renewal fees and late renewals shall apply, if appropriate. The provisions of G.S. 143-151.16(c) shall not apply. This section does not affect the Board's powers under G.S. 143-151.17. (1977, c. 531, s. 1; 1993 (Reg. Sess., 1994), c. 678, s. 35; 1999-78, s. 4.)

§ 143-151.16. Certification fees; renewal of certificates; examination fees.

(a) The Board shall establish a schedule of fees to be paid by each applicant for certification as a qualified Code-enforcement official. Such fee shall not exceed twenty dollars ($20.00) for each applicant.

(b) A certificate, other than a probationary certificate, as a qualified Code-enforcement official issued pursuant to the provisions of this Article must be renewed annually on or before the first day of July. Each application for renewal must be accompanied by a renewal fee to be determined by the Board, but not to exceed ten dollars ($10.00). The Board is authorized to charge an extra four dollar ($4.00) late renewal fee for renewals made after the first day of July each year.

(c) Any person who fails to renew his certificate for a period of two consecutive years may be required by the Board to take and pass the same examination as unlicensed applicants before allowing such person to renew his certificate.

(d) The Board may contract with persons for the development and administration of the examinations required by G.S. 143-151.13(a), for course development related to the examinations, for review of a particular applicant's examination, and for other related services. The person with whom the Board contracts may charge applicants a reasonable fee for the costs associated with the development and administration of the examinations, for course development related to the examinations, for review of the applicant's examinations, and for other related services. The fee shall be agreed to by the Board and the other contracting party. The amount of the fee under this subsection shall not exceed one hundred seventy-five dollars ($175.00). Contracts for the development and administration of the examinations, for course development related to the examinations, and for review of examinations shall not be subject to Article 3, 3C, or 8 of Chapter 143 of the General Statutes or to Article 3D of Chapter 147 of the General Statutes. However, the Board shall: (i) submit all proposed contracts for supplies, materials, printing, equipment, and contractual services that exceed one million dollars ($1,000,000) authorized by this subsection to the Attorney General or the Attorney General's designee for review as provided in G.S. 114-8.3; and (ii) include in all proposed contracts to be awarded by the Board under this subsection a standard clause which provides that the State Auditor and internal auditors of the Board may audit the records of the contractor during and after the term of the contract to verify accounts and data affecting fees and performance. The Board shall not award a cost plus percentage of cost agreement or contract for any purpose. (1977, c. 531, s. 1; 2005-289, s. 1; 2008-124, s. 8.2; 2009-451, s. 21.3; 2010-194, s. 25; 2011-326, s. 15(z).)

§ 143-151.17. Grounds for disciplinary actions; investigation; administrative procedures.

(a) The Board shall have the power to suspend any or all certificates, revoke any or all certificates, demote any or all certificates to a lower level, or refuse to grant any certificate issued under the provisions of this Article to any person who:

(1) Has been convicted of a felony against this State or the United States, or convicted of a felony in another state that would also be a felony if it had been committed in this State;

(2) Has obtained certification through fraud, deceit, or perjury;

(3) Has knowingly aided or abetted any person practicing contrary to the provisions of this Article or the State Building Code or any building codes adopted by a federally recognized Indian Tribe under G.S. 153A-350.1;

(4) Has defrauded the public or attempted to do so;

(5) Has affixed his signature to a report of inspection or other instrument of service if no inspection has been made by him or under his immediate and responsible direction; or,

(6) Has been guilty of willful misconduct, gross negligence or gross incompetence.

(b) The Board may investigate the actions of any qualified Code-enforcement official or applicant upon the verified complaint in writing of any person alleging a violation of subsection (a) of this section. The Board may suspend, revoke, or demote to a lower level any certificate of any qualified Code-enforcement official and refuse to grant a certificate to any applicant, whom it finds to have been guilty of one or more of the actions set out in subsection (a) as grounds for disciplinary action.

(c) A denial, suspension, revocation, or demotion to a lower level of a certificate issued under this Article shall be made in accordance with Chapter 150B of the General Statutes.

(d) The Board may deny an application for a certificate for any of the grounds that are described in subsection (a) of this section. Within 30 days after receipt of a notification that an application for a certificate has been denied, the applicant may make a written request for a review by a committee designated by the chairman of the Board to determine the reasonableness of the Board's action. The review shall be completed without undue delay, and the applicant shall be notified promptly in writing as to the outcome of the review. Within 30 days after service of the notification as to the outcome, the applicant may make a written request for a hearing under Article 3A of Chapter 150B of the General Statutes if the applicant disagrees with the outcome.

(e) The provisions of this section shall apply to Code-enforcement officials and applicants who are employed or seek to be employed by a federally recognized Indian Tribe to perform inspections on tribal lands under G.S. 153A-350.1. (1977, c. 531, s. 1; 1987, c. 827, s. 228; 1993, c. 504, s. 36; 1993 (Reg. Sess., 1994), c. 678, s. 36; 1999-78, s. 5; 2007-120, s. 3.)

§ 143-151.18. Violations; penalty; injunction.

On and after July 1, 1979, it shall be unlawful for any person to represent himself as a qualified Code-enforcement official who does not hold a currently valid certificate of qualification issued by the Board. Further, it shall be unlawful for any person to practice Code enforcement except as allowed by any currently valid certificate issued to that person by the Board. Any person violating any of the provisions of this Article shall be guilty of a Class 1 misdemeanor. The Board is authorized to apply to any judge of the superior court for an injunction in order to prevent any violation or threatened violation of the provisions of this Article. (1977, c. 531, s. 1; 1993, c. 539, s. 1012; 1994, Ex. Sess., c. 24, s. 14(c); 2007-120, s. 4.)

§ 143-151.19. Administration.

(a)   The Division of Engineering and Building Codes in the Department of Insurance shall provide clerical and other staff services required by the Board, and shall administer and enforce all provisions of this Article and all rules promulgated pursuant to this Article, subject to the direction of the Board, except as delegated by this Article to local units of government, other State agencies, corporations, or individuals.

(b)   The Board shall make copies of this Article and the rules adopted under this Article available to the public at a price determined by the Board.

(c)   The Board shall keep current a record of the names and addresses of all qualified Code-enforcement officials and additional personal data as the Board deems necessary. The Board annually shall publish a list of all currently certified Code-enforcement officials.

(d)   Each certificate issued by the Board shall contain such identifying information as the Board requires.

(e)   The Board shall issue a duplicate certificate to practice as a qualified Code-enforcement official in place of one which has been lost, destroyed, or mutilated upon proper application and payment of a fee to be determined by the Board. (1977, c. 531, s. 1; 1987, c. 827, ss. 224, 229.)

§ 143-151.20. Donations and appropriations.

(a) In addition to appropriations made by the General Assembly, the Board may accept for any of its purposes and functions under this Article any and all donations, both real and personal, and grants of money from any governmental unit or public agency, or from any institution, person, firm or corporation, and may receive, utilize, disburse and transfer the same, subject to the approval of the Council of State. Any arrangements pursuant to this section shall be detailed in the next regular report of the Board. Such report shall include the identity of the donor, the nature of the transaction, and the conditions, if any. Any moneys received by the Board pursuant to this section shall be deposited in the State treasury to the account of the Board.

(b) The Board may provide grants as a reimbursement for actual expenses incurred by the State or political subdivision thereof for the provisions of training programs of officials from other jurisdictions within the State. The Board, by rules, shall provide for the administration of the grant program authorized herein. In promulgating such rules, the Board shall promote the most efficient and economical program of Code-enforcement training, including the maximum utilization of existing facilities and programs for the purpose of avoiding duplication. (1977, c. 531, s. 1; 1987, c. 827, s. 224.)

§ 143-151.21. Disposition of fees.

Fees collected by the Commissioner under this Article shall be credited to the Insurance Regulatory Fund created under G.S. 58-6-25. (1991, c. 689, s. 295; 2003-221, s. 10.)

§§ 143-151.22 through 143-151.25. Reserved for future codification purposes.

Article 9D.

Enforcement of Building Code Insulation and Energy Utilization Standards.

§§ 143-151.26 through 143-151.41. Repealed by Session Laws 1999-393, s. 3, effective August 4, 1999.

Article 9E.

Master Electrical and Natural Gas Meters Prohibited.

§ 143-151.42. Prohibition of master meters for electric and natural gas service.

(a)   From and after September 1, 1977, in order that each occupant of an apartment or other individual dwelling unit may be responsible for his own conservation of electricity and gas, it shall be unlawful for any new residential building, as hereinafter defined, to be served by a master meter for electric service or natural gas service. Each individual dwelling unit shall have individual electric service with a separate electric meter and, if it has natural gas, individual natural gas service with a separate natural gas meter, which service and meters shall be in the name of the tenant or other occupant of said apartment or other dwelling unit. No electric supplier or natural gas supplier, whether regulated public utility or municipal corporation or electric membership corporation supplying said utility service, shall connect any residential building for electric service or natural gas service through a master meter, and said electric or natural gas supplier shall serve each said apartment or dwelling unit by separate service and separate meter and shall bill and charge each individual occupant of said separate apartment or dwelling unit for said electric or natural gas service. A new residential building is hereby defined for the purposes of this section as any building for which a building permit is issued on or after September 1, 1977, which includes two or more apartments or other family dwelling units. Provided, however, that any owner or builder of a multi-unit residential building who desires to provide central heat or air conditioning or central hot water from a central furnace, air conditioner or hot water heater which incorporates solar assistance or other designs which accomplish greater energy conservation than separate heat, hot water, or air conditioning for each dwelling unit, may apply to the North Carolina Utilities Commission for approval of said central heat, air conditioning or hot water system, which may include a central meter for electricity or gas used in said central system, and the Utilities Commission shall promptly consider said application and approve it for such central meters if energy is conserved by said design. This section shall apply to any dwelling unit normally rented or leased for a minimum period of one month or longer, including apartments, condominiums and townhouses, but shall not apply to hotels, motels, hotels or motels that have been converted into condominiums, dormitories, rooming houses or nursing homes, or homes for the elderly.

(b) The provisions of this section requiring that service and meters for each individual dwelling unit be in the name of the tenant or other occupant of the apartment or other dwelling unit shall not apply in either of the following circumstances:

(1) The Utilities Commission has approved an application under G.S. 62-110(h).

(2) The tenant and landlord have agreed in the lease that the cost of the electric service or natural gas service or both shall be included in the rental payments and the service shall be in the name of the landlord. (1977, c. 792, s. 9; 2007-98, s. 1; 2011-252, s. 5; 2013-168, s. 1.)

Article 9F.

North Carolina Home Inspector Licensure Board.

§ 143-151.43. Short title.

This Article is the Home Inspector Licensure Act and may be cited by that name. (1993 (Reg. Sess., 1994), c. 724, s. 1.)

§ 143-151.44. Purpose.

This Article safeguards the public health, safety, and welfare and protects the public from being harmed by unqualified persons by regulating the use of the title "Licensed Home Inspector" and by providing for the licensure and regulation of those who perform home inspections for compensation. (1993 (Reg. Sess., 1994), c. 724, s. 1.)

§ 143-151.45. Definitions.

The following definitions apply in this Article:

(1) (Effective until October 1, 2013) Associate home inspector. - An individual who is affiliated with or employed by a licensed home inspector to conduct a home inspection of a residential building on behalf of the licensed home inspector.

(2) Board. - The North Carolina Home Inspector Licensure Board.

(3) Compensation. - A fee or anything else of value.

(4) Home inspection. - A written evaluation of two or more of the following components of a residential building: heating system, cooling system, plumbing system, electrical system, structural components, foundation, roof, masonry structure, exterior and interior components, or any other related residential housing component.

(5) Home inspector. - An individual who engages in the business of performing home inspections for compensation.

(6) Residential building. - A structure intended to be, or that is in fact, used as a residence by one or more individuals. (1993 (Reg. Sess., 1994), c. 724, s. 1; 1998-211, s. 33; 2009-509, s. 3.3.)

§ 143-151.46. North Carolina Home Inspector Licensure Board established; members; terms; vacancies.

(a) Membership. - The North Carolina Home Inspector Licensure Board is established in the Department of Insurance. The Board shall be composed of the Commissioner of Insurance or the Commissioner's designee and seven additional members appointed as follows:

(1) A public member who is not actively engaged in one of the professional categories in subdivisions (2) through (4) of this subsection, appointed by the General Assembly upon the recommendation of the Speaker of the House of Representatives.

(2) Four home inspectors, two of whom shall be appointed by the General Assembly upon the recommendation of the President Pro Tempore of the Senate, one of whom shall be appointed by the General Assembly upon the

recommendation of the Speaker of the House of Representatives, and one of whom shall be appointed by the Governor.

(3)   A licensed general contractor appointed by the Governor upon the recommendation of the North Carolina Home Builders Association.

(4)   A licensed real estate broker appointed by the Governor upon the recommendation of the North Carolina Association of Realtors.

All members of the Board must be citizens of the State. Appointments by the General Assembly must be made in accordance with G.S. 120-121.

(b)   Terms. - The members shall be appointed for staggered terms and the initial appointments shall be made prior to August 1, 1995. The appointees shall hold office until July 1 of the year in which their respective terms expire and until their successors are appointed and qualified.

Of the members initially appointed, the home inspector appointed by the Governor shall serve a one-year term. The home inspector appointed by the General Assembly upon the recommendation of the Speaker of the House of Representatives and the licensed real estate broker shall serve two-year terms. One home inspector appointed by the General Assembly upon the recommendation of the President Pro Tempore of the Senate and the licensed contractor shall serve three-year terms. The remaining home inspector appointed by the General Assembly upon the recommendation of the President Pro Tempore of the Senate and the citizen of the State shall serve four-year terms.

Thereafter, as the term of each member expires, a successor shall be appointed for a term of four years.

(c)   Vacancies. - Vacancies in the Board occurring for any reason shall be filled for the unexpired term by the appointing official making the original appointment. Vacancies in positions appointed by the General Assembly upon the recommendation of the President Pro Tempore of the Senate or the Speaker of the House of Representatives shall be filled in accordance with G.S. 120-122. (1993 (Reg. Sess., 1994), c. 724, s. 1; 2011-412, s. 6.)

§ 143-151.47. Compensation of Board members.

Members of the Board shall receive no salary for serving on the Board. Members may be reimbursed for their travel and other expenses in accordance with G.S. 93B-5 but may not receive the per diem authorized by that statute. (1993 (Reg. Sess., 1994), c. 724, s. 1.)

§ 143-151.48. Election of officers; meetings of Board.

(a) Officers. - Within 30 days after making appointments to the Board, the Governor shall call the first meeting of the Board. The Board shall elect a chair and a vice-chair who shall hold office according to rules adopted by the Board.

(b) Meetings. - The Board shall hold at least two regular meetings each year as provided by rules adopted by the Board. The Board may hold additional meetings upon the call of the chair or any two Board members. A majority of the Board membership constitutes a quorum. (1993 (Reg. Sess., 1994), c. 724, s. 1.)

§ 143-151.49. Powers and responsibilities of Board.

(a) General. - The Board has the power to do all of the following:

(1) Examine and determine the qualifications and fitness of applicants for a new or renewed license.

(2) Adopt and publish a code of ethics and standard of practice for persons licensed under this Article.

(3) Issue, renew, deny, revoke, and suspend licenses under this Article.

(4) Conduct investigations, subpoena individuals and records, and do all other things necessary and proper to discipline persons licensed under this Article and to enforce this Article.

(5) Employ professional, clerical, investigative, or special personnel necessary to carry out the provisions of this Article.

(6) Purchase or rent office space, equipment, and supplies necessary to carry out the provisions of this Article.

(7) Adopt a seal by which it shall authenticate its proceedings, official records, and licenses.

(8) Conduct administrative hearings in accordance with Article 3A of Chapter 150B of the General Statutes.

(9) Establish fees as allowed by this Article.

(10) Publish and make available upon request the licensure standards prescribed under this Article and all rules adopted by the Board.

(11) Request and receive the assistance of State educational institutions or other State agencies.

(11a) Establish education requirements for licensure.

(12) Establish continuing education requirements for persons licensed under this Article.

(13) Adopt rules necessary to implement this Article.

(b) Education Requirements. - The education program adopted by the Board may not consist of more than 200 hours of instruction. The instruction may include field training, classroom instruction, distance learning, peer review, and any other educational format approved by the Board. (1993 (Reg. Sess., 1994), c. 724, s. 1; 2009-509, s. 2.1.)

§ 143-151.50. License required to perform home inspections for compensation or to claim to be a "licensed home inspector".

(a) Requirement. - To perform a home inspection for compensation or to claim to be a licensed home inspector, an individual must be licensed by the Board. An individual who is not licensed by the Board may perform a home inspection without compensation.

(b) Form of License. - The Board may issue a license only to an individual and may not issue a license to a partnership, an association, a corporation, a firm, or another group. A licensed home inspector, however, may perform home inspections for or on behalf of a partnership, an association, a corporation, a firm, or another group, may conduct business as one of these entities, and may enter into and enforce contracts as one of these entities. (1993 (Reg. Sess., 1994), c. 724, s. 1; 2009-509, s. 3.4.)

§ 143-151.51. Requirements to be licensed as a home inspector.

(a) Licensure Eligibility. - To be eligible to be licensed as a home inspector, an applicant must do all of the following:

(1) Submit a completed application to the Board upon a form provided by the Board.

(2) Pass a licensing examination prescribed by the Board.

(3) Repealed by Session Laws 2009-509, s. 2.2, effective October 1, 2011.

(4) Pay the applicable fees.

(5) Meet one of the following three conditions:

a. Have a high school diploma or its equivalent and satisfactorily complete an education program approved by the Board. The program must be completed within three years of the date the applicant submits an application for licensure under this section.

b. Have education and experience the Board considers to be equivalent to that required by sub-subdivision a. of this subdivision.

c. Be licensed for at least six months as a general contractor under Article 1 of Chapter 87 of the General Statutes, as an architect under Chapter 83A of the General Statutes, or as a professional engineer under Chapter 89C of the General Statutes. A person qualifying under this sub-subdivision on or after October 1, 2011, must remain in good standing with the person's respective licensing board.

(b) License. - Upon compliance with the conditions of licensure under subsection (a) of this section, to be eligible to be licensed as a home inspector, an applicant must meet all of the insurance requirements of this subsection.

(1) General liability insurance in the amount of two hundred fifty thousand dollars ($250,000), which insurance may be individual coverage or coverage under an employer policy, with coverage parameters established by the Board.

(2) One of the following:

a. Minimum net assets in an amount determined by the Board, which amount may not be less than five thousand dollars ($5,000) nor more than ten thousand dollars ($10,000).

b. A bond in an amount determined by the Board, which amount may not be less than five thousand dollars ($5,000) nor more than ten thousand dollars ($10,000).

c. Errors and omissions insurance in the amount of two hundred fifty thousand dollars ($250,000), which insurance may be individual coverage or coverage under an employer policy, with coverage parameters established by the Board. (1993 (Reg. Sess., 1994), c. 724, s. 1; 2009-509, s. 2.2.)

§ 143-151.52. (Repealed effective October 1, 2013) Requirements to be licensed as an associate home inspector.

To be licensed as an associate home inspector, a person must do all of the following:

(1) Submit a completed application to the Board upon a form provided by the Board.

(2) Pass a licensing examination prescribed by the Board.

(3) Pay the applicable fees.

(4) Have a high school diploma or its equivalent.

(5) Be employed by or affiliated with or intend to be employed by or affiliated with a licensed home inspector and submit a sworn statement by that licensed home inspector certifying that the licensed home inspector will actively supervise and train the applicant. (1993 (Reg. Sess., 1994), c. 724, s. 1; 1998-211, s. 34; 2009-509, s. 3.3.)

§ 143-151.53. Notification to applicant following evaluation of application.

If the Board finds that the applicant has not met fully the requirements for licensing, the Board shall refuse to issue the license and shall notify in writing the applicant of the denial, stating the grounds of the denial. The application may also be denied for any reason for which a license may be suspended or revoked or not renewed under G.S. 143-151.56. Within 30 days after service of the notification, the applicant may make a written demand upon the Board for a review to determine the reasonableness of the Board's action. The review shall be completed without undue delay, and the applicant shall be notified promptly in writing as to the outcome of the review. Within 30 days after service of the notification as to the outcome, the applicant may make a written demand upon the Board for a hearing under Article 3A of Chapter 150B of the General Statutes if the applicant disagrees with the outcome. (1993 (Reg. Sess., 1994), c. 724, s. 1; 1998-211, s. 35.)

Vision Books Order Form

Fax Orders:	1-980-299-5965
Phone Orders:	1-704-898-0770
E-mail Orders:	www.visionbooks.org
Mail Orders:	Vision Books, LLC P.O. Box 42406 Charlotte, NC 28215

Shipp To:
Name_____
Address_____
City_____State_____Zip_____
Phone_____Fax_____
Email_____@_____

Bill To: We can bill a third party on your behalf.
Name_____
Address_____
City_____State_____Zip_____
Phone____(_____)_____Fax_____
Email_____@_____

Pamphlet Number ($15.00 Each)	Qty	Total Cost
_____	_____	_____
_____	_____	_____
_____	_____	_____
_____	_____	_____
_____	_____	_____
_____	_____	_____
_____	_____	_____
_____	_____	_____
<u>Full Volume Set 1-92</u>	<u>92 Pamphlets</u>	<u>1,380.00</u>

Free Shipping & Handling on Full Volume Orders
Add $1.00 Shipping & Handling per pamphlet $_____

Total Cost $_____

Thank you for your support. Mmanagement!

DID YOU ENJOY THIS BOOK?

Vision Books, LLC would like to hear from you! If you or someone you know has been fasely imprisoned, we would like to hear your story. If the 'North Carolina Criminal Law and Procedure' has had an effect in your life or if you have suggestions, we would like to hear from you. Send your letters to:

Vision Books, LLC
Attn: Staff Writers
P.O. Box 42406
Charlotte, NC 28215
Email: staff@visionbooks.org

Order Additional Copies:

Fax Orders:	1-980-299-5965
Phone Orders:	1-704-898-0770
E-mail Orders:	www.visionbooks.org
Mail Orders:	Vision Books, LLC P.O. Box 42406 Charlotte, NC 28215

www.ingramcontent.com/pod-product-compliance
Lightning Source LLC
Chambersburg PA
CBHW051630170526
45167CB00001B/130